T

DINKY TOY
Price Guide

4th edition

Frank Thompson

Also by Frank Thompson

The Corgi Toy Price Guide

The Matchbox Toy Price Guide

The Space Toy Price Guide

The Tri-ang, Minic & Spot-On Price Guide

1343701

Fourth edition 1995
Third edition 1989
A & C Black (Publishers) Limited
35 Bedford Row, London WC1R 4JH

ISBN 0-7136-4245-9

First published 1982
Second edition 1987
Ernest Benn Ltd

Copyright © 1995, 1982, 1987, 1989 Frank Thompson

Photographs by kind permission of Christie's
South Kensington.

A CIP catalogue record for this book is available from the
British Library.

Typeset in 8½ on 9½pt Palatino

Printed in Great Britain by
Bell & Bain Limited, Thornliebank, Scotland

CONTENTS

IMPORTANT NOTICE

The prices given in this guide are the prices that you should expect to pay in order to buy an item. They are not necessarily what you should expect to receive when selling to a dealer. Although every care has been taken in compiling this guide, neither the publishers nor the author can accept any responsibility whatsoever for any financial loss or other inconvenience that may result from its use

INTRODUCTION

No. 930   Bedford Pallet Jekta Van

HISTORY

Dinky Toys were the forerunner of all modern diecast items and the man we have to thank was Frank Hornby, who started it all.

In his early years in Liverpool, Frank Hornby saved his pocket money and made a few trips to London, by train, of course. He used to visit a place known at the time as 'the finest toyshop in the world' and made friends with several of the staff, especially one of the sons of Walter Lines, who invited him to visit the Lines factory at Merton, in south London, where approximately fifty million wheels a year were made and fixed to toys that were exported to countries all over the world. It took a whole day to tour the 25-acre plant; there were eight thousand employees who included craftsmen in the mould of Herbert Staines and Charles Rathbone.

Later, while working in the office of a Liverpool firm of importers, he never abandoned his mechanical and model making pursuits. As the years went by he gradually acquired some useful equipment in the way of tools and wrote a book on the principles of model engineering. As his two sons grew up, he delighted in making toys for them, initially with a sheet of copper and watchmaker's bolts and screws.

The great day came when he built his first model – for his son Roland G. Hornby. He thus invented the first Meccano plaything while making a train journey, after seeing the great cranes on the Liverpool docks. The great Hornby Crane runs on wheels and luffs and jibs in the same manner as the real thing. It gives endless pleasure because it can be taken apart and built up again. With a jib it is a genuine crane; without a jib but with a few more pieces (supplied with the model), it becomes a truck which can be made to run on rails formed by yet more pieces. And, like no other toy before it, its parts can be used to construct a whole range of other models.

Development of Hornby and Meccano manufacturing and repertoire followed, leading eventually to the great factory in Binns Road, Liverpool.

When this crane came into production in September 1907, several hundred cranes were made, one of the first original Meccano products which, depending on condition, is now worth several hundred pounds. The names of Meccano, Hornby and Dinky were over the years to belong to the same company.

It was about the year 1911 that the Fairy Cycle was made in the form of a moving toy which had Hornby stamped all over it (without any number). In the 1930s, this was to become a Meccano Dinky model in green and dark brown with a railway company logo, very much connected with the delivery bicycles seen on railway stations and in the streets of Liverpool. Still without a number, it was presented in a plain box of six, at a price of 2/11, or in a limited number of boxed gift sets that also contained passenger and rail staff figures. The price likely for such a set at today's auction prices is hard to forecast.

Not the least of Frank Hornby's achievements was his success in organising and welding together Meccano enthusiasts of many countries into the worldwide fellowship of the Meccano Guild in 1918. Ten years later, in 1928, he founded the Hornby Trains Organisation, the purpose of which was to guide young people who were enthusiastic about his famous models. Trains and trams were joined by buses and vans which were to become Dinky when he brought the name into being. The first of the Dinky Dublo models are among the most sought after by collectors. The very rare No. 060 Milk Wagon is the one to look for.

By the early 1930s, Frank Hornby had developed Hornby Model Miniatures to go with Hornby Electric train sets (of 00 and 0 gauges). The following sets had platform machines, name boards, animals and figures:

No. 1	Station Staff Set
No. 2	Farmyard Animals Set
No. 21	Train Set
No. 22	Motor Vehicles Set

The inclusion of advertisements brought realism to the railway station. While the first sets were 4/-, single items were on sale from 1d to 1/- in pre-decimal currency.

Odd models and even sets of racers, commercial vehicles and ordinary cars were smuggled out of the Binns Road factory. They were announced in the December 1933 issue of the *Meccano Magazine*. A few Meccano Dinky models were on sale in shops in the pre-Christmas period of 1933 and others were being sold in the clubs and pubs of the four northern counties of England. Models quickly travelled to London, Leeds, Birmingham and Glasgow, and even overseas. At the early stage of Meccano Dinky, models had no letters and were cast in lead (actually an alloy containing considerably more lead than the later Zamak formula), the vehicles having metal wheels.

If any of you come across miniatures which seem unidentifiable, they may possibly be models for the real-rare-miniature series, which the Hornby Company had lost interest in before April 1934 when the same models were renamed Dinky Toys. They were then given distinguishing letters as follows:

'22' series issued 1934

No. 22a	Sports Car
No. 22b	Sports Coupé

No. 22c   Motor Truck
No. 22d   Delivery Van
No. 22e   Farm Tractor
No. 22f   Army Tank

Other names around at the same period have long since vanished, but you may occasionally come across models from Electron, Kemex or Hamleys.

PRE-WAR YEARS

1934 was the official first year for Dinky. The most important thing to remember in dealing with any of the pre-war series, especially when trying to differentiate between them, is the fact that the parts may at some time have been mixed up in the factory. For example, the Town Sedan in its second form may still retain the hole in the body for the pin of the spare wheel which did not remain a part of this model; the tinplate windscreens of Nos. 24g and 24h Tourers may be solid or open; a No. 30f Ambulance may carry an earlier plain radiator or be attached to a '36' series chassis. This makes things a little difficult for buying and selling; a misunderstood model was sold around 1960 for only 10/- when it was worth over £250. The same model today would be worth between £1000 and £5000. In general, however, the system holds.

The '24' and '36' series of motor cars were issued between 1934 and 1938. The very first '24' series models were an extremely important issue and have become unobtainable apart from a few No. 24d Vogue models which had no names despite being based on actual cars of the period; their body castings were used for Rover and Bentley models of the later '36' series.

Red and grey ambulances of the '24' and '30' series seem at first sight to be much the same. The original No. 24a has high front wings. The '30' series ambulance has wings well down over the tyres and a moulded chassis.

The '25' series of commercial motor vehicles was a first-class investment in earlier years mainly because collectors were more interested in the sports series. The series lasted a long time and has been found in many places in very good condition. The set consists of

No. 25a   Wagon
No. 25b   Covered Wagon
No. 25c   Flat Truck
No. 25d   Petrol Tank Wagon
No. 25e   Tipping Wagon
No. 25f   Market Gardener's Van

The only common feature of the '25' series of vehicles is a black chassis. The fairly solid chassis is pierced at the rear for a tipping mechanism (whether or not intended for the tipping wagon). The cab casting is standard (except for the Petrol Tank Wagon which has a broader radiator, a divided screen and a slightly different window system, with different rear ends attached). Every model has a hook cast at the rear of the chassis, apart from the Petrol Tank Wagon where the chassis is cut short and the rear of the tank fitted over the cut end. The Covered Wagon is simply the wagon with a tinplate cover over the back. In the Tipping Wagon, the body extends behind the cab to provide anchorage for the tipping rear end where there is a hinged tailboard held in place on the chassis by a wire axle flattened at the ends.

Between 1934 and 1950 there were four main types:

1. The original issues had a chassis with three shield shaped openings. Wheels are plated and tyres are white; the cab has fairly fine lines – no representation of door hinges, casting lines above and below the door handles, 18 fine louvres on the bonnet (except for the Petrol Tank Wagon which has a single line above the handle and 13 louvres). The radiator is a single tinplate stamping without headlights, slotted into the front of the radiator which is slightly longer than on later models. Some collectors believe that the first type of castings with tinplate radiators came out only as the Petrol Tank Wagon, the Tipping Wagon and the Market Gardener's Van. My research suggests that this is not correct.

2. The second type was introduced between 1937 and 1938. At first sight there is little difference apart from the radiator. The chassis casting is the same or very similar, but the wheels are not plated and the tyres are usually black. There is a new cab: the bonnet is shorter with 10 coarser louvres and die-cast radiator with headlights instead of the former tinplate stamping.

3. The third type is more the post-1945 version: the most obvious feature is the new chassis casting which, from below, is almost featureless with one tiny hole in the middle. The wheels are ridged.

4. The fourth type is definitely post-1945. The main difference lies in the chassis casting which is flat; the moulding beneath includes a ribbed sump, gearbox, prop-shaft and differential with a deeper mudguard at the front which comes well down over the wheel and incorporates a front bumper. The mudguards have small side-light bumps. The bodies remain as before and the radiators are almost identical.

Some of the '25' series of vehicles carried advertising and command higher prices. Hand-painted examples of the first type can be very valuable if valued by an expert. Petrol tank wagons of the second type had many attractive transfers. Covered wagons sometimes had Meccano or Carter Paterson transfers.

The '28' series of delivery vans is another difficult one to sort out unless the following basic facts are kept in mind.

Vans originally had no numbers. When numbers were issued later, it was obvious that the delivery vans with lettering on the sides could not all be listed as the '22d' series, so they were grouped in four sets: '28/1', '28/2', '28/3' and '280'. Three different castings were used and advertising motifs and transfers were sometimes carried from one to the next: Wakefield's Castrol Oils can be seen on the examples of the first three types. '28/1' was produced in 1934. It is difficult to know when one type was replaced by another, but I am almost certain that '28/2' had arrived by the end of 1934 and '28/3' in 1936.

The first type of casting is virtually the old No. 22d Delivery Van with rubber tyres, open rear-wheel arches and rather square, sharp-edged bodywork. The second type has a very different shape with a rounded roof line, open rear windows and covered-in rear-wheel arches. The radiator is plain and slightly recessed and resembles that of the Ford 8 or 10. Oddly, one of the '28/2' series, with Meccano lettering, is numbered 22d. The third type has a much cruder radiator. This was the criss-cross type seen in the post-1945 loudspeaker van with the rear windows filled in. This casting, known simply as the '280', was later reissued without any advertising.

The '28/1' series, brought out in 1934, is a rare set:

No. 28a   Hornby Trains Van
No. 28b   Pickford's Removals Van
No. 28c   Manchester Guardian Van
No. 28d   Oxo Van
No. 28f   Palethorpes Sausages Van
No. 281   Ensign Cameras Van

There was a revised set in the '28/1' series issued in 1935 as follows:

No. 28a   Hornby Trains Van
No. 28b   Pickford's Removal Van
No. 28c   Manchester Guardian Van
No. 28e   Firestones Tyre Van
No. 28f   Palethorpe's Sausages Van
No. 28n   Atco Lawn Mowers Van

1934 also saw the appearance of the '28/2' series which is rare as well but worth looking out for:

No. 28g   Kodak Cameras Van
No. 28h   Sharps Toffee Van
No. 281   Crawfords Biscuits Van
No. 28m   Wakefield's Oil Van
No. 28n   Marsh & Baxter's Sausages Van
No. 22o   Meccano Van

There is also a '28/2' revised set issued in 1935:

No. 28d   Oxo Van
No. 28g   Kodak Cameras Van
No. 28h   Dunlop Van
No. 28k   Marsh and Baxter's Sausages Van
No. 28m   Wakefield's Castrol Oil Van
No. 28p   Crawfords Biscuits Van

Finally there was a '28/3' series issued in 1936:

No. 28r   Swan's Van
No. 28s   Fry's Van
No. 28t   Ovaltine Van
No. 28w   Osram Van
No. 28x   Hovis Van
No. 28y   Exide/Drydex Van

The '30' series appeared in August 1935. No. 32 Chrysler Airflow Saloon had already appeared and was now renumbered 30a.

Cars in the '30' series were the first to be given their proper names. Those issued before the Second World War are rare but were all reissued later. This series consists of:

No. 30a   Chrysler Airflow Saloon
No. 30b   Rolls Royce
No. 30c   Daimler
No. 30d   Vauxhall
No. 30e   Bedford Breakdown Van
No. 30f   Ambulance

The Vauxhall presents certain problems. The first version had the usual open chassis with a spare wheel mounted in the nearside wing, which was the practice at that time. The metal radiator was perforated with a 'squared-off' appearance resembling an eggbox (similar to that of the '28' series van casting, Type 3). The spare wheel in the wing was abandoned around 1938/39 and the radiator became shield shaped about the same time. But there are one or two examples of the shield shaped radiator used on the spare wheel chassis. Such factory faults add value to the model.

The Chrysler Airflow Saloon appeared again after the war, though not for long; therefore the model is rarer and more valuable than the other three saloons. Rolls Royce, Daimler and Vauxhall bodies and chassis often carry the faint markings of the deleted pin holes or wheel slots. They were reissued after the war with the same open chassis painted black, although this became a solid casting with one small hole (similar to the '25' series of lorries). The early Vauxhall windows were all cut out, but more recent rear windows were filled in. The '30' series ambulance has heavier front wings further over the wheels than the '24' series ambulance where the front wings are high and slender.

The '33' series appeared in 1935, consisting of the Mechanical Horse and five assorted trailers. The 'horse' was a simple casting with three wheels and could be articulated to the trailers, all of which were fitted with a tinplate pressing which swivelled and represented the small front wheels of this type of vehicle.

      No. 33a   Mechanical Horse
      No. 33b   Flat Truck
      No. 33c   Open Wagon
      No. 33d   Box Van
      No. 33e   Dust Wagon
      No. 33f   Petrol Tank Trailer

The Dust Wagon was a tinplate pressing on the open wagon casting with an open door flap. Similarly the Petrol Tank Trailer was a tinplate casting on the Flat Truck; about 1937/1938 advertising was added on the sides, either Esso or Wakefield Castrol Motor Oil. The Box Van was initially high, closed and plain but two years later carried Meccano Engineering or Hornby Trains advertising. Such models led to the issue of tugs and trailers in railway liveries, these being called the '33R' series. There were four main liveries (LMSR, LNER, GWR and SR) and occasional specials, the rarest being the cream and brown of the GWR.

THE FABULOUS FIFTIES

Throughout the war years the *Meccano Magazine* continued to be published. This kept alive the name of Frank Hornby and his inventions in the minds of collectors worldwide. Toys were no longer made from 1940 to 1945; any sold were from warehouse stock.

In 1950 a directors' meeting of the Hornby Railway Company made the public a special offer: for the price of one shilling, a badge, a certificate and a copy of the rare Hornby Railway catalogue, together with an official typed letter signed by 'your sincere friend, the Secretary'. This enrolled members into either the Junior Section or the Senior Section with the very important membership number.

The set I possess is No. 184976 with the certificate dated the seventh day of December 1950. The set consists of:

badge of membership
certificate signed by Roland G. Hornby
letter signed by the Secretary
Hornby Company catalogue
Meccano price list of 1 February 1950
advertising for Dinky Toys, Meccano and Hornby Railway

The value of the set is £2000 (without badge £1500).

1951 saw the appearance of some good models, though not in vast quantity. The first came in February, the start of the Hillman Minx saloons, No. 40F. There followed No. 30R Fordson Thames Flat Truck and No. 31A 15cwt Trojan Van (in red with Esso lettering) which was to be a first-class basis for later vans. Then came No. 40E Standard Vanguard, for the first time with closed rear-wheel covers, No. 106 Austin A90 Atlantic and No. 140B Rover 75 Saloon.

In 1952 appeared the great No. 532, Leyland Comet with Hinged Tailboard and No. 505 Foden Flat Truck with Chains. There were also a number of sets of figures made for the railway enthusiast, some to 0 and others to 00 gauge.

1953 was unique for the fantastic racing cars which were issued from March onwards. The '23' Series Racing Car Set contained:

No. 23F   Alfa Romeo
No. 23G   Cooper Bristol
No. 23H   Ferrari
No. 23J   HWM
No. 23K   Talbot Lago
No. 23N   Maserati

In October of the same year came the tractor as the basis of country-interest models, such as No. 27N Field Marshall Farm Tractor – it was then what every little boy wanted for Christmas and has become one of the best investments.

1953 was also the final year in which models were identified by combined digits and letters. In 1954 the company decided to replace the combination by all-digit identification. The 1954 catalogue showed both old and new forms, the old in brackets. By 1955 the old system had been abandoned and only the all-digit numbers were used.

1954 is known for some extra-good models which lasted and which lifted production. The first issues which really made the headlines were the military vehicles:

No. 622   10-Ton Army Truck
No. 621   3-Ton Army Wagon
No. 623   Army Covered Wagon
No. 641   Army 1-Ton Cargo Truck
No. 651   Centurion Tank
No. 670   Armoured Car
No. 673   Scout Car
No. 674   Austin Champ

The return of the Supertoys in 1955 made the early collector jump for joy. The same year also saw the start of the production of the sports car range with newer and brighter paint which made the logos stand out more.

The first issue came in February with No. 676 Armoured Personnel Carrier. In March there followed the Military Gift Set No. 1 and the first of the competition cars, No. 133 Cunningham C5R, a model based on the big American sports racer sponsored and driven by Briggs Cunningham. One of these cars came third in the 1954 Le Mans race, making the model one of the biggest sellers of 1955; it is still highly sought after more than thirty years later.

April 1955 saw the issue of the sports car, No. 108 MG Midget Competition Model. There were also No. 260 Royal Mail Van and No. 972 Coles 20-Ton Lorry Mounted Crane. In June came No. 109 Austin Healey 100 and the masterpiece, No. 942 Regent Foden Tanker.

July was a lean month with just the issue of No. 781 Esso Petrol Pump Station, but then after an interval came No. 255 Mersey Tunnel Poice Van Special, No. 481 Ovaltine Bedford Van and No. 692 5.5 Medium Gun.

The last quarter of 1955 saw the appearance of No. 965 Euclid Rear Dump Truck, No. 471 Nestlés Austin Van, No. 107 Sunbeam Alpine Competition Finish and No. 132 Packard Convertible. The final models were two vans in December: No. 918 Ever Ready Guy Van and No. 923 Heinz Big Bedford Van. The latter had 'Heinz 57 Varieties' and a tin of baked beans on the sides; in 1958 the tin of baked beans was replaced by a tomato ketchup bottle.

In 1956 old models, originally in single colours, were reissued in two colours. This idea worked better in some cases than others. The first models to receive the new treatment were No. 156 Rover 75 Two-Tone (in blue and cream, or two shades of green); No. 159 Morris Oxford Two-Tone (green and cream or white and red); No. 171 Hudson Commodore Two-Tone (in red and blue or grey and blue); and No. 254 Austin Taxi Two-Tone (in green and yellow).

The end of 1957 saw the introduction of several Dublo Dinkies:

No. 064   Austin Lorry
No. 065   Morris Pick-Up
No. 066   Bedford Flat Truck

In the same year Roland G. Hornby announced the Dinky Toys Club, the logical development of the Meccano Guild of 1918 and similar Hornby Trains Organisation of 1928. Collectors of model cars received a badge and a scroll for one shilling. They could also purchase the model of the month, in the first instance No. 443 National Benzole Petrol Tanker, based on the Studebaker tanker, painted yellow with the lettering in black. The set of badge, scroll and model, with the signature of Roland G. Hornby, was a top-class investment for the future. I would now value the collection at £10000 (without signature £2000).

1958 came in with a bang. No. 643 Army Water Tanker arrived in January. This was followed in February by No. 956 Turntable Fire Escape with Windows Supertoy. This began the interest in police, fire and ambulance models and in the rescue models which became popular through the TV adventures of many favourites. The best investment of the year was No. 943 Esso Leyland Octopus Tanker Supertoy.

In April 1958 the company proudly announced the development of Dinky Toys with glazed windows, the first of which was No. 176 Austin A105 Saloon, a striking model in two-tone finish. Corgi had models with glazed windows in 1956 but not in the class or quality of the Dinky range.

In July 1958 there appeared a very large Supertoy, No. 983 Dinky Car Carrier and Trailer which was also sold as No. 984 Dinky Car Carrier and No. 985 Dinky Trailer.

Later in 1958 the Guy trucks were modified, but the model numbers remained the same. No. 431 Guy Warrior 4-Ton Lorry and No. 432 Guy Warrior Flat Truck had completely new cab castings and had the Guy Warrior chassis although No. 433 Guy Flat Truck with Tailboard did not have its cab changed. The Warrior chassis was also used later in 1959/60 as the basis of No. 920 Heinz Guy Warrior Van which replaced No. 923 Heinz Big Bedford Van. The prices of the Heinz models go up and down but remain my tips for top investments.

1959 was a year when an interesting variety of models came out. Dinky had rather belatedly added so-called independent suspension in an effort to keep up with their competitors. The finish on all Dinky models improved rapidly through the efforts of engineers and workshop artists. The two models for January were No. 178 Plymouth Plaza and No. 168 Singer Gazelle. The prestige model, issued at a bargain price but now worth double on all valuations, was undoubtedly No. 150 Rolls Royce Silver Wraith in two-tone grey with glazed windows, suspension, plated parts and treaded tyres. Then came No. 191 Dodge Royal Sedan.

The taxi of 1959 took everyone's eye: No. 067 Austin Taxi. Even more popular was No. 068 Royal Mail Van. There was also the reintroduction of the AA Motor Cycle Patrol (No. 270) and later came No. 189 Triumph Herald shortly after the actual car reached the garage forecourts and other selling outlets in the UK.

The same year saw the introduction of several models connected with television: No. 967 BBC TV Mobile Control Room, No. 968 BBC TV Roving Eye Vehicle, and No. 969 BBC TV Extending Mast Vehicle. The value of the set in mint boxed condition is £750, while value is added to any of these models if there is an accompanying official autograph by a star personality involved in the BBC at the time.

During this period I toured shows around Britain with my double-decker bus and a collection of models. At the same time I became involved with radio and television programmes. I was also giving serious consideration to the preparation of a price guide for Dinky Toys.

THE GREAT SIXTIES

1960 was certainly the year of the commercial vehicle. Models were all good 'buys'. After so many American sedans, the company decided to make No. 930 Bedford Pallet Jekta Van. Then came cement lorries and No. 667 Missile Servicing Platform Vehicle. Two petrol stations and No. 966 Multi-Bucket Unit were issued. The end of 1960 saw the making of No. 256 Police Patrol Car from No. 165 Humber Hawk.

1961 brought the first issue of the larger format of the *Meccano Magazine* which was more lavish but more difficult to store and to keep clean. No. 949 Wayne School Bus Special and various caravans were issued.

In 1962 Dinky produced a more interesting and diverse range of models in the UK, with many new features. Again there were many American models. No. 264 RCMP Police Patrol Car was a good quality investment. Other police vehicles sold well and there was an increasing demand for colourful gift sets. Several models were released simultaneously with the actual vehicles: No. 113 MGB was one. This fed the search for boxes autographed by car manufacturers and salesmen.

The French branch of the Dinky Company became very active. The first of their models were released in the UK, namely No. 579 Simca Glaziers Lorry, No. 581 Berliet Truck with Container and No. 893 Unic Pipe Line Transporter. These were followed in July 1962 by:

No. 518   Renault
No. 535   2cv Citroën
No. 550   Chrysler Saratoga
No. 553   Peugeot 404
No. 555   Ford Thunderbird Convertible
No. 561   Citroën Delivery Van
No. 563   Renault Pick-Up Truck
No. 815   Panhard Armoured Car
No. 817   AMX 13-Ton Truck
No. 822   M3 Half-Track
No. 884   Brockway Truck with Bridge
No. 894   Unic/Boillot Car Transporter

All the models came in their original French boxes.

There were some bright models for Christmas 1962: No. 145 Singer Vogue and No. 277 Superior Criterion Ambulance.

A new bubblepack was announced in 1962, particularly for the packaging of racing models: a transparent moulded plastic cover backed by card. Diecast wheels were now being replaced by plastic ones. But this form of packaging scratched many models and was not a success.

In January 1963 two reissues of previous models appeared in certain shops: No. 146 Daimler V8 2½ litre (from the old Jaguar 3.4) and No. 953 Continental Touring Coach (originally the Wayne School Bus Special). Things improved as the year went ahead with No. 140 Morris 1100. Then came the first Dinky racing car to have suspension, No. 242 Ferrari Racing Car. This gave collectors the chance to visit racing tracks and to meet racing drivers of the period.

July 1963 saw No. 944 Shell BP 4000-Gallon Tanker Supertoy. There was excellent advertising material because this was a joint venture with Shell BP. The writing was on the wall, so to speak, and a takeover loomed.

August brought out more variations on old themes such as No. 117 Caravan.

No. 292 Atlantean Bus in red (from 1962) came out with two transfers, Corporation or Ribble. The same casting was then issued in a green livery as No. 293. About the same time No. 114 Triumph Spitfire was issued with a lady driver. The price today is very different if that driver has been lost.

In late 1963 at the time of the Motor Show, the Dinky Company brought out No. 135 Triumph 2000 – the model was in the shops before the actual car was on sale, not the normal procedure. (The same thing happened to the model of the Hillman Imp, No. 138.)

Several gift sets came on the scene in November for Christmas sale:

No. 121   Goodwood Racing Set
No. 122   Touring Set
No. 123   Mayfair Set

No. 298   Emergency Services Set
No. 299   Motorway Services Set

In 1964, the last year before the takeover, some of the best Dinky models ever produced came on the market. The first was No. 952 Vega Major Luxury Coach, very well finished inside and out with flashing indicators that worked as the model was steered along.

The *Meccano Magazine* Vol. 49, No. 1, which was slightly larger than the previous Dinky Meccano catalogues, contained an article called 'How They All Began', a clever Dinky history by Toyman.

No. 196 Holden Special Sedan was a great success in the Australian market, nicely finished with an opening bonnet and jewelled headlights, a feature loved by the makers but regarded with mixed feelings by the collector. The children of the time almost refused to buy them. I remember quite distinctly kids saying, 'Hey, mister, that doesn't look anything like a real car, they're rubbish.' At about this time the decline in sales at many of the smaller shops became prominent.

Production lines did not come to a halt until 1980. During the years between 1964 and 1980 many good toys were made, especially the wonderful models seen on television. James Bond models and those of the Thunderbirds and of the Muppet Show, even those used for Tom and Jerry, Basil Brush and Dougal's Roundabout (in Magic Roundabout), have become great boons to investors.

Models have been made of royal events, movie stars, sporting personalities, firms worldwide (such as Mars and Coca Cola) and all kinds of sweets, biscuits and chocolate. Walt Disney's films have led to the development of many models.

THE CREAM OF DINKY INVESTMENTS

THE RAREST

One of the rarest models ever produced is No. 31 Holland Coachcraft Van (Box No. A2031). The original van was designed by W. H. Holland and because of its unusual appearance and reliability drew crowds when on exhibition in 1935 at Olympia, London, and on tour in Glasgow. The following report comes from the July 1932 *Automobile and Carriage Builders Journal*:

> Mr Holland has been engaged in the body building industry since 1924 in various capacities commencing with three years spent on actual body construction with Messrs McIntyre Ltd of Greenock.
>
> This was followed by an intensive study of engineering drawing on the completion of which he was appointed Assistant Manager and in 1929 finally became Manager of the body works of the above firm.
>
> As a skilled draughtsman with a good knowledge of engineering principles, Mr Holland has been involved in a new type of body construction and, in 1931, started business on his own account as Holland Coachcraft at Kintra Street, Govan. A speciality is made of commercial bodywork having a streamline formation. The construction of the body is designed on scientific principles in order that all strains are well distributed with economy of weight. Holland Coachcraft has attracted widespread

notice and the shops are actively engaged with bodywork for various trades.

DUBLO DINKIES
    No. 060   Milk Wagon

GIFT SETS
    No. 307   New Avengers Set
    No. 309   Star Trek Gift Set

LORRIES, TRUCKS AND COMMERCIAL VEHICLES
    No. 25b   Carter Paterson Covered Wagon
    No. 25d   Redline Glico Petrol Wagon
    No. 504   Mobilgas Foden 14-Ton Tanker
    No. 505   Foden Flat Truck with Chains
    No. 908   Mighty Antar with Transformer
    No. 935   Leyland Octopus Flat Truck with Chains
    No. 941   Mobilgas Foden Tanker
    No. 942   Regent Foden Tanker
    No. 983   Dinky Car Carrier and Trailer
    No. 991   AEC Shell Chemicals Tanker

MILITARY VEHICLES AND ACCESSORIES
    No. 301   Daimler Military Ambulance
    No. 624   Daimler Ambulance
    No. 666   Missile Erector Vehicle and Corporal Missile
    No. 668   Foden Army Truck
    No. 674   Austin Champ (Promotional Special)

MODELS FROM TV, SPACE ETC.
    No. 354   The Pink Panther
    No. 357   Klingon Battle Cruiser
    No. 358   USS Enterprise
    No. 602   Armoured Command Car

SPORTS CARS AND SALOONS
    No. 32   Chrysler Airflow Saloon (Box No. A2032)
    No. 100A Lady Penelope's Fab 1
    No. 100B Lady Penelope's Fab 1
    No. 101   Thunderbird 4

VANS
The following Trojan vans are examples of valuable investments:
    No. 452   Chivers
    No. 455   Brooke Bond
These Guy vans are also valuable investments:
    No. 514   Slumberland
    No. 514   Lyons
    No. 514   Weetabix

No. 514   Spratts
No. 917   Spratts
No. 918   Ever Ready
No. 919   Golden shred
No. 920   Heinz

TIPS FOR FUTURE INVESTMENTS

I have selected items that are reasonably priced in the collector market, though prices will, of course, vary from place to place.

AGRICULTURAL VEHICLES
Dinky has produced many models over the years. All vehicles, especially tractors or combine harvesters, are reasonable in price and should make good investments. Models are usually available at agricultural shows (farming journals will give dates and places).

BUSES AND COACHES
Any bus coach or hire vehicle in model form should become a good investment. Advertisements on them can make a large difference to the collector's price.

LORRIES, TRUCKS AND COMMERCIAL VEHICLES AND VANS
Commercial models often have higher investment potential than ordinary car models. Actual large container vehicles (petrol, milk, sugar) have usually had models made from them. Garage shops often sell their own special model or exchange it for the vouchers given against payment for petrol etc.

MODELS FROM TV, SPACE ETC.
Buy now at bargain prices. Thunderbird models led the way for investments in this field: Kermit and Miss Piggy models (from the Muppets show) are still at a reasonable price and should soon make a profit – but you must avoid panic selling.

TAXIS
Models are often offered by mail order firms at Christmas and Easter.

EMPTY BOXES AND CATALOGUES
In the early 1950s nobody knew that these things would become so valuable, but I was already collecting. Many are now impossible to find. Buy any that you see, especially since many empty boxes are fetching more than the models themselves. Where the numbering of boxes is doubtful and where catalogues have misprints, there is additional interest. As with postage stamps, mistakes eventually make money.

MATCHBOX DINKY COLLECTION
Any model in a special box will prove a good investment. The hardest model to find will be No. DY-10 Mercedes Benz 03500 Stuttgart Bus.

GENERAL HINTS FOR COLLECTORS

STARTING AND BUILDING A COLLECTION
The best place to find a collector or to start your own collection is a swapmeet or fleamarket. Sometimes they are a combination of the two. Although the major auction houses such as Sotheby's and Christie's are now only too willing to sell diecast toys, most business is still conducted at toy collectors' fairs which have sprung up all over Europe and the United States. Many have become established as annual events, some are monthly and a few are even weekly. In 1976/7 there might have been about 400 swapmeets a year, now there are probably 400 a month in the United Kingdom alone.

National and particularly local newspapers give details of swapmeets and fleamarkets all the time. *The Collectors' Gazette, Exchange and Mart*, local radio and television as well, of course, as collectors' shops are all useful sources of information.

Another, and perhaps unexpected, place which attracts collectors is the traction engine rally. At most of these there are trade stands with dealers buying and exchanging models. Many are special promotional models, advertising a particular show. A publication called *The World's Fair* lists all the traction engine rallies to be held.

Similarly the major agricultural shows attract many model enthusiasts as do meetings held by various car clubs and bus and coach preservation societies. Information on meetings is usually available locally. The possibility of buying a special promotional model at some of these events is an added incentive for attending.

It is well to remember that a collector should, whenever possible, buy an additional model as these can become exchangeable and thus a better means of finding those items which may be necessary to complete a collection.

ODD COLOURS AND DISCREPANCIES
Wrong colours, misspelt advertisements – even missing wiper blades on a car, van or bus – may not immediately be noticed but are important. Models with the wrong tyres, wheels or other significant faults may become good investments. Look very carefully whenever you are considering buying.

RECOGNITION OF DINKY TOYS
Models carry the words 'Meccano' or 'Dinky Meccano' in 99 per cent of cases. To avoid fakes or to be sure, take an expert with you to major sales or seek advice.

CARE AND PRESERVATION

Care for your models yourself – **never** trust any job to anyone in the family or outside. If you cannot do it yourself, wait until you can.

PURCHASE
Most genuine collectors carry a magnifying glass to inspect any goods. They look for any kind of dirt, scratch or stain; some collectors will want only the perfect mint model and the perfect box, free from any marks whatsoever.

Look for signs of damp and also for signs of fading due to sunlight. Never pay the full price for models taken from a shop window. They may have been there for a long time so that the colouring of both box and model has suffered.

If it is raining, keep everything as dry as possible. Keep an old umbrella handy to help protect packages that you acquire unexpectedly or that you need to deliver in good condition.

HANDLING

Models and boxes should be touched as little as possible and never cleaned before an expert has looked at them. When they are handled, it should be with medical gloves of the kind that are made of silk or satin, and, if the model has to be picked up, it should be done so gently but firmly by the wheels, held between a thumb and the finger which is most comfortable to use.

PACKING AND STORING

Wrap carefully in nothing but soft tissue paper or gunpaper. Any type of newspaper should be avoided at all cost, so that no print can possibly be transferred to the model or to the box.

Toys that move are usually more difficult to transport than the static type. If an item has movable parts, take the pieces and wrap them carefully, making sure that you remember how to put things back together again.

Store in a place with an even temperature and where the atmosphere is neither damp nor too dry. This should stop any motif or paint coming off the model itself. The box should remain in better condition, too.

DESPATCH

Be very careful about the organization you select for delivering an item, particularly for more valuable pieces. You can give specific instructions for the care of what you are sending. At the same time, make certain about the insurance arrangements. If something unfortunate should occur before delivery or, worse of all, the packet becomes lost, you will at least receive financial compensation.

SELLING

Recommendations for handling and storage underline the importance of your model's condition when you want to sell. Serious collectors examine all models and boxes extremely carefully.

On many boxes you may find instructions, names, addresses etc. Even if they have grown faint, never write over them. A lady once found a toy box containing an old train set. It had been sent from London to Leeds in 1901. Before selling it, she wrote carefully with a ballpoint pen over the name of the mail order company who had made and sent the box – and lost more than £250 at the sale.

MARKET MALPRACTICE

When buying a model, particularly one with some form of mechanical movement, keep your eye on it from the moment of first view or demonstration. If there is anything wrong with it, the retailer should report to the manufacturer and then destroy or return for replacement. But models can be sold by unscrupulous people who display a good model but wrap a reject. The reject may be difficult to prove and therefore to return.

Be very careful when buying privately, especially, say, from a stranger in a public house. You may have to return the model if it is found to be stolen and you lose your money as well.

Models are sometimes repainted and there may be special reasons for this. Model shops may be asked to add names to commercial vans. (If you have such a thing done, have the fact documented, even through a solicitor.) Generally it is better to buy a model in fair condition than one that has been repainted. Tyres and wheels can differ through a mistake in the original assembly, but more often they have been added incorrectly at a later date. This is difficult for even an expert to determine. Straight fakes tend to be larger than the genuine models and to have been assembled carelessly.

Some models have been made privately, craftsman built or even semi-mass-produced in areas where labour is cheap. Many of them are not true-to-scale models and often have sides that are too thick, lengths that are excessive, paintwork that is too bright and wording on boxes that looks different. Sellers of such models tend to be nervous, to discard fake models if they make an escape and to keep a bicycle or car nearby for that purpose. If you have good reason to suspect anyone, inform the police at once.

There are a thousand and one things that can go wrong in the world of collecting, far too many to list here, but if any of you want to write to me care of my publishers, please do so, not forgetting to include a stamped addressed envelope. Perhaps you have tips of your own which you would be happy to send me.

A NOTE ON THE PRICES

Any price guide is certain to cause controversy, especially in an area of collecting where prices are often rising very rapidly. There will always be variations of opinion, and you may find that a model which is selling for £50 in one place is available for £5 in another. This is not as true as it was, but I hope very much that this guide will set a general standard to be followed.

The prices were as accurate as possible at the time of going to press, but variations may have occurred in the months it has taken for the book to be produced. Often an item is as valuable as the amount the person can afford to pay, and this is particularly true of rare models where cost can become unimportant to the buyer.

USER'S GUIDE

To make it as easy as possible for the collector to find his or her model, I have divided the book into sections, each one devoted to a particular class or type of product. Within each section the models have been listed in numerical order, with all the necessary details of colour, tyres etc. Entries give the date that the model was issued, deleted or had its number changed for some reason. Lengths and heights of models are also given. Prices are given for Mint Boxed, Mint Unboxed and Good Condition. Some models never had individual boxes as they were sold in sets of six or twelve, or as boxed sets. Therefore only Mint Unboxed and Good Condition prices apply.

As many numbers were duplicated several times and became rather confusing, I have set out such numbers to the best of my ability. For instance, if the number 198 had more than one colour scheme attached to it, I would call one of them 198/A or just give a higher or lower price to that particular item.

If the model happened to be issued in both pre- and post-war years, it will be distinguished by being given a small letter suffix pre-war and a capital letter suffix post-war. For example, the Reconnaissance Car which was issued in 1938 (officially 152b) is called 152b; the same model which was reissued in 1946 and still classed as 152b in the catalogue is now indicated as 152B.

If the same number is given to two different models, I have used an oblique stroke, but the details themselves should be sufficient for identification.

Lengths are given in millimetres. Remember, however, that models are affected by expansion during manufacture or through metal fatigue in the case of old models.

The date of introduction will indicate the time when the model was first mentioned in a Dinky catalogue or magazine. Release dates for promotional items are as accurate as possible, and checks have been made with the relevant company or event associated with that model. Normally these models were produced in very limited editions and were sold out on the day and date in question. Deletion dates are also given, though these are sometimes uncertain. However, the information is as accurate as I can make it.

The original prices given are correct at the time a particular model was released. However, prices were often altered at a later date and not all shops sold toys at the recommended price.

There are various ways to identify models and you will find that on practically all Dinky Toys the maker's name was shown, but there are exceptions: 'Dinky Toys', 'Meccano Ltd', 'Made in England', 'Supertoys', 'Made Overseas under Special Licence' and patent numbers were used. In these cases the letters M N mean 'Maker's Name'. Words in inverted commas such as 'Taxi' or 'Firestone Tyres' indicate the wording of a transfer or special paint job and have nothing to do with the words that were cast in metal. Many models are identified by authentic transfers and liveries of their large counterparts.

The wheels of many models were either smooth or ridged and sometimes this can be misleading in trying to date models.

ABBREVIATIONS

MB	**Mint Boxed**
MU	**Mint Unboxed**
GC	**Good Condition**
BOR	Opening boot at rear
D	Driver. Separate, static or movable
DC	Diecast alloy. Usually Zamak except for early '22' series
DH	Dual headlights
FTS	Finger tip steering, or Prestomatic as the factory called it
H	Hook for towing. Either cast into body, or as separate attachment
HG	Hook guard against weather
IP	Imitation plastic
LHD	Left hand drive position for steering wheel
MN	Manufacturer's name
OA	Open attachment for hauling
OB	Bonnet opens to reveal engine
OD	Doors open
OR	Quick reverse mechanism
P	Plastic. Either transparent in windows or on other parts of body

PW	Plastic wheels
QT	Quick tipping action
RI	Red indicators
RT	Rubber tyres. Does not include wheels or axles
RW	Solid rubber wheels
S	Seats or interior fittings
SD	Striped decor
SS	Independent suspension, springing etc
SW	Steering wheel separate and not cast in
SWIP	Side wood imitation panels
T	Tin
TP	Tinplate
TPO	Tinplate ovals
TPS	Tinplate step system
TS	Triple sidelights
TW	Tough windowglass
W	Windows
WD	Wider doors
WS	Separate plastic windscreen

THE FAMOUS
ATLANTEAN BUS

No. 292   Atlantean Bus

Of all the models made by Dinky none is more popular than the Atlantean Bus. There were three casting variations of the much admired and sought after first Atlantean bus. The first casting was the Corporation Transport model where the front entrance doors were fully extended to the bottom of the casting and the livery was a pinkish red or Post Office red and off-white with white interior seats. The second casting had a small extension added to the main chassis which protruded into a space where the space immediately underneath the doors was recessed; this alteration continued until this model was withdrawn in 1966. The third casting was the green Corporation Transport model with the ribbed roof.

These models were brought out in the following livery order. No. 1 was red and off-white with white interior; it was first described in the 10th edition of the Dinky small catalogue in May 1962. No. 2 was red and off-white with white interior, Regent adverts and the 'Ribble' name on the sides. No. 3 was red and off-white with no advertisements but still had the word 'Ribble' on the sides. No. 4 was first issued in green, with pale yellow and 'BP is the Key to Better Motoring' on sides and with red interior seating. No. 5 was the second issue in green, with 'BP is the Key to Better Motoring' in bright orange and with red interior seating. No. 6 was the third issue in green, with red interior seating.

In 1973 the first casting came out in red and white with Regent adverts but no Corporation Transport Transfers. The first advertising for the No. 292 in the 1962 Dinky catalogue showed the Corporation lettering and displayed a driver behind the wheel, but in the 11th edition of the Dinky catalogue of January and July 1963 a different bus illustration was used. This model had a single line route indicator and Regent adverts, but the Corporation lettering and the driver were missing.

The 12th edition of the Dinky catalogue in January 1964 had the same illustration in red and the driver was shown once more. The No. 293 green version was advertised at 7/11 but not illustrated. Both the February and August issues of the 1965 Dinky catalogue showed a green bus with a much larger route indicator panel and with BP adverts and Corporation lettering.

By 1966 the style of the Dinky catalogues had changed altogether as the new ideas of Lines Bros were introduced. The catalogues now had one model to a small page (pocket size) while the red Atlantean Bus had disappeared and in its place a new view of the offside of the green model appeared with full lettering. This model also featured in the No. 2 issue of the 1966 Dinky catalogue, in the No. 3 issue of 1967, and in the No. 4 issue of 1968.

The model was neither illustrated nor listed as a model in the No. 5 (May) issue of the 1969 Dinky catalogue. The green Atlantean with the ribbed roof was first illustrated in 1967 and the box had a fine picture of the model on it. Boxes are very important when getting a good price for models. The first bus issue had a full colour illustration on the front of its box, while on the back there were important notes about the public service aspects of the vehicle. The Ribble version used the same box, but the word 'Ribble' was stamped in ink in the bus style of printing on the opening flap. The later No. 293 box had a smart colour illustration which showed the red seating and occupied almost the whole of the front cover and rear, but this illustration was different as far as model appearance was concerned.

I hope this additional information will help satisfy the great number of bus collectors, although I would be pleased to receive comments and variations from any of the readers of this guide.

ACTION KITS

The range of Dinky Toys called 'Action Kits' came in unpainted form with a tiny holder of paint. The colours usually differ from the normal models, and also many collectors bought other paints and used a range of colours. However, in good condition and perfectly constructed these models are worth a lot of money to the real enthusiast. The correct colours are mentioned if I am positive about them, as it is very important to note the kit colours from the standard models. Made-up models should always be regarded as 'repaints' since they will not be a factory job. Prices for these models can vary according to the quality of the work done. I give the number of the regular Dinky model from which the kit derived if there was one.

MODEL	MB	MU	GC
No. 1001 Rolls Royce Phantom V Limousine The first of the range. From No. 152. Colours: black, royal blue, maroon or silver-grey. Jewelled headlights, opening doors, boot and bonnet. Price £1.45. Issued 1971. Deleted 1978.	£100	—	—
No. 1002 Volvo 1800S Coupé From No. 116. Colours: lemon or lime-green. All-opening doors, boot, bonnet and folding seats. Price £1.25. Issued 1971. Deleted 1975.	£75	—	—
No. 1003 Volkswagen 1300 Colours: red or white. Opening doors, bonnet, boot and jewelled headlights. Price £1.25. Issued 1971. Deleted 1975.	£75	—	—
No. 1004 Ford Escort Police Panda Car From No. 270. Colours: blue or white. Authentic police transfers. Opening doors, bonnet, boot and folding seats. Colour on all models by Humbrol. Price £1.25. Issued 1971. Deleted 1977.	£100	—	—
No. 1005 Peugeot 504 Cabriolet Kit From French Dinky No. 1423 which was never released. Very rare model in green or black. Price £1.50. Issued 1971. Deleted 1978. Note: Only a few models were given to private collectors by reps or work staff.	£75	—	—
No. 1006 Ford Escort Mexico Kit From No. 168. Colour: red. Mexico transfer stripes. Price £1.50. Issued 1973. Deleted 1978.	£75	—	—

No. 1007 Jensen FF
From No. 188. Colours: blue, dark green or silver.
Opening doors and bonnet. Price £1.50. Issued 1971.
Deleted 1975.

| | £75 | — | — |

No. 1008 Mercedes Benz 600
From No. 128. Colours: dark green or lemon. Price £1.35.
Issued 1973. Deleted 1977.

| | £75 | — | — |

No. 1009 Lotus F1
From No. 225. Colours: red and gold, white and red, and
green. John Player racing team transfers. Detailed rear
engine and racing driver. Price £1.76. Issued 1971.
Deleted 1975.

| | £75 | — | — |

No. 1012 Ferrari 213-B2
From No. 226. Transfers in red and white with red paint
and black '9' in white circle. Price £1.25. Issued 1973.
Deleted 1975.

| | £75 | — | — |

No. 1013 Matra Simca M530
A few of these models were made but never released for
sale to the general public. From French Dinky No. 1403.
See comments for No. 1005.

| | £75 | — | — |

No. 1014 Beach Buggy
From No. 227. Colours: mid-blue with dark red band
down bonnet and silver-grey top. Red, white and blue
star transfers. Price 95p. Issued 1975. Deleted 1977.

| | £75 | — | — |

No. 1017 Routemaster London Bus
From No. 289. Colours: red. Esso advert transfers,
although other transfers are known to exist. Price 75p.
Issued 1971. Deleted 1977.

| | £100 | — | — |

No. 1018 Leyland Atlantean Bus
From No. 295. Colours: various (see below). Price £1.25.
Issued 1973. Deleted 1977. Issued with several paints and
I will list the prices given for the various transfers.

White with national emblems	£100	—	—
Silver with 'Silver Jubilee' transfers	£250	—	—
Red with 'See London by Night' transfers	£250	—	—
Dark blue with 'Fly by British Airways' transfers	£300	—	—

Other transfers in good make-up condition worth
between £50 and £75 mint.

No. 1023 AEC Merlin Single Decker Bus
From No. 283. Colours: green. Green Line Bus transfers.
Also with green paint and white and red markings.
Watch for unusual transfers and colours on this model as

worth double normal livery. Automatic doors, button
bell and moulded seats. Price £1.25. Issued 1972. Deleted
1977.   £100   —   —

No. 1025 Ford Transit Van
From No. 407. Colours: red. 'Avis' transfers. Sliding door,
opening rear doors and opening side door. Again this
model was made up by several firms as a promotional
gimmick. Many of these are now worth £70, although I
advise caution and the advice of an expert. Price £1.25.
Issued 1971. Deleted 1976.   £70   —   —

No. 1027 Lunar Rover Kit
From No. 355. Blue and white. Front and rear wheels
steered by pivoting central control column. Model
astronauts and simulated energy cells. Price 75p. Issued
1972. Deleted 1975.   £100   —   —

No. 1029 Ford D800 Tipper Truck
From No. 438. Colours: red for cab and yellow for tipper
with opening doors, tip-up body and opening tail-board.
Also green and grey (worth double). Price 99p. Issued
1971. Deleted 1977.   £75   —   —

No. 1030 Land Rover Breakdown Truck
From No. 442. Colours: red and white. Price £1.25. Issued
1974. Deleted 1977.   £75   —   —

No. 1032 Army Land Rover
From No. 344. Green army livery and transfers. Price 75p.
Issued 1977.   £50   —   —

No. 1033 USA Army Jeep
From No. 615. Colours: lime green or mustard. US stars.
Extra large model with driver, spare wheel, radio aerial
etc. Price £1.75. Issued 1971. Deleted 1977.   £50   —   —

No. 1034 Mobile Gun
From No. 654. Colours: military green. Price 55p. Issued
1974. Deleted 1977.   £35   —   —

No. 1035 Striker Anti-Tank Vehicle
From No. 691. Army livery and military transfers. Price
£1.35. Issued 1975. Deleted 1975.   £50   —   —

No. 1036 Leopard Tank
From No. 692. Military livery and transfers. Price £2.25.
Issued 1974. Deleted 1977.   £75   —   —

No. 1037 Chieftain Tank
From No. 683. Full army transfers and army livery. Price
£2.25. Issued 1974. Deleted 1977.   £75   —   —

No. 1038 Scorpion Tank
From No. 690. Military transfers and paint. Price £2.25.
Issued 1975. Deleted 1977.   £75   —   —

No. 1039 Leopard Recovery Tank
From No. 699. Military transfers and paint. Price £1.75.
Issued 1975. Deleted 1977.   £75   —   —

No. 1040 Sea King Helicopter
From No. 724. Colours: white and orange with red
stripes. Battery operated main rotor, finger operated
lifting gear and moulded seats. Price £1.25. Issued 1971.
Deleted 1977.   £50   —   —

No. 1041 Hawker Hurricane Mk IIC
From No. 718. RAF transfers and paint for camouflage.
Price 75p. Issued 1973. Deleted 1976.   £50   —   —

No. 1042 Spitfire Mk II
From No. 719. RAF transfers and livery paint. Price 75p.
Issued 1971. Deleted 1977.   £75   —   —

No. 1043 SEPECAT Plane
From No. 731. Colours: dark green and blue. Transfers
and livery. Price 75p. Issued 1973. Deleted 1976.   £50   —   —

No. 1044 Messerschmitt BF 109E
From No. 726. Colours: brown or bronze and blue.
Transfers. Price 75p. Issued 1972. Deleted 1976.   £50   —   —

No. 1045 Multi-Role Combat Aircraft
From No. 729. Transfers and livery. Price 75p. Issued
1973. Deleted 1976.   £50   —   —

No. 1050 Motor Patrol Boat
From No. 675. Colours: white and blue. Transfer. Price
£1.00. Issued 1975. Deleted 1977.   £45   —   —

No. C1 Motor Car Outfit
A range of super cars can be built with this set. Parts
supplied can build four cars in a colour combination of
red and light blue. Powerful clockwork motor included.
Price 10/-. Issued 1935. Deleted 1940.   £200   £100 £50

No. C2 Motor Car Outfit
Larger models of a superior type can be built with this
set. Colours include red, light blue and black. Enough

	MB	MU	GC
parts to build 6 sports cars and 2 racing cars. Two powerful clockwork motors, each giving a run of more than 150ft on one winding. Price £1. Issued 1936. Deleted 1940.	£350	£200	£150

No. C3 Two Seater Sports Car (Non-Constructional)
This is a realistic model of a two seater sports car, beautifully made and finished by factory craftsmen, fitted with a strong clockwork motor. Blue body, black chassis and cream mudguards. Price 6/6. Issued 1936. Deleted 1940. 234mm long x 95mm wide x 57mm deep.

	MB	MU	GC
	£250	£150	£100

No. C4 Clockwork Sports Car
Red body with cream mudguards and blue interior. Seats and silver headlights. Bumpers and black grille. Solid red wheels and white rubber tyres with spare wheel on rear. Sidelights and reflector on rear. Price 7/6. Issued 1937. Deleted 1940. 236mm long x 96mm wide x 59mm deep.

	MB	MU	GC
	£400	£250	£100

No. C5 Sports Tourer with Hood
Red and cream with black outline and black hood. Cream interior, black mudguards and running board. Long running clockwork motor. Price 9/6. Issued 1937. Deleted 1940. 240mm long x 94mm wide x 59mm deep.

	MB	MU	GC
	£400	£200	£100

No. C6 Road Racer No. 1
Red and blue with black chassis and black seats with white driver (tinplate). Long running clockwork motor and '1' in black on sides and nose. Price 1/3. Issued 1937. Deleted 1940. 117mm long x 91mm wide x 53mm deep.

	MB	MU	GC
	£400	£250	£150

No. C7 Saloon Coupé
Red with blue interior and cream mudguards. Long running clockwork motor. Tinplate driver. Bumpers. Headlights, sidelights, tail light and sounding horn, all worked by battery. Price 10/-. Issued 1938. Deleted 1940. 240mm long x 99mm wide x 101mm deep.

	MB	MU	GC
	£300	£150	£75

No. C8 Sports Tourer
Red, light blue or cream. Long running clockwork motor. Headlights, sidelights, tail lights and horn, all worked by battery. Opening doors and dicky seat in rear. Price 9/-. Issued 1938. Deleted 1940. 240mm long x 99mm wide x 59mm deep.

	MB	MU	GC
	£400	£200	£50

No. C10 Road Racer Special
Red body and light blue interior. '10' on black discs on sides, rear and nose. Long running clockwork motor. Tinplate driver in black suit, red helmet and goggles. Price 9/-. Issued 1939. Deleted 1940. 235mm long x 97mm wide x 56mm deep.

	MB	MU	GC
	£350	£150	£75

No. C11 Motor Van without Adverts
Red body and light blue mudguards. Running board and
long running clockwork motor. Opening doors at rear
and opening cab doors. Black steering wheel. Thick grey
tyres, rear light and horn. Strong bumper bars and black
grille. Price 15/-. Issued 1939. Deleted 1940. 300mm long
x 99mm wide x 76mm deep.

	£500	£250	£100

No. C12 Dinky Garage and Car
Cream garage with red doors and black workbench with
vice. Contains blue sports car with cream mudguards and
seats with black steering wheel. Long running clockwork
motor. Lights and horn worked by battery. White tyres.
Price 4/11. Issued 1938. Deleted 1940. Garage 115mm
high x 132mm long x 102mm wide. Car 117mm high x
91mm wide x 53mm deep.

	£350	£200	£150

AGRICULTURAL VEHICLES

No. 301   Field Marshall Tractor

MODEL	MB	MU	GC
No. 22e Farm Tractor			
Green, yellow and red, and in blue. Metal wheels. Price 9d. Issued December 1933. Deleted 1940. 70mm. SW/H/DC.	£850	£450	£150
Blue and white with red wheels. Otherwise as above.	£850	£450	£150
No. 27A Massey Harris Farm Tractor			
Red and yellow. Front swivel. Price 5/-. Issued June 1948. Renumbered 300 in 1954. Deleted 1960. 89mm. SW/DH/DC/TP.	£75	£40	£20
No. 27AK Farm Tractor and Hay Rake			
Red and yellow. Price 8/6. Issued March 1953. Renumbered 310 in 1954. Deleted 1960. 157mm. DC/TP/Wire.	£150	£75	£45
No. 27B Halesowen Harvest Trailer			
Brown and red with tow-bar and removable front and back supports. Price 2/10. Issued June 1949. Renumbered 320 in 1954. Deleted 1960. 121mm. DC/H.	£45	£20	£10

No. 27C Massey Harris Manure Spreader
Red. Complete with tow-bar and working parts in red.
'Massey Harris Manure Spreader' on sides. Price 3/9.
Issued October 1949. Renumbered 1954. Deleted 1960.
113mm. DC. Late examples PW/RI.

£65   £25   £10

No. 27G Moto-Cart
Brown and green. SW/D with tipping rear. Price 4/6.
Issued December 1949. Renumbered 342 in 1954. Deleted
1960. 110mm. DC/RT.

£45   £25   £5

No. 27H Disc Harrow
Red and yellow with discs which rotate. Price 2/6. Issued
April 1951. Deleted 1960. Renumbered 322 in 1954.
86mm. DC.

£35   £20   £5

No. 27J Triple Gang Mower
Red, yellow and green with working blade. Price 6/6.
Issued October 1952. Renumbered 323 in 1954. Deleted
1960. 114mm. DC.

£55   £25   £10

No. 27K Hay Rake
Red and yellow. Rake raises and lowers. Price 2/11.
Issued 1953. Renumbered 324 in 1954. Deleted 1960.
77mm. DC.

£40   £20   £5

No. 27M Land Rover Trailer
Orange or green with tow-bar, clip and two wheels. Price
2/6. Issued April 1950. Renumbered 341 in 1954. Deleted
1960. 79mm. DC/TP.

£35   £15   £5

No. 27N Field Marshall Farm Tractor
Orange with front axle which swivels. Price 4/4. Issued
October 1953. Renumbered 301 in 1954. Deleted 1960.
79mm. DC/TP/SW/D/H.

£95   £50   £30

No. 27N Field Marshall Farm Tractor (Special)
Black with tow-bar and special front axle which swivels.
Price 4/4. Issued October 1953. Deleted 1954. Definitely
produced in 1953 and not when renumbered. 75mm.
DC/TP.

£2500   —   —

No. 30N Farm Produce Wagon
Green and yellow, and blue and red. Price 3/3. Issued
July 1950. Renumbered 343 in 1954. Deleted 1960. 107mm.
DC/TP/RT.

£75   £45   £20

No. 300 Massey Ferguson Tractor
Red with yellow wheels and blue driver. Front axle
swivel. Price 4/11. Issued 1960. Deleted 1965. 89mm.
DC/P.

£50   £25   £10

No. 300 Massey Harris Tractor
Red and yellow. 'Massey Harris' on sides. Price 4/-.
Issued 1954. Deleted 1976. 89mm. DC.

£50   £25   £10

No. 300 Massey Ferguson Tractor
Red and orange. Latter is rarer with 'Massey Ferguson'
on sides. SW/D/H and plastic wheels at front. Front axle
swivel. Price 4/11. Issued 1960. Deleted 1965. This is the
rubber tyred version. 89mm. DC/TP/P/RT.

£45   £20   £10

No. 301 Field Marshall Tractor
Orange with adjustable steering. Front axle swivel. Price
4/2. Issued 1954. Deleted 1964. 75mm.
DC/TP/SW/D/H.

£60   £30   £15

No. 301 Field Marshall Tractor (Special)
Black livery discovered in 1955. Adjustable steering.
SW/D/H. Price 4/2. Deleted 1956. 75mm. DC/TP. Rare.

£3000   —   —

No. 305 David Brown Tractor
Red and yellow with brown or grey driver and movable
front wheels. Price 9/11. Issued 1965. Deleted 1970.
83mm.

£75   £30   £10

No. 305 David Brown Tractor
Black, red and white. Colour discovered in 1972. Lift-off
hatch and swivelling wheels. With or without grey or
brown driver. Price 9/11. Issued 1965. Deleted 1970.
83mm.

£100   £50   £20

No. 305 David Brown Tractor
Black with red wheels and blue driver. This model
appeared in 1967, but only a few of this rare colour
known. Price 9/11. Issued 1965. Deleted 1970. 83mm.
DC/P.

£500   £250   £100

No. 308 Leyland 384 Tractor
Purple and cream with blue driver, with 'Leyland' on
sides. Price 76p. Issued 1971. Deleted 1977. 86mm. DC/P.

£75   £40   £25

No. 308 Leyland 384 Tractor
Orange and black with white plastic wheels and driver.
New colour for 1978. Price 87p. Issued 1977. Deleted 1980.
86mm. P.

£250   £100   £50

No. 310 Farm Tractor and Hay Rake
Red and yellow. Price 7/11. Issued 1954. Deleted 1960.
157mm. DC/TP/Wire.

£100   £50   £30

No. 319 Week's Tipping Trailer
Red and yellow. Two wheels, tow-bar and tipping body
with hinged tailboard. Price 4/6. Issued June 1961.
Deleted 1968. 105mm. DC/RT.
Also found with red top, with dark red wheels and
yellow chassis. Rare.

	MB	MU	GC
	£50	£20	£10
	£500	—	—

No. 320 Halesowen Harvest Trailer
Red and brown. Tow-bar. Price 3/6. Issued 1954. Deleted
1960. 120/121mm. DC.

	£50	£25	£10

No. 321 Massey Harris Manure Spreader
Red with silver blades which rotate. Tow-bar and
working parts at rear. Price 4/5. Issued 1954. Deleted
1960. 113mm. DC.
Later with yellow plastic wheels, with very dark red body
and white blades.

	£50	£35	£15
	£50	£35	£15

No. 322 Disc Harrow
Red and yellow. Tow-bar and rotating discs. Price 2/-.
Issued 1954. Deleted 1966. 86mm. DC.
White and blue. Otherwise as above. Rare.

	£40	£20	£10
	£30	£10	£5

No. 322 Disc Harrow
Red and white with full working parts. Price 2/11. Issued
1966. Deleted 1971. 79mm.

	£30	£15	£10

No. 323 Triple Gang Mower
Red, yellow and green with working blades. Price 5/3.
Issued 1954. Deleted 1963. 114mm. DC.

	£30	£15	£10

No. 324 Hay Rake
Red, yellow and silver. Rake raises and lowers by lever.
Price 3/9. Issued 1954. Deleted 1954.

	£30	£15	£10

No. 325 David Brown Tractor
White, red and black with red pipe. 'David Brown' on
sides. Price 9/11. Disc harrow optional as set. Price 12/11.
Issued 1966. Deleted 1974. 152mm. DC/P.
Tractor only
Set with harrow

	£35	£25	£15
	£35	£25	£15

No. 325 David Brown Tractor and Disc Harrow
Red with white flash. Perfect matching pair. Only a few
known in these colours. Price 12/11. Discovered 1967.
Deleted 1974. 152mm. DC/P with working parts.

	£150	£75	£30

No. 342 Moto-Cart
Green and brown. S/W/D end tipper. Price 4/3. Issued
1955. Deleted 1960. 110mm. DC/RT.

	£50	£25	£10

AGRICULTURAL VEHICLES	MB	MU	GC

No. 343 Farm Produce Wagon
Green and yellow. Dodge type. Price 3/6. Issued 1954.

	MB	MU	GC
Deleted 1964. 107mm. DC/TP/RT.	£75	£30	£10
Red and blue	£55	£20	£10
Red and black. Very rare.	£350	—	—

No. 381 Convoy Farm Truck
Cab and chassis with lemon and black bumpers. Dropping tailboard. Price £1.35. Issued 1977. Deleted 1980. 110mm. DC.

	£25	£10	£5

No. 381 Convoy Farm Truck
Yellow and brown with black bumper, silver wheels and dark yellow chassis. Price £1.35. Issued 1978. Deleted 1980. 110mm. DC.

	£35	£15	£10

No. 399 Farm Tractor and Trailer Set
A 300 Massey FerFerguson tractor and trailer. Price 13/11. Issued 1969. Deleted 1975. 188mm. DC/P.

	£100	£50	£25

No. 563 Very Heavy Tractor
Red. Price 6/9. Issued 1948. Renumbered 963 in 1954.

	MB	MU	GC
Deleted 1959. 116mm. Rubber tracks. DC/TP.	£150	£60	£25
Later in yellow.	£15	£10	£5

No. 973A Eaton Vale Articulated Tractor Shovel
Yellow and red, and later in yellow. Silver lifting and lowering bucket, articulated main body action. Simulated hydraulic ram action. Price 15/11. Issued 1971. Deleted 1975. 116mm.

	£30	£15	£10

AIRCRAFT AND ACCESSORIES

No. 999 DH Comet Airliner

This very interesting section covers the many aircraft which have proved popular with collectors since they were first introduced. Although the information has been very difficult to obtain, I am pleased to be able to include it in this guide.

MODEL	MB	MU	GC
No. 60a Imperial Airways Liner Red fuselage and wing tips, white wing, nose and tail, blue and gold with 'sunburst' effect on wings. Other colours exist. This model and all the '60' series, with the exception of the autogiro, have cast fuselages and tin wings. Price 9d. Issued 1934. Deleted 1940. Wing span 127mm. Not boxed except in set.	—	£125	£55
No. 60ab Imperial Airways Liner Gold or silver with registration G-AB7. Otherwise as above.	—	£175	£50

AIRCRAFT AND ACCESSORIES	MB	MU	GC

No. 60b DH Leopard Moth
Light green with yellow wing tips and tail; blue with orange wing tips and tail; or bright green, gold or silver with registration G-ACP7. Open cockpit windows. From 1938 the side windows were filled in and also from 1938 there was a No. 66b Dive Bomber Fighter in dark green and brown camouflage. Model was introduced in July 1940 with RAF markings and was deleted soon afterwards. Price 6d. Issued 1934. Deleted 1940. Wing span 76mm.

	MB	MU	GC
With open windows	—	£65	£35
With closed windows	—	£55	£25
No. 66b	—	£75	£45

No. 60c Percival Gull Plane
Up to 1938 the model had pierced windows. Then from 1938 to 1940 and from 1946 to 1948 it had solid windows. The pre-war model was either marked 'Percival Gull' or not at all. The post-war markings were 'Percival Tower'. The model was also brought out in 1940 as No. 66c, as a two seater fighter in camouflage with roundels. Colours for No. 60c with open windows are white with blue wing tips and tail or buff with orange wing tips and tail. Colours for the solid window version were silver, red or white. Registration G-ADZO. Price 6d. Issued 1934. Deleted 1940. Wing span 76mm.

	MB	MU	GC
With open windows	—	£65	£25
With closed windows	—	£55	£15
With post-war windows	—	£45	£5

No. 60c Commemorative Special, Percival Gull
Known as No. 60k which was a version of No. 60c, it was a commemorative model made for Amy Johnson's 1936 record breaking flight. Light flue fuselage, silver wings and blue registration G-ADZO. Also to be found with black G-ADZO to commemorate H. L. Brooke's 1937 record breaking flight to South Africa. Price 1/6. Wing span 76mm. Special boxes. Very rare. Each model.

	MB	MU	GC
	£275	£100	£50

No. 60d Low Wing Monoplane
Red with cream wing tips and tail without pilot. Then yellow, orange and red with pilot from 1936. Also No. 66D. Torpedo dive bomber in camouflage with roundels from July to December 1940. Price 6d. Issued June 1934. Deleted 1940. Wing span 76mm.

	MB	MU	GC
Without pilot	—	£75	£35
With pilot	—	£65	£25
Box of six	£350	—	—

No. 60e General Monospar Plane

First version (1934) was gold with red wing tips and tail
or silver with royal blue wings tips and tail. Second
version (1936) was gold or silver with registration
G-ABVP. In July 1940 the model came out as No. 66e
Medium Bomber in camouflage with roundels price 9d,
compared with the others which were originally priced
6d. Issued June 1934. Deleted 1940. Wing span 80mm.

First version	—	£175	£75
Second version	—	£150	£50

No. 60f Cierva Autogiro

Gold with royal blue stabiliser tips and no pilot. Later
gold or silver with pilot. Also No. 66f Army Operational
Autogiro in camouflage with roundels from July to
September 1940. Price 6d. Issued 1934. Deleted 1940. Pilot
after 1937. Rotor diameter 72mm and length of fuselage
49mm.

Without pilot	—	£75	£35
With pilot	—	£65	£25

No. 60g DH Comet Aeroplane

First version had red and gold ailerons and rudder;
gold/red ailerons and rudder; or silver with blue ailerons
and rudder with no name stamped on the wing. Second
version was gold, silver or red, with registration G-ACSR
and 'DH Comet' under wings. Reissued from 1946 to 1949
in red, yellow or silver with registration G-RACE and
'Light Racer' under wings. Price 6d. Issued 1936. Deleted
1940. Wing span 86mm. Model of plane used by C. W. A.
Scott and T. C. Black in their Australian flight.

First version	—	£75	£25
Second version	—	£55	£15
Post-war version	—	£45	£10

No. 60h Short Singapore III Flying Boat

Silver with RAF roundels. Also a No. 60m Four Engined
Flying Boat in silver, blue or green with non-existent
registrations. Price 1/-. Issued 1936. Deleted 1940. Wing
span 126mm.

No. 60h in special box	£150	£100	£50

No. 60n Fairey Battle Bomber

Silver with RAF rounbels. 'Fairy Battle Bomber' under
wing from 1938. Also issued as No. 60s Medium Bomber
in camouflage between 1938 and 1940. Price 4½d. Issued
1936. Deleted 1940. Wing span 75mm.

No. 60n without name	—	£40	£15
No. 60n with name	—	£60	£20
No. 60s	—	£40	£15

No. 60p Gloster Gladiator Biplane
Light biplane in silver with RAF roundels. 'Gloster
Gladiator' under wing from 1937. Price 2/-. Issued 1936.
Deleted 1940. Wing span 44mm.

	MB	MU	GC
Without name	—	£80	£30
With name	—	£60	£20

No. 60r Empire Flying Boat
Silver. Price 9d. Issued 1935. Deleted 1940. Wing span
126mm.

	—	£80	£20

No. 60t Douglas DC3
Red and cream or silver with black wing tips. 'Douglas
Airliner' under wing and registration PM-ALI. Price
2/11. Issued 1938. Deleted 1940. Wing span 132mm.

	£400	£150	£50

No. 60v Armstrong Whitworth Whitley
Civilian aircraft in red and silver or blue and silver. Price
6d. Issued 1935. Deleted 1940. Wing span 86mm.

	—	£60	£30

No. 60w Sikorsky Clipper III
Red and silver or all-gold. Price 6d. Issued 1935. Deleted
1940. Wing span 126mm.

	—	£75	£35

No. 60x Atlantic Flying Boat
Silver and black. Price 9d. Issued 1935. Deleted 1940.
Wing span 126mm.

	—	£60	£30

No. 62a Spitfire
Camouflage. Price 9d. Issued 1939. Deleted 1940. Wing
span 80mm. Quite rare and sought after.

	—	£150	£35

No. 62a Spitfire
Issued in a variety of colours and made as a pendant.
Neatly boxed with references and information on lid.

	—	£75	£35

No. 62b Blenheim
Silver. Price 9d. Issued 1938. Deleted 1940. Wing span
75mm.

	—	£60	£30

No. 62d Blenheim
Camouflage. Otherwise as above.

	—	£60	£30

No. 62e Spitfire
Silver with RAF roundels. Otherwise as No. 62a.

	—	£100	£35

No. 62g Hawker Hurricane
Silver. Also a No. 62s in camouflage. Price 9d. Issued 1938.
Deleted 1940. Wing span 188mm.

	—	£65	£25

|---|---|---|---|

No. 62k King's Flight
Colours vary. Price 9d. Issued 1938. Deleted 1940. Wing span 126mm. £500 £150 £85

No. 62m Airspeed Envoy
Colours vary. Price 6d. Issued 1938. Deleted 1940. Wing span 126mm. — £60 £30

No. 62n Junkers Ju90
German Air Force colours. Price 9d. Issued 1938. Deleted 1940. Wing span 126mm. £320 £50 £20

No. 62p The Ensign
Colours vary. Price 1/-. Issued 1938. Deleted 1940. Wing span 126mm. — £50 £20

No. 62q Flying Fortress
Silver and black. Price 1/-. Issued 1935. Deleted 1940. Wing span 126mm. £175 £65 £35

No. 62r DH Albatross
Authentic company liner colours. Price 1/-. Issued 1938. Deleted 1940. Wing span 140mm. £130 £50 £20

No. 62t Armstrong Whitworth Whitley Bomber
Camouflage. Price 9d. Issued 1938. Deleted 1940. Wing span 86mm. £140 £50 £20

No. 62x 40 Seater Airliner
Silver. Price 1/-. Issued 1938. Deleted 1940. 140mm. — £75 £25

No. 62y Frobisher
Grey. Price 1/-. Issued 1938. Deleted 1940. Wing span 88mm. — £50 £20

No. 62y High Speed Monoplane
Colours vary. Price 9d. Issued 1938. Deleted 1940. Wing span 126mm. — £50 £20

No. 63 Mayo Composite
Colours vary. Price 1/-. Issued 1938. Deleted 1940. Wing span 88mm. £220 £50 £20

No. 66a Imperial Airways Liner
Issued as a heavy bomber in dark green and brown camouflage colours. Although issued in 1934 it was not made into a bomber until 1940 when it had a very short run. Otherwise as No. 60a. — £175 £75

| --- | --- | --- | --- |

No. 67a Junkers Ju89 Bomber
German Air Force colours. Price 9d. Issued 1938. Deleted
1940. Wing span 188mm. — £50 £20

No. 68a 40 Seater Airliner
Camouflage. Otherwise as No. 62x. — £50 £20

No. 68b Frobisher
Camouflage. Otherwise as No. 62y. — £50 £20

No. 700 Sea Plane
Originally issued as No. 63b Mercury Sea Plane. With the
top half of the Mayo Composite and registration
G-ADMJ. 'Mercury Sea Plane' under wings. Issued 1939.
Deleted 1940. Registration G-AVKX from 1946 to 1949
and also in reissue from 1952 to 1954 when it was
renumbered 700. Finally deleted in 1957. No casting
changes on post-war version. Price 1/5. Wing span
102mm. Pre-war version not boxed; post-war version
boxed.

	MB	MU	GC
No. 63b	—	£50	£20
No. 700	£75	£35	£15

No. 700 Commemorative Special Issue, Spitfire Mk II
Silver with RAF roundels on a special green onyx stand.
Only 5000 made for Diamond Jubilee of the Royal Air
Force. Stamped with medallion and 'Gilby Jubilee
Collection'. Also 'Per Ardua Ad Astra 1918–1978'.
'Diamond Jubilee of the Royal Air Force' on base. Price
£8.50. Issued and deleted 1978. Wing span 135mm.
Special blue presentation box. £750 £300 £175

No. 701 Short Shetland Aircraft
Silver and blue design. Price 6/6. Issued 1956. Deleted
1965. Wing span 126mm. £150 £85 £45

No. 704 Avro York Air Liner
Silver with white, red or blue trim and black letters.
Originally No. 704 from 1952 to 1954. Deleted 1960. Only
No. 704 has number stamped under wing. Registration
always G-AGJC. Price 2/11.Wing span 102mm. £120 £60 £25

No. 705 Vickers Viking Airliner
Originally issued as No. 70C in 1947 in grey with silver
windows or in silver with blue windows. Registration
always G-AGOL. Renumbered 705 in 1954 and made in
silver thereafter. Finally deleted in 1963. Price 2/-. Wing
span 140mm. Not individually boxed and delivered to
shops in boxes of six.

	MB	MU	GC
Grey	—	£55	£25
Silver	—	£45	£15

No. 706 Air France Viscount
Blue and silver. Registration F-BGNL. Price 5/6. Issued
1956. Deleted 1957. Wing span 408mm.

	MB	MU	GC
	£100	£55	£25

No. 708 Vickers Viscount 800 Airliner
BEA aircraft in silver with red trim lines along centre and
red bull tip design on nose with red propellers and decals
in red. Registration G-AOJA. Price 4/11. Issued 1957.
Deleted 1965. Wing span 408mm.

	MB	MU	GC
	£95	£55	£25

No. 710 Beechcraft S35 Bonanza Aircraft
Red and white with black plastic wheels. From 1970
bronze and yellow with black engine cover. From 1975
red, white and blue. Price 7/11. Issued 1965. Deleted
1977. Wing span 133mm.

	MB	MU	GC
First version	£45	£25	£15
Second version	£35	£15	£10
Third version	£25	£10	£5

No. 712 US Army T/42A
Dark green with black interior and US stars and stripes
decals. Same basic casting as No. 715 but with wing tip
tanks. Price 49p. Issued 1973. Deleted 1977. Wing span
153mm.

	MB	MU	GC
	£45	£25	£10

No. 715 Bristol 173 Helicopter
Turquoise with rotors. Registration G-AUXR. Price 2/8.
Issued 1956. Deleted 1963. Wing span 127mm.

	MB	MU	GC
	£60	£30	£15

No. 715 Beechcraft C55 Baron
White, yellow and black with green trim lines. Yellow
engine covers and prop. The number '715' was originally
that used for the helicopter model. There was a colour
change in 1972 when it became dark orange with yellow
centre line flash with the same markings on the rail and
wing tips. Price 9/6. Issued 1967. Deleted 1978. Wing
span 150mm. DC/P.

	MB	MU	GC
White, yellow and black	£50	£30	£15
Dark orange and yellow	£40	£20	£10

No. 716 Westland Sikorsky Helicopter
Red body with silver cockpit, red rotors, cream letters and
silver wheels. Registration G-ATWX. Price 2/5. Issued
1957. Deleted 1963. Wing span 89mm.

	MB	MU	GC
	£50	£30	£15

No. 717 Boeing 737 Plane
Fawn with silver tips on nose and wings. Dark blue line
along centre jets and tail fins. Black wheels. Lufthansa
decals in light blue. Price 8/11. Issued 1970. Deleted 1976.
Wing span 152mm.

	MB	MU	GC
	£40	£20	£10

AIRCRAFT AND ACCESSORIES	MB	MU	GC

No. 718 Hawker Hurricane Fighter
Camouflage green and grey. Price 55p. Issued 1973.
Deleted 1976. Wing span 188mm.

	£100	£50	£25

No. 719 Spitfire Mk II
Green, brown and grey with RAF decals and motor
driven propeller. Price 17/11. Issued 1970. Replaced in
1977 by No. 741 with same casting but no motor. Deleted
1980. Wing span 173mm.

	MB	MU	GC
No. 719	£100	£60	£25
No. 741	£75	£35	£15

No. 721 Junkers Ju87B Stuka Fighter
Camouflage green and sky-blue with German decals etc.
Cap firing bomb. Price 15/11. Issued 1970. Deleted 1980.
Wing span 191mm.

	£50	£25	£10

No. 722 Hawker Harrier Jump Jet
Camouflage green and grey with all-folding wheels.
Price 17/11. Issued 1971. Deleted 1980. Wing span
125mm.

	£50	£25	£15

No. 723 Hawker Siddeley HS125 Executive Jet
Red, white and blue with opening door. Price 17/11.
Issued 1975. Deleted 1975. Wing span 132mm.

	£50	£25	£15

No. 724 Sea King Helicopter
Silver and medium blue with US Stars and Stripes. Motor
driven rotor blade. Price £1/1/-. Issued 1972. Deleted
1980. Wing span 179mm.

	£50	£25	£15

No. 725 F4K Phantom II
Dark blue. Royal Navy livery signs etc. Stand-off firing
missiles. Price £1.65. Issued 1972. Deleted 1978. Wing
span 132mm.

	£50	£25	£15

No. 726 Messerschmitt BF109E
Olive green with mustard tips and engine cover. Black
letters, German cross and swastika. Motor driven
propeller. Price 89½p. Issued 1972. Deleted 1976. Wing
span 165mm.

	£75	£50	£25

No. 728 RAF Dominie
Dark green, medium blue and grey battle colours and
RAF decals. Same basic casting as No. 723. Price 89p.
Issued 1972. Deleted 1975. Wing span 132mm.

	£50	£20	£10

No. 729 MRCA Swing Wing Fighter
Multi-role combat aircraft. Grey, green, dark blue and dark yellow battle colours with red and blue circle decals. Black nose top. Price 89p. Issued 1973. Deleted 1976. Wing span 164mm. — £40 £20 £10

No. 730 Tempest Fighter
RAF battle livery. Also silver with red, white and blue roundels. Price 9d. Issued as No. 701 from 1946 to 1948 and from 1952 to 1954, when it was renumbered 730. Deleted 1957. 51mm. Not boxed. Good investment. — £45 £25

No. 730 US Navy Phantom Fighter
Silver, black and blue with US decals and stars etc. Price 75p. Issued 1972. Deleted 1976. Wing span 132mm. — £40 £20 £10

No. 731 Twin Engined Fighter
Silver with no markings. Model of a Messerschmitt 119, the model having being planned in 1940, but never released. Then released as a twin-engined fighter as No. 70D from 1946 to 1948 and from 1950 to 1954, when it was renumbered 731. Price 8d. Deleted 1956. 51mm. Not boxed. — £35 £15

No. 731/A SEPECAT Jaguar
Jaguar fighter in green, grey, blue and dark blue battle colours and RAF decals. Opening cockpit and pilot ejector seat. Price 65p. Issued 1973. Deleted 1976. Wing span 106mm. — £40 £20 £10

No. 732 Meteor Twin Jet Fighter
Price 1/-. Originally issued as No. 70E from 1946 to 1948. Reissued between 1952 and 1954 as No. 732. Deleted 1963. Wing span 66mm. Not boxed. — £50 £20

No. 732/A Bell Helicopter
White, red and dark blue with black props. Red skis and blue cap interior with pilot. Black police decals. Price £1.75. Issued 1973. Deleted 1980. 211mm long. — £35 £15 £7

No. 733 Shooting Star Jet Fighter
Silver body, white stars and blue circles. Price 1/-. Issued as No. 70F from 1947 to 1949 and from 1952 to 1954, when it was renumbered 733. Deleted 1963. Wing span 60mm. Not boxed. — £35 £15

No. 734 Supermarine Swift Fighter
Authentic RAF battle colours and decals. Metal wheels. Price 1/9. Issued 1955. Deleted 1963. Wing span 51mm. — £35 £15 £7

No. 734/A P47 Thunderbolt
Silver blue metallic with mustard tail, black and orange
nose and propeller design. Red bombs under wings with
US Stars and Stripes decals. Black letters and numbers.
Price £1.25. Issued 1975. Deleted 1978. Wing span 190mm.   £35   £15   £10

No. 735 Gloster Javelin Delta Wing Fighter
Blue, green and grey battle colours and RAF decals. Silver
cockpit. Metal wheels became plastic in 1963. Price 2/5.
Issued 1956. Deleted 1965. Wing span 82mm.   £45   £25   £10

No. 736 Hawker Hunter Fighter
Green, grey and dark blue battle livery with RAF decals.
Metal wheels. Price 1/9. Issued 1955. Deleted 1964. Wing
span 54mm.   £55   £25   £10

No. 736/A Bundesmarine Helicopter
Silver, red and gold with black wheels and propellers
with motor driven main rotor blades and finger operated
winch. Price £2.25. Issued 1973. Deleted 1978. 179mm.   £35   £15   £7

No. 737 Lightning P1B Fighter
Silver with RAF roundels, black plastic radar cone and
probe fitted to nose. Metal wheels from 1963 and plastic
from 1965. Later paint finish changed to metallic
silver-grey. Price 2/-. Issued 1959. Deleted 1976. Wing
span 64mm.
Silver metal wheels   £45   £25   £10
Silver-grey metal wheels   £35   £15   £7
Plastic wheels   £25   £10   £5

No. 738 DH 110 Sea Vixen
Silver-grey. Price 7/11. Issued 1956. Deleted 1965. Wing
span 184mm.   £45   £15   £7

No. 739 A6M5 Zero-Sen-Fighter Plane
Dark green with wide black nose band and wheels. Red
Japanese decals and nose point and motor driven
propellers. Price 89p. Issued 1975. Deleted 1978. Wing
span 184mm.   £25   £10   £5

No. 997 Sind Caravelle Plane
Colours vary. Authentic Caravelle markings and
numbers. Price 7/6. Issued October 1956. Deleted 1965.
Wing span 126mm. Very good investment.   £35   £15   £7

No. 998 Bristol Britannia
Silver with white upper fuselage and rudder. Canadian
Pacific livery, blue letters and registration CF-CZA. Later
paint changed to metallic silver-grey. Metal wheels. Price
9/3. Issued 1959. Deleted 1975. Wing span 225mm.

	MB	MU	GC
Silver	£55	£35	£15
Metallic silver-grey	£35	£15	£10

No. 999 DH Comet Airliner
First colours were blue line trim and silver with wide
strip design, black numbers and letters. Then from 1963
metallic silver-grey finish. Originally issued as No. 702
De Havilland Comet. Renumbered 999 in 1955 with
G-ALYX. Deleted 1965. Price 6/4. Wing span 184mm.

	MB	MU	GC
No. 702	£50	£30	£15
No. 999 Silver	£40	£20	£10
No. 999 Silver-grey	£30	£15	£10

No. 1040 Sea King Helicopter
Diecast metal kit with screws and paint and no glue
required. Price £1.25. Issued 1972. Deleted 1977. Only
mint boxed price given for these models. Good prices
given for finished planes, depending on how good the
work is, although collectors like to buy the kits in original
condition.   £75   —   —

No. 1041 Hawker Hurricane Mk II
Diecast metal kit. Price £1.25. Issued 1973. Deleted 1976.   £75   —   —

No. 1042 Spitfire Mk II
Diecast metal kit. Price £1.25. Issued 1972. Deleted 1977.   £100   —   —

No. 1043 SEPECAT Jaguar
Diecast metal kit. Price £1.25. Issued 1974. Deleted 1976.   £50   —   —

No. 1044 Messerschmitt BF109E
Diecast metal kit of No. 726. Price £1.25. Issued 1972.
Deleted 1975.   £50   —   —

AEROPLANE CLOCKWORK MOTORS

No. 1 Aeroplane Clockwork Motor
Long running motor specially designed to fit fuselage of
models made with Nos. 1 and 2 Aeroplane Outfits and
Nos. 1 and 2 Special Aeroplane Outfits. Rotates at high
speed, greatly adding to the realism of the model it fits.
Price 1/9. Issued 1934. Deleted 1940.   £200   —   —

No. 2 Aeroplane Clockwork Motor
Powerful motor which, in addition to rotating the propeller, drives the landing wheels of Nos. 1 and 2 Aeroplane Outfits and Nos. 1 and 2 Special Aeroplane Outfits to make the machine taxi along the floor in a very realistic manner. Adjustable tail-wheel also supplied. Price 3/6. Issued 1935. Deleted 1940.   £200   —   —

AEROPLANE OUTFITS

No. 0 Aeroplane Outfit
Red and cream or blue and white. One of the first Dinky outfits produced. Designed for educational purposes and a great favourite in many schools. One could make an interesting range of aeroplane models, including high and low wing monoplanes, seaplanes and standard light biplanes. Price 4/6. Issued 1934. Deleted 1940. Neat picturesque box.   £350   —   —

No. 00 Aeroplane Outfit
Red and cream or blue and white. Contains good selection of aeroplane parts with which delightful models can be made. Price 3/3. Issued 1935. Deleted 1940.   £350   —   —

No. 00/a Aeroplane Outfit
Red and blue, red and gold or blue and gold. Price 4/6. Issued 1935. Deleted 1940.   £500   —   —

No. 1 Aeroplane Outfit
Red and cream or blue and white. Parts for making high standard quality planes etc. Price 7/6. Issued 1935. Deleted 1940.   £500   —   —

No. 1/a Aeroplane Constructor Access Outfit
Spare wings, wheels etc. Price 6/-. Issued 1936. Deleted 1940.   £400   —   —

No. 1/b Access Outfit
Spare parts to use with No. 1 Aeroplane Outfit. Price 5/6. Issued 1936. Deleted 1940.   £300   —   —

No. 2 Aeroplane Outfit
Blue and white or red and cream. This kit can make a much larger range of models than the No. 1 Aeroplane Outfit, including triple engined monoplanes and biplanes; a racing seaplane of the type which was used in the pre-war Schneider Trophy Contests; the particularly interesting Giant Plane Bombing Machine; and amphibians. Price 12/6. Issued 1936. Deleted 1940.   £750   —   —

No. 1 Special Aeroplane Outfit
Red and cream or blue and white. This kit could build
over 20 realistic models of various types of aircraft. The
range of special parts included mainplanes, fitted
ailerons, tail planes with elevators, movable rudder,
radial engine cowling etc. Special manual. Price 12/6.
Issued 1937. Deleted 1940.

£750 — —

No. 1a Special Aeroplane Accessory Outfit
Converts No. 1 Aeroplane Outfit into No. 2 Special
Aeroplane Outfit. Price 10/-. Issued 1937. Deleted 1940.

£400 — —

No. 2 Special Aeroplane Outfit
Rd and cream or blue and white. Contains a large range
of aircraft parts with which practically any type of model
aircraft of the pre-war period could be built. Rare manual
(worth £25) shows 44 examples of model aircraft with full
instructions. Price £1/1/-. Issued 1937. Deleted 1940.

£1250 — —

AMBULANCES

No. 253   Daimler Ambulance

MODEL	MB	MU	GC
No. 24a Ambulance Red chassis with grey body. Criss-cross chassis, plain radiator, open windows with high frontage wings. Price 9d. Issued April 1934. Deleted 1938. 102mm. DC/RT.	£350	—	—
No. 24a Ambulance Red chassis with grey body. Criss-cross chassis, open windows, high front wings and radiator with badge. Price 6d. Issued 1938. Deleted 1940. 102mm. DC/RT.	£200	—	—
No. 30f Ambulance Red chassis with grey body. Red crosses painted on sides and solid moulded chassis with holes for passengers. All windows open. Plain radiator. Price 9d. Issued August 1935. Deleted 1938. 101mm. DC/RT.	£150	£100	£75
No. 30f Ambulance Red chassis with grey body. Red crosses painted on sides with solid moulded chassis with holes for passengers. All windows open. Radiator with badge. Price 6d. Issued 1938. Deleted 1940. 101mm. DC/RT.	£150	£100	£75
No. 30F Ambulance Black chassis with grey or cream body. Red crosses painted on sides. Moulded chassis. All windows open. Price 4/11. Issued 1946. Deleted 1947. 99mm. DC/RT.	£200	£150	£75
No. 30F Ambulance Cream with slotted chassis for passengers. Price 4/11. Issued 1946. Deleted 1947. 99mm. DC/RT.	£30	£20	£15

No. 30F Ambulance
Dark grey. Otherwise as above. Rare. £70 £60 £50

No. 30F Ambulance
Black slotted chassis and white tyres. Otherwise as above. £30 £25 £20

No. 30F Ambulance
Black chassis with cream body. Red crosses painted on
sides, moulded chassis and no windows. Price 4/11.
Issued 1947. Deleted 1948. 99mm. DC/RT. £65 £50 £40

No. 30F Ambulance
Slotted chassis holes for passengers. White tyres. Green
chassis and no crosses on sides. Otherwise as above. Rare. £200 £150 £100

No. 30H Daimler Ambulance
Cream with red crosses. Price 3/3. Issued January 1950.
Renumbered 253 in 1954. Deleted 1960. 96mm.
DC/RT/TP. £75 £35 £15

No. 253 Daimler Ambulance
White with red crosses on sides. Also in cream with red
crosses. Price 2/9. Issued 1954. Deleted 1954. 96mm.
DC/T/RT. £60 £25 £15

No. 253 Daily Service Daimler Ambulance
Models which have the red cross missing are worth
perhaps five times more than the normal model. Price
3/11. Issued 1960. Deleted 1969. 96mm. DC/TP/RT. £50 £20 £5

No. 263 Superior Criterion Ambulance
'Ambulance' on windows. Two attendants, dummy roof
light and patient on stretcher. Opening doors. Price 8/6.
Issued September 1962. Deleted 1964. 127mm.
DC/TP/P/RT/LHD/SW/SS/FTS/S/W. Also made for
the US market. £55 £30 £10

No. 263A Superior Criterion Ambulance
White and cream with red side flashes, roof light, driver
and attendant and patient on stretcher. Opening rear
doors, silver hubs, bumpers etc. Price 8/11. Issued 1964.
Deleted 1972. 127mm. DC/RT/P. £65 £30 £10

No. 267 Superior Cadillac Ambulance
Cream and red with patient on stretcher. Opening doors
and roof light. Two-tone sides and red bonnet with silver
bumpers, headlights etc. 'Ambulance' on front, sides and
top. Price 13/11. Issued 1964. Deleted 1970. 152mm.
DC/P/RT. £55 £30 £15

No. 267A Superior Cadillac Ambulance
Completely all-red model, apart from cream flashes on
sides. Otherwise as above.

	MB	MU	GC
	£55	£30	£15

No. 268 Range Rover Ambulance
White. Price 15/6. Issued 1973. Deleted 1978. 109mm.
DC/P.

	MB	MU	GC
	£45	£25	£10

No. 274 Ford Transit Ambulance
White with opening side and rear doors, complete with
patient on stretcher. Ambulance roof sign and red cross
with 'Ambulance' on side. Three windows on each side
blacked out. Red cab interior. Price £1.25. Issued 1977.
Deleted 1980. 133mm. DC/P.

	MB	MU	GC
	£45	£25	£10

No. 276 Ford Transit Ambulance
White and orange with black cab interior. Red crosses on
side. 'Ambulance' on sides and roof sign. Opening doors.
Price 99p. Issued 1971. Deleted 1976. 129mm. DC/P.

	MB	MU	GC
	£50	£30	£10

No. 276 Ford Transit Ambulance
White. Price 99p. Issued 1971. Deleted 1978. 129mm.
DC/P.

	MB	MU	GC
	£45	£20	£5

**No. 277 Superior Criterion Ambulance with Flashing
Light**
Two-tone colours of dark blue and cream with two
drivers. Flashing red light on roof. White tyres. Silver
trim on bumpers, grille etc. Opening rear doors. Price
8/11. Issued 1969. Deleted 1972. 127mm. DC/P.

	MB	MU	GC
	£55	£30	£15

No. 277A Superior Criterion Ambulance
Metallic blue with white roof. 'Ambulance' on windows.
Two drivers and opening rear door. Flashing red light on
roof. Price 8/11. Issued December 1962. Deleted 1969.
127mm. TP/P/RT/DC/LHD/SS/FTS/SW.

	MB	MU	GC
	£60	£25	£10

No. 277B Superior Criterion Ambulance
All-blue body. Issued 1962. Deleted 1969. Otherwise as
above. Very rare.

	MB	MU	GC
	£75	£40	£20

No. 278 Vauxhall Ambulance
White with blue roof light. Red crosses on sides and
'Ambulance' on the front. Driver and silver bumpers,
grille etc. Price 7/-. Issued 1964. Deleted 1972. 87mm.
DC/P/RT.

	MB	MU	GC
	£30	£15	£10

No. 278A Vauxhall Victor Ambulance
White with red crosses on sides. Dummy blue roof light.
Opening rear doors. Patient on stretcher. Price 6/11.
Issued July 1964. Deleted 1972. 91mm.
SW/SS/FTS/S/DC/TP/RT.

	MB	MU	GC
	£25	£15	£10

No. 288 Superior Cadillac Ambulance
White with orange panels along bottom sides. Roof light
and ambulance sign with orange panel on bonnet. Patient
on stretcher. Price 4/11. Issued 1964. Deleted 1970.
152mm. DC/P.

	£50	£30	£15

No. 288 Superior Cadillac Ambulance
White with red base line and silver bumpers, hubs etc.
Patient on stretcher and opening doors at side and rear
The model with the opening side door is a factory flaw
and is rare. Price 4/11. Issued 1964. Deleted 1977. 142mm.
DC/P.

	MB	MU	GC
Without flaw	£45	£25	£10
With flaw	£150	—	—

No. 288 Superior Cadillac Ambulance
Cream, white and red. With opening rear doors, roof
lights and siren. Patient on stretcher. White interior. Price
7/11. Issued 1971. Deleted 1978. 152mm. DC/RT.

	£45	£20	£10

**No. 288A Denmark Special Superior Cadillac
Ambulance**
Black and white with roof light and sign, patient on
stretcher and opening doors at rear. Made for Danish
market. Equivalent price 8/11. Issued 1964. Deleted 1971.
152mm. DC/P. This rare model would be brought back
to Britain by tourists or sent by collectors on an exchange
basis.

	£150	—	—

BUSES AND COACHES

No. 949   Wayne School Bus Special

MODEL	MB	MU	GC
No. 27 Tram Car Red and white, advertising 'Lipton's Tea' on the sides. Price 6d. Issued July 1934. Deleted 1938. 77mm. DC. Very rare.	£300	£200	£100
No. 27 Tram Car Red and cream with Ovaltine adverts. Otherwise as above.	£300	£200	£100
No. 27 Tram Car Green and cream with Ovaltine adverts. Otherwise as above.	£400	£300	£200
No. 29 Double Decker Bus Green or yellow with white roof. 'Marmite' on sides. This model also had various other adverts connected with it. The models with really high values are those advertising special events such as exhibitions and 'The Great Circus Coming to Town'. The models have metal wheels and even though suffering greatly from metal fatigue they bring a fantastic price in the swapmeets and top-class sale rooms throughout the world. Price 6d. Issued July 1934. Deleted 1938. 69mm. DC.	£500	£400	£300

No. 29 Double Decker Bus
Various two-tone colours exist in this model range. The
most common are blue and green, although prices vary
according to colours. Open rear window. Price 6d. Issued
April 1935. Deleted 1940. 88mm. DC/RT.

	MB	MU	GC
Blue and green	£350	£250	£150
Yellow and brown	£500	£400	£250
Red and cream	£650	£500	£350

No. 29 Double Decker Bus
Yellow with 'Marmite' on sides. Otherwise as above. £400 £350 £250

No. 29b Streamlined Bus
No advertising on this model. Open rear windows. Price
6d. Issued April 1936. Deleted 1937. 88mm. DC/RT. £90 £50 £10

No. 26B Streamlined Bus
Cream and red or green. No rear windows. Price 2/6.
Issued January 1948. Deleted 1950. 88mm. DC/RT. £250 £150 £50

No. 29c Double Decker Bus
Blue with white or cream roof. 'Dunlop Tyres' on sides.
Stairs on rear platform. Type 1 radiator (AEC). Price 1/-.
Issued early 1938. Deleted 1939. 100mm. DC/RT. Highly
sought after. £500 — —

No 29c Double Decker Bus
Red and cream, or green and white, or red and grey
(which is very rare). Stairs on rear platform. Type 1
radiator (AEC). Adverts on sides: 'Beecham Pills' and
'Wild Woodbine the Great Little Cigarette'. Price 1/-.

	MB	MU	GC
Issued March 1938. Deleted 1940. 100mm. DC/RT.	£600	—	—
Red and grey (with Woodbine advert)	£5000	—	—

No. 29C Double Decker Bus
Green or red bodywork and cream or grey top. Model has
type 1 radiator (AEC) and cutaway front mudguard with
no stairs. Various adverts connected with model, and
many with no adverts at all. The models with adverts are
worth considerably more than those without. Price 2/10.
Issued October 1947. Deleted 1955. 101mm. DC/RT. £150 £75 £35

No. 29C Double Decker Bus
Green with cream top. 'Dunlop the World's Master Tyre'
on sides. With type 2 radiator (Guy). Straight front
mudguards. Price 3/9. Issued 1950. Deleted 1954.
Renumbered 290 in same year. Deleted 1964. 101mm.
DC/RT. £100 £50 £30

No 29dz Autobus
Dark brown or silver. Model was advertised in the
Meccano Magazine in the 1930s, but it was never officially
sold in England. Advertised price 10d. Issued 1937/39.
Deleted 1940. Very rare.

£1000 — —

No 29E Single Decker Bus
Cream with blue flashes, or green with dark green
flashes, or blue with dark blue flashes. Price 3/3. Issued
March 1948. Deleted 1952. 113mm. DC/RT/TP.

£130 £60 £25

No. 29F Single Decker Bus
Red with dark red and silver flashes. This observation
coach has 'Airport Special' on sides. Price 3/3. Issued July
1950. Deleted 1951. 112mm. DC/TP/RT. Rare.

£75 £35 £25

No. 29F Observation Coach
Grey with red flashes. 'Observation Coach' on sides. Price
3/3. Issued July 1950. Renumbered 280 in 1954. Deleted
1964. 112mm. DC/TP/RT.

£160 £80 £30

No. 29G Luxury Coach
Fawn with orange flashes. Price 3/1. Issued April 1951.
Renumbered 281 in 1954. Deleted 1964. 113mm.
DC/TP/RT.

£250 £90 £35

No. 29H Duple Roadmaster Coach
Blue with silver flashes. Prices 4/4. Issued November
1952. Renumbered 282 in 1954. Deleted 1964. 119mm.
DC/TP/RT.

£65 £30 £20

No. 111 Cinderella's Coach
Gold with four white horses and driver. Driver in pink
with girl figure inside. Made because of the film The
Slipper and the Rose. Price £3.75. Issued 1977. Deleted
1978. 242mm. DC/P.

£50 £15 £10

No. 111 Cinderella's Coach
Gold with four black or white horses. Driver and girl
figure inside. Special one-off model. Price £7.50. Issued
1977. Deleted 1978. 242mm. DC. Very rare.

£100 £75 £50

No. 248 Continental Touring Coach
One of the best investments Dinky produced in the 1970s
period. Coach is the type which carried the various
football teams around the country. Model is available in
the various soccer-team liveries. Collect them all if you
are lucky enough to find them. Basic colour is white. The
value depends on what soccer-club colours are connected
with it. Price £1.95. Issued 1978. Deleted 1980. 164mm.
DC/P.

£100 £50 £20

No. 280 Observation Coach
Cream with red flashes. Renumbering of 29F. Price 3/1.
Issued 1954. Deleted 1960. 112mm. DC/TP/RT.   £100   £50   £30

No. 281 Modern Coach
Fawn with orange flashes or maroon with cream flashes.
Price 2/11. Issued 1954. Deleted 1960. 113mm.
DC/TP/RT.   £100   £50   £30

No. 281 Luxury Coach
Blue with orange or fawn flashes. Deep yellow wheels,
black tyres, silver radiator grille and lights. Price 3/6.
Issued 1954. Deleted 1960. 113mm. DC/TP/RT.   £100   £50   £30

No. 282 Duple Roadmaster Coach
Blue with silver flashes, or red with silver flashes. Known
as the 'Leyland Royal Tiger Bus'. Price 3/5. Issued April
1954. Deleted 1961. 119mm. DC/TP/RT.
Blue with silver flashes   £150   £75   £25
Red with silver flashes   £150   £100   £50

No. 283 BOAC Coach
Blue with white roof. 'British Overseas Airways
Corporation' and 'BOAC' on sides. Price 4/2. Issued
October 1956. Deleted 1963. 120mm. DC/TP/RT.   £100   £50   £25

No. 283 Single Decker Bus
Red with long wide white flashes on sides and with 'Red
Arrow'. Silver wheels, headlights etc. Price 99p. Issued
1971. Deleted 1977. 167mm. DC/P.   £75   £45   £25

No. 283 Single Decker Bus
Metallic red with automatic opening doors and bell. Price
99p. Issued 1971. Deleted 1977. 167mm. DC/RT/P.   £100   £50   £25

No. 289 London Transport Routemaster Bus
Red with driver and conductress. There are many adverts
connected with this model. Although there are other
colours or liveries, the general colour is red. Any collector
should consult an expert, or write to me c/o the
publishers with regard to the various values on adverts
etc. The more common adverts are 'London Transport',
'Esso Petrol', 'Tern Shirts' and 'Dunlop'. Price 4/2.
Increased to 8/11 after first year. Issued June 1964.
Deleted 1966. 121mm. SW/DC/P/RT.   £75   £35   £20

No. 289 London Routemaster Bus
Red with driver and conductress. Full destination signs
on front and rear. Promotional models were a great
attraction and this edition is very rare. 'Festival of

	MB	MU	GC
London Stores' on sides. Price 9/11. Issued 1965. Deleted 1966. 121mm. DC/RT/P.	£500	—	—

No. 289 Routemaster Bus
Red with 'Esso Safety Grip Tyre' on sides. Price £1.25. Issued 1971. Deleted 1978. 121mm. DC/P.

	£50	£25	£15

No. 289 Routemaster Bus
Red with 'Kenning Car...Van & Truck Rental' or 'Hire' placed on a wide purple background with silver and plastic trim. Price £1.25. Issued 1971. Deleted 1978. 121mm. DC/P.

	£75	£35	£20

No. 289 London Routemaster Bus
Red with 'Esso Grip' or 'Esso Safety Grip Tyres'. Also a new introduction of the three-colour variations of 'Schweppes' advert. Cream, white or grey. Otherwise as above. Price £1.50. Issued 1976. Deleted 1978. 121mm. DC/P.

	£30	£20	£15

No. 289 London Routemaster Bus (Promotional)
Only a very limited number of these models were made. Otherwise as above except where indicated.

	MB	MU	GC
Gold with 'Madame Tussaud'	£200	£150	£75
Red with 'Madame Tussaud'	£250	£100	£75
Red with 'Jackson's the Tailor'	£500	£250	£100
Red with 'Woolworth's Stores the Wonder Store for All the Family'	£600	£300	£150

No. 289 London Routemaster Bus
Red with driver and conductress. 'Schweppes' and 'London Transport' on sides. Price £1.50. Issued 1976. Deleted 1978. 121mm. DC/P.

	£100	£50	£25

No. 289 London Routemaster Bus
Red with 'Schweppes' and designs on the side. Model has thick black or gold lines around wording. Only a few finished in this style for a special order. Price £1.50. Issued 1976. Deleted 1978. 121mm. DC/P.

	£100	£75	£30

No. 290 Double Decker Bus
Red with cream roof and 'Dunlop the World's Master tyre' on sides. This was a type 2 radiator (Guy). These models come with or without small headboards on the roof at the front; however, the values are almost the same. Collectors look for these models in all parts of the world. Price 4/2. Issued 1957. Deleted 1963. 103mm. DC/TP/RT.

	£75	£50	£25

No 290 Dunlop Double Decker Bus
Green with cream roof. Type 3 radiator (Leyland). Price
4/2. Issued 1957. Deleted 1963. 103mm. DC/RT/TP.

	£250	£100	£50

No 291 London Bus (Exide)
Red with 'Exide Batteries' on sides. No. '73' on
destination plates. Type 3 radiator (Leyland). Price 4/2.
Issued 1960. Deleted 1963. 103mm. DC/RT.
Note: For more details on the Atlantean Bus see page 1.

	£250	£100	£50

No. 291 Atlantean City Bus
Orange and white with opening doors. Price 8/11. Issued
1960. Deleted 1966. 123mm. DC/RT/TP.

	£75	£50	£25

No. 291A Atlantean City Bus (Kennings)
Red and white with opening doors. Price 8/11. Issued
1960. Deleted 1966. 123mm. DC/RT/TP.

	£100	£50	£25

No. 292 Atlantean Bus
Red and white with 'Regent', 'Corporation Transport'
etc. Price 7/10. Issued August 1962. Deleted 1966.
120mm. DC/P/RT/SW/D/S/W.

	£150	£75	£35

No. 292A Atlantean Bus
Red and white with 'Ribble Transport' or 'Midland Red'.
Price 7/10. Issued July 1962. Deleted 1966. 120mm.
DC/P/RT/SW/D/S/W.

	£100	£50	£25

No. 293 Atlantean Bus
Green and white with 'BP is the Key to Better Motoring'
and 'Corporation Transport'. Price 7/10. Issued August
1963. Deleted 1966. 120mm. SW/D/S/W/DC/RT/P.

	£100	£50	£25

No. 293 Atlantean Bus
Green and cream with 'BP is the Key to Better Motoring'
in yellow and cream. Price 7/11. Issued 1963. Deleted
1966. 121mm. D/DC/P/RT.

	£75	£50	£25

No. 293A Swiss Postal Bus
Green with orange or cream roof and white interior. Also
yellow with cream roof. Price £1.35. Issued 1975/6.
Deleted 1978. 119mm. DC/P.

	£500	£150	£50

No. 295 Atlantean Bus
Yellow and black with the first version of 'Yellow Pages,
Let Your Fingers do the Talking'. 'Yellow Pages' in
reverse on the headboard. Price £1.35. Issued 1973.
Deleted 1976. 121mm. DC/P.

	£100	£50	£35

No. 295 Atlantean Bus
Yellow and black. As previous model but with 'Yellow
Pages' correct on headboard. Price £1.35. Issued 1973.
Deleted 1976. 121mm. DC.

| | £75 | £35 | £25 |

No. 295 Atlas Standard Kenebrake Bus
Light blue and grey. Windows, steering wheel, seating
and four-wheel suspension. Price 3/9. Issued May 1960.
Deleted 1969. 86mm. DC/P/RT.

| | £75 | £35 | £25 |

No. 295 Atlantean Bus
Yellow and black. Black band around the bus
immediately above the doors with 'Yellow Pages' in
white. Price £1.35. Issued 1976. Deleted 1977. 121mm.
DC/P. Very rare.

| | £500 | £250 | £75 |

No. 295A Atlas Kenebrake Bus
Silver with 'Butlins Holiday Camp Special' on sides. Price
7/11. Issued 1968/69. Deleted 1971. 90mm. DC/P.

| | £500 | £150 | £75 |

No. 296 Luxury Coach
Royal blue with white or cream interior. Silver wheels
and trim. Price 75p. Issued 1972. Deleted 1975. 119mm.
DC/P.

| | £75 | £45 | £25 |

No. 297 Silver Jubilee Bus
Silver and black with 'The Queen's Silver Jubilee 1977' on
sides. Price £1.50. Issued and deleted 1977. 123mm.
DC/P.

| | £100 | £50 | £25 |

No. 297 Silver Jubilee Bus
Silver with 'National' in red and blue letters on each side.
Otherwise as above. Price £1.50. Issued and deleted 1977.
123mm. DC/P.

| | £100 | £50 | £25 |

No. 297 Silver Jubilee Bus
Silver with 'Woolworth's Stores, Everybody Needs One!'
Promotional model. Price £1.50. Issued and deleted 1977.
123mm. DC/P.

| | £100 | £50 | £25 |

No. 306 Luxury Coach Viceroy
Metallic red. Price 96p. Issued 1973. Deleted 1975.
119mm. DC/P.

| | £100 | £50 | £25 |

No. 949 Wayne School Bus Special
Orange with red trim and 'School Bus' on front. Price
12/9. Issued 1961. Deleted 1964. 195mm. DC/P/TP/RT.

| | £250 | £100 | £50 |

Green with white trim. Very rare.

| | £500 | £200 | £75 |

No. 952 Vega Major Luxury Coach
Grey and maroon. 'Lowland' on sides. Six wheels,
flashing indicators and opening boot. Price £1/1/-.
Issued January 1964. Deleted 1969. 242mm.

SW/SS/S/W/DC/P/RT.	£150	£50	£25
Metallic	£75	£50	£25

No. 952 Vega Major Luxury Coach
Cream and chocolate or very dark brown with blue and
white seats. Silver bumpers, grille etc. Opening boot and
flashing indicators. Price £1/1/-. Issued 1968. Deleted

1971. 245mm. DC/P/RT.	£250	£100	£50
Metallic. Rare.	£400	£150	£75

No. 952 Vega Major Luxury Coach
White or off-white and dark red. Flashing indicators.
Opening boot. Price £1/1/-. Issued 1971. Deleted 1973.

245mm. DC/P.	£100	£50	£25

No. 953 Continental Touring Coach
Pale blue with white roof. Also medium red with cream
roof and pale green with white roof. Both with 'Dinky
Continental Tours' on sides. Six wheels and the same
casting as No. 949. Price 13/6. Issued January 1963.

Deleted 1964. 242mm. SW/W/S/DC/P/RT/TP.	£100	£75	£50
Medium red with cream roof. Rare.	£450	£300	£150
Pale green with white roof. Rare.	£500	£350	£200

CARAVANS

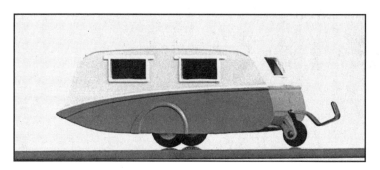

No. 190 Caravan

MODEL	MB	MU	GC
No. 30g Caravan			
Two-tone green with two wheels and towing hook. Price 6d. Issued April 1936. Deleted 1940. 81mm. DC/RT/H.	£100	£50	£30
No. 30G Caravan			
Orange and cream with two wheels and tow-bar. 'Caravan Club' shown on small plaque in front. Price 2/6. Issued January 1948. Deleted 1950. 81mm. DC/RT.	£130	£60	£40
No. 117 Caravan			
Blue and cream. Four berth type with glass roof and full interior fitments. Price 6/-. Issued August 1963. Deleted 1965. 118mm. DC/RT/P/TP/SS/H.	£35	£15	£10
No. 117 Four Berth Caravan with Transparent Roof			
Yellow with red interior, white door and tow-bar. Fine interior fittings. Price 7/-. Issued 1965. Deleted 1968. 132mm. DC/P/TP/RT.	£30	£15	£10
No. 188 Four Berth Caravan			
Green and yellow with windows and interior fittings. Price 5/6. Issued April 1961. Deleted 1963. 132mm. DC/TP/P/RT/SS/W/OD/S/HG. Rare.	£50	£20	£10
No. 188A Four Berth Caravan			
Cream and blue or white and blue. Price 5/6. Issued 1961. Deleted 1963. 132mm. DC/TP/P/RT.	£55	£30	£20

No. 190 Caravan
Cream and orange with tow-bar. Suitable for attachment
to almost every model car or Land Rover that Dinky ever
made. Price 3/8. Issued May 1956. Deleted 1960. 118mm.

	MB	MU	GC
DC/TP/P/RT.	£35	£15	£10
Red and brilliant white. Rare.	£150	£75	£50

No. 190A Caravan
Cream and yellow with tow-bar. Price 3/8. Issued July
1956. Deleted 1961. 118mm. DC/TP/P/RT.   £40   £20   £10

CRANES, EXCAVATORS, BULLDOZERS AND CONSTRUCTION SITE VEHICLES

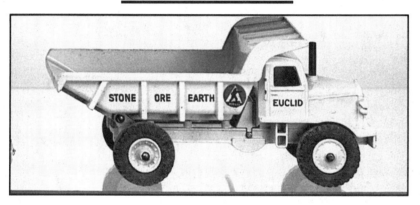

No. 965   Euclid Rear Dump Truck

MODEL	MB	MU	GC
No. 25c Flat Truck Dark brown or green with open chassis and tinplate radiator (Type 1) and no lights. Price 9d. Issued 1934. Deleted 1940. 105mm. DC/TP/RT. Never individually boxed.	—	£350	£150
No. 25c Flat Truck Green with open chassis, diecast radiator (Type 2) and lights. Price 9d. Issued 1938. Deleted 1940. 105mm. DC/RT/TP. Never individually boxed.	—	£250	£100
No. 25C Flat Truck Green with plain chassis, diecast radiator (Type 3) and lights. Price 1/6. Issued 1946. Deleted 1947. 105mm. DC/RT. Never individually boxed.	—	£125	£50

BUILDING AND CONSTRUCTION VEHICLES	MB	MU	GC

No. 25C Flat Truck
Orange with moulded chassis, diecast radiator (Type 4), lights and bumpers. Price 2/-. Issued 1947. Deleted 1950. 110mm. DC/RT. Never individually boxed.

	—	£95	£45

No. 25M Bedford End Tipper
Orange, red and cream with tail board hinges and tipping handle. Price 5/9. Issued March 1948. Deleted 1954 when renumbered 410. 98mm. DC/TP/RT/ Never individually boxed.

	—	£95	£45

No. 25X Breakdown Lorry with Working Crane
Orange and green with 'Dinky Service' on sides. Price 5/6. Issued 1950. Deleted 1954 when renumbered 430. 123mm. DC/TP/RT.

	£250	£100	£50

No. 30e Bedford Breakdown Van
Red, green or grey with rear window in cab and wire hook on crane. Price 9d. Issued August 1935. Deleted 1940. 92mm. DC/RT. Never individually boxed.

	—	£275	£100

No. 30E Bedford Breakdown Van
Red, green or grey. No rear window, although I have seen models which have. Wire hook on crane. Price 5/11. Issued 1946. Deleted 1948. 92mm. DC/RT.

	£95	£40	£20

No. 30M Rear Tipping Wagon
Orange with handle tips and tailboard hinges. Price 2/11. Issued 1950. Deleted 1954 when renumbered 414. 99mm. DC/TP/RT.

	£65	£20	£10

No. 380 Convoy Skip Truck
Green and orange with thick black bumpers. Yellow chassis with orange rear from 1978. First of five large toys. Price 97p. Issued 1977. Deleted 1980. 112mm. D.

	£50	£20	£10

No. 382 Convoy Dumper Truck
Yellow chassis and cab with white interior and orange body. Black bumpers. Price 75p. Issued 1977. Deleted 1980. 118mm.

	£50	£20	£10

No. 382 Convoy Dumper Truck
Red cab and red chassis with fawn body. Price 95p. Issued 1978. Deleted 1980. 118mm.

	£40	£15	£5

No. 410 Bedford End Tipper
Brown and yellow or blue and yellow. Rear tips by handle and tailboard hinges. Renumbering of 25M. Price 5/3. Issued 1954/55. Deleted 1963. 97mm. DC/TP/RT.

	£95	£40	£20

No. 410 Bedford End Tipper
Red and cream. Exactly as No. 410 but new colours and
windows. Price 6/11. Issued 1963/64. Deleted 1970.
97mm. DC/TP/RT.   £85   £20   £10

No. 430 Commer Breakdown Lorry
Working crane. Orange and green with 'Dinky Service'
on sides. Renumbering of 25X. Price 4/11. Issued 1954.
Deleted 1964. 123mm. DC/TP/RT.   £125   £50   £25

No. 430 Commer Breakdown Lorry
Red and grey with windows and 'Dinky Service' on sides.
Price 7/6. Issued 1964. Deleted 1969. 123mm.
DC/TP/RT/P.   £95   £30   £15

No. 430 Johnson 2-Ton Dumper
Orange chassis, red skip, blue driver and silver hubs.
Price £1.75. Issued 1976. Deleted 1980. 106mm. DC/P. £55   £20   £10

No. 432 Foden Tipping Lorry
White cab, lemon body and lemon plastic wheels on black
chassis and lemon bumpers. Price £1.25. Issued 1976.
Deleted 1980. 175mm. DC/P.   £55   £20   £10

No. 434 Bedford TK Crash Truck
White with green flash. 'Top Rank Motorway Services'
on sides. Operating winch and four wheels. Price 7/11.
Issued April 1964. Deleted 1970. 122mm. DC/RT/P.   £85   £40   £20

No. 435 Bedford TK Tipper
Light grey, blue and orange. Rear tips and three flaps let
down. Six wheels. Price 7/11. Issued May 1964. Deleted
1971. 120mm. DC/RT/P.   £95   £40   £20

No. 437 Muir Hill 2WL Loader
Yellow with red wheels and driver. Silver-grey or grey
trim. Also black plastic wheels. Price 12/11. Issued 1970.
Deleted 1978. 121mm. DC/P.   £50   £20   £10

No. 437 Muir Hill 2WL Loader
Red with full working parts. Price 8/6. Issued 1962.
Deleted 1979. 121mm. DC/P.   £50   £20   £10

No. 438 Ford D800 Tipper Truck
Yellow body on tipper. Grey chassis with yellow wheels.
Red cab with opening doors and white interior. Hinged
tailboard. Price 12/11. Issued 1970. Replaced in 1977 by
No. 440 which had sealed doors. Deleted 1978. 132mm. £50   £20   £10

	MB	MU	GC
No. 439 Ford D800 Snow Plough Tipper Truck Purple, red and yellow with white wheels and tipping body. Price 12/11. Issued 1971. Deleted 1977. 194mm. DC/P.	£95	£50	£20
No. 440 Ford D800 Tipper Truck Orange and lemon with white cab interior and grey chassis. Price £1.25. Issued 1977. Deleted 1978. 132mm. DC/P.	£50	£20	£10
No. 442 Land Rover Breakdown Crane White and red with 'Motorway Rescue' on sides. Price £1.25. Issued 1973. Deleted 1980. 121mm. DC/P.	£75	£40	£20
No. 442 Land Rover Breakdown Crane White and red. Made for Dutch market only. Issued 1974. Deleted 1978. 121mm. DC/P.	£275	£150	£50
No. 561 Blaw Knox Bulldozer Red with lifting blades and rubber treads. Price 11/6. Issued January 1949. Deleted 1949. Renumbered 961 in 1954. Deleted 1975. 138mm. DC/TP.	£60	£30	£15
No. 562 Muir Hill Dumper Truck Yellow. Price 9/-. Issued September 1948. Deleted 1954 when renumbered 962. 105mm. DC/TP.	£65	£30	£15
No. 563 Heavy Tractor Red. Also blue with pale blue wheels and green tracks (worth double). Rubber tracks. Price 6/9. Issued 1948. Deleted 1954 when renumbered 963.	£65	£30	£15
No. 564 Elevator Loader Yellow and blue with all working parts and rubber treads. Price £1/2/6. Issued 1962. Renumbered 964 in 1954. 230mm. DC.	£45	£20	£10
No. 571 Coles Mobile Crane Yellow and black. Crane works by handle. Price 9/11. Issued December 1949. Renumbered 971 in 1954. 160mm. DC/TP/RT.	£95	£50	£25
No. 752 Goods Yard Crane Blue and yellow with working crane. Price 13/9. Issued February 1953. Renumbered 973 in 1954. Base 100mm. 195mm high. DC.	£85	£30	£15
No. 924 Aveling Barford Centaur Dump Truck Red cab, white interior and yellow tipper with hydraulic system. Red hubs and thick black ribbed wheels. Price £1.25. Issued 1973. Deleted 1978. 180mm. DC/P.	£65	£30	£15

No. 958 Snow Plough with Guy Warrior Chassis
Yellow and black. Four wheels with one spare and blue
roof light. Lifting plough blade and hinged tailboard.
Price 12/6. Issued January 1961. Deleted 1966. 195mm.
DC/TP/RT.   £75   £30   £15

No. 959 Foden Dump Truck with Bulldozer Blade
Red and silver with six wheels and lifting blade. Rear tips.
Price 16/3. Issued October 1961. Deleted 1969. 169mm.
DC/RT.   £95   £50   £25

No. 960 Albion Lorry Concrete Mixer
Orange, yellow and blue or red, yellow and blue (worth
at least double). Cement hopper rotates and tips. Six
wheels and one spare. Price 8/9. Issued August 1960.
Deleted 1969. 128mm. DC/TP/RT/P.   £75   £40   £20

No. 961 Blaw Knox Bulldozer
Red and later yellow. Also green and orange (worth
double). Driver, elevating blade and rubber tracks.
Renumbering of 561. Price 12/6. Issued January 1955.
Deleted 1964. 138mm. DC/TP.   £75   £50   £20

No. 962 Muir Hill Dumper Truck
Yellow model had metal hubs and black rubber tyres
from 1962. Price 6/9. Issued 1955. Deleted 1964. 105mm.   £65   £30   £15

No. 963 Blaw Knox Heavy Tractor
Red, then yellow and later orange. Rubber tracks and
driver. Renumbering of 563. Price 7/9. Issued January
1955. Deleted 1959. 116mm. DC/TP.   £65   £40   £20

No. 963 Road Grader
Red, yellow and black with silver shovel and hubs. Price
£1.55. Issued 1970. Deleted 1978. 238mm. DC/P.   £55   £20   £10

No. 964 Elevator Loader
Yellow or blue (worth double). All-working parts and
rubber tracks on loader. Renumbering of 564. Price 18/-.
Issued January 1955. Deleted 1969. 230mm. DC.   £65   £30   £15

No. 965 Euclid Rear Dump Truck
Yellow with background of red or grey (worth double).
'Euclid Stone Ore Earth' on door and sides. Price 9/6.
Issued 1955. Deleted 1956. 142mm. DC/RT.   £95   £50   £20

No. 966 Multi-Bucket Unit
Yellow with grey buckets. Six wheels and all working
parts. Price 10/9. Issued December 1960. Deleted 1964.
115mm. DC/RT.   £65   £30   £15

BUILDING AND CONSTRUCTION VEHICLES	MB	MU	GC

No. 967 Muir Hill Loader and Trencher
Orange and black or yellow and black. Price £1.45. Issued
1973. Deleted 1978. 163mm. DC/P.

| | £65 | £30 | £15 |

No. 970 Jones Fleetmaster Cant Crane
Red and white or metallic red and white from 1971. 'Jones
Fleetmaster' on side and 'Jones' shown clearly on red disc
on spare wheel. Price £1/1/-. Issued 1967. Deleted 1977.
Red and white
Metallic red and white

| Red and white | £75 | £40 | £20 |
| Metallic red and white | £60 | £30 | £15 |

No. 971 Coles Mobile Crane
Yellow and black. Crane worked by handle.
Renumbering of 571. Price 9/11. Issued January 1955.
Deleted 1966. 160mm. DC/TP/H.

| | £60 | £30 | £15 |

No. 972 Coles 20-Ton Lorry Mounted Crane
Red and orange with black and white stripes. Driver,
working crane, orange wheels and black tyres. 'Coles
Giant Crane' on sides. Price £1/0/3. Issued 1955. Deleted
1970. 245mm. DC/RT/TP.

| | £95 | £50 | £25 |

No. 973 Goods Yard Crane
Yellow or blue (worth double). Price 11/6. Issued January
1955. Deleted 1959. Base 100mm. 195mm high. DC.

| | £75 | £30 | £15 |

No. 973 Eaton Vale Articulated Tractor Shovel
Red and mustard yellow with silver hubs and large black
ribbed wheels. Price £1.35. Issued 1973. Deleted 1978.
178mm. DC/P.

| | £55 | £20 | £10 |

No. 975 Ruston Bucyrus Excavator
Red, yellow and grey with rubber tracks. Price £1/7/6.
Issued October 1963. Deleted 1968. 190mm. DC/TP/P.

| | £175 | £50 | £30 |

No. 976 Michigan 180-111 Tractor Dozer
Yellow and orange with driver. Removable cab and
engine hatch. 'Michigan' on sides. Price 18/11. Issued
1968. Deleted 1977. 147mm. DC/P.

| | £75 | £30 | £15 |

No. 977 Servicing Platform Vehicle
Red and cream with folding down side supports,
elevating crane etc. Six wheels and one spare. The chassis
is an international size. Price 13/6. Issued September
1960. Deleted 1964. 197mm. DC.

| | £125 | £50 | £25 |

No. 977 Shovel Dozer
Yellow and black with red roof and red and silver shovel.
Silver or black plastic tracks. Price £1.99. Issued 1973.
Deleted 1978. 151mm. DC/P.

| | £50 | £20 | £10 |

BUILDING AND CONSTRUCTION VEHICLES	MB	MU	GC

No. 980 Coles Hydra Truck 150T
Dark grey and mustard. Silver hubs and working crane.
Price £2.25. Issued 1973. Deleted 1978. 210mm. DC/P.

	£75	£30	£15

No. 984 Atlas Digger
Yellow. Price £2.25. Issued 1974. Deleted 1978. 247mm.
DC/P.

	£75	£40	£20

No. 986 Mighty Antar Low Loader and Propeller
Red and grey with driver and plastic propeller load. 6 x
6 wheels. Price 14/11. Issued June 1959. Deleted 1964.
295mm. DC/RT/P.

	£175	£80	£40

No. 3209 Mogul Heavy Duty Dumper
Orange and black with white plastic wheels. Price £1.75.
Issued 1974. Deleted 1980. 330mm. DC/P.

	£50	£20	£10

No. 3299 Mogul Mobile Crane
Bright lemon and black with silver wheels. Price £2.25.
Issued 1974. Deleted 1980. 337mm. DC/P.

	£50	£20	£10

DINKY FIGURES

MODEL	MB	MU	GC
No. 12D Telegraph Messenger Blue. Price 3d. Issued 1939. Deleted 1940. 35mm. Never individually boxed. Delivered to shops in boxes of six.	£40	—	—
No. 12E Postman Blue with bag and badge. Price 3d. Issued 1938. Deleted 1940. 35mm. DC. Box of six.	£40	—	—
No. 42C Point Duty Policeman in White Coat Price 3d. Issued August 1936. Deleted 1940. 42mm. DC. Box of six.	£40	—	—
No. 42D Point Duty Policeman in Blue Uniform Price 4d. Issued August 1936. Deleted 1940. 40mm. DC. Box of six.	£40	—	—
No. 43C RAC Guide Directing Traffic Red sash etc. Price 3d. Issued October 1935. Deleted 1940. 37mm. DC. Box of six.	£40	—	—
No. 43D RAC Guide Saluting Red sash etc. Price 3d. Issued October 1935. Deleted 1940. 36mm. DC. Box of six.	£40	—	—
No. 44C AA Guide Directing Traffic Blue sash etc. Price 3d. Issued October 1935. Deleted 1940. Box of six.	£40	—	—
No. 44D AA Guide Saluting Blue sash etc. Price 3d. Issued October 1935. Deleted 1940. 36mm. DC. Box of six.	£40	—	—
No. 007 Set of Two Petrol Pump Attendants Male and female with white coats. Price 10d. Issued October 1960. Deleted 1967. Average height 35mm. P.	£15	£8	£4
No. 008 Fire Station Personnel Set of six figures in blue uniforms. Length of hose. Price 3/-. Issued April. Deleted 1964. 35mm. P.	£25	£10	£5
No. 009 Service Station Personnel Set of eight figures mainly in white. Price 3/9. Issued June 1962. Deleted 1967. Average height 35mm. P.	£35	£15	£10

No. 010 Road Maintenance Set
Six figures in various colours with set of road signs etc.
Price 5/-. Issued May 1962. Deleted 1964. Average height
35mm.

	MB	MU	GC
No. 010 Road Maintenance Set	£15	£10	£5

No. 012 Postman
Blue with bag and badge etc. Price 9d. Issued April 1952.
Deleted 1960. Average height 35mm. DC. Box of six. — £40 — —

Set No. 1 Station Staff
Six figures. Price 1/6. Issued 1934. Deleted 1940. — £30 — —

Set No. 2 Farmyard Animals
Six figures. Price 2/-. Issued 1934. Deleted 1940. Reissued
1948. Deleted 1956. — £30 — —

Set No. 3 Passengers
Price 1/-. Issued 1934. Deleted 1940. — £30 — —

Set No. 4 Engineering Staff
Six figures. Price 1/6. Issued 1934. Deleted 1940. — £30 — —

Set No. 5 Train and Hotel Staff
Six figures. Price 2/-. Issued 1934. Deleted 1940. Reissued
1948. Deleted 1960. — £30 — —

Set No. 6 Shepherd Set
Six figures. Price 2/-. Issued 1934/35. Deleted 1940.
Reissued 1948. Deleted 1960. — £50 — —

DUBLO DINKIES

The Dublo Dinky models were first made with the railway enthusiast in mind. In no way were the little toys copied from the Matchbox series, as was believed by many people. Frank Hornby had thought of tiny pocket toys long before the Matchbox range had been conceived. It so happened that plans were found by the takeover firm of Lines Bros and the Dublo Dinky was born. They had a two year production and the run was very successful. Today the models are always in constant demand by collectors and, in fact, very hard to come by. To me these little items were special, particularly No. 068 Royal Mail Van. They are equally special to thousands of collectors in many parts of the world and will be a real investment to anyone who has the set mint boxed.

MODEL	MB	MU	GC
No. 060 Milk Wagon One of the first Meccano-Dinky models to go with train sets and railway items. Reported but not verified in dark brown or cream. Possibly pre-war. Very rare.	£1000	£200	£100
No. 061 Ford Prefect Fawn or grey (worth at least treble). Smooth grey plastic wheels and tyres. Price 1/6. Issued March 1958. Deleted 1960. 58mm. DC/TP/PW.	£65	£20	£10
No. 062 Singer Roadster Orange or fawn with red seats (worth double). Smooth grey plastic wheels and tyres. Price 1/6. Issued 1958. Deleted 1960. 50mm. DC/PW.	£65	£20	£10
No. 063 Commer Van Blue with plastic wheels. Price 1/6. Issued March 1958. Deleted 1960. 53mm. DC/TP.	£95	£30	£15
No. 064 Austin Lorry Green with smooth grey or ribbed black plastic wheels and tyres. Price 1/6. Issued December 1957. Deleted 1962. 64mm. DC/PW.	£75	£30	£15
No. 065 Morris Pick-Up Red with smooth grey plastic wheels and tyres. Price 1/9. Issued December 1957. Deleted 1960. 54mm. DC/PW.	£55	£20	£10

No. 066 Bedford Flat Truck
Grey or brown (worth at least treble). Smooth grey plastic
wheels and tyres. Price 1/11. Issued December 1957.
Deleted 1960. 107mm. DC/PW.   £65   £20   £10

No. 067 Austin Taxi
Blue and cream with ribbed grey or black plastic wheels.
Price 2/5. Issued March 1959. Deleted 1967. 60mm.
DC/PW. One of the more sought after models and a good
investment.   £95   £30   £15

No. 068 Royal Mail Van
Red with 'Royal Mail' and 'E2R' on the side. Plastic
windows and ribbed black plastic wheels and tyres. Price
2/2. Issued April 1959. Deleted 1964. 48mm. DC. I
consider this to be the best investment of all the Dublo
range.   £95   £30   £15

No. 069 Massey Harris Ferguson Tractor
Various shades of blue; also black (rare). Grey ribbed
plastic wheels and hook. Driver in some models though,
surprisingly, quite rare as the hole in the seat was meant
specifically for this purpose. Price 1/6. Issued September
1959. Deleted 1965. 37mm. DC.   £55   £30   £15

No. 070 AEC Shell Tanker
Red and green. Black ribbed plastic wheels. Windows.
'Shell Petroleum Products BP' on sides. Price 2/6. Issued
October 1959. Deleted 1964. 91mm. DC/TP/PW.   £75   £40   £25

No. 071 VW Delivery Van
Yellow with 'Hornby Dublo' on sides. Black ribbed
plastic wheels. Windows. Price 2/-. Issued March 1960.
Deleted 1967. 54mm. DC/TP/PW.   £55   £20   £10

No. 072 Bedford Articulated Truck
Orange cab and red trailer. Windows. Price 2/6. Issued
June 1959. Deleted 1964. 116mm. DC/TW.   £55   £20   £10

No. 073 Land Rover and Trailer
Green Land Rover with windows and orange trailer with
black plastic door. Smooth grey or ribbed black plastic
wheels and tyres. Tin baseplate. Price 4/3. Issued 1960.
Deleted 1967. 103mm. DC.   £55   £20   £10

No. 076 Lansing Bagnall Tractor and Trailer
Maroon. Tractor has driver and hook. Hook also on
trailer. Price 2/9. Issued June 1960. Deleted 1d 1964.
75mm. DC/TP/PW.   £65   £25   £15

No. 078 Lansing Bagnall Tractor
This is for the trailer only and for some unknown reason,
this item remained in the catalogues until 1971. Price 1/4.
Issued June 1960. Officially deleted 1964. 49mm.
DC/TP/PW.   £55   £20   £10

FIRE ENGINES
AND STATIONS

No. 956   Turntable Fire Escape with Windows

Fire engines have always played an important part in the world of collectors. Having one of every model in this range, I known how magnificent the models and stations look when fully displayed. Some of the first models were never individually boxed, and for these I quote prices for mint unboxed and good condition only.

MODEL	MB	MU	GC
No. 25h Streamlined Fire Engine Red. Price 9d. Issued April 1936. Deleted 1940. 101mm. DC/RT/TP.	—	£65	£20
No. 25H Streamlined Fire Engine Red. Price 2/9. Issued 1948. Renumbered 250 in 1954. Deleted 1960/62. 101mm. DC/RT/TP. Box of six.	—	£45	£5
No. 25k Streamlined Fire Engine Red with six tinplate firemen. Price 5/6. Issued 1938. Deleted 1940. 101mm. DC/RT/TP.	—	£175	£50
No. 250 Streamlined Fire Engine Red with silver ladder and grey bell. Price 3/2. Reissue of No. 25H. Issued 1954. Deleted 1962. 99mm. DC/TP/RT.	£95	£25	£15

No. 259 Fire Engine
Red with 'Fire Brigade' on each side. Bell and detachable
ladder. Price 5/9. Issued November 1961. Deleted 1970.
115mm. DC/TP/P/RT.

£65   £20   £10

No. 263 Airport Fire Rescue Tender
Golden yellow with ladder. 'Airport' and 'Rescue' on
sides in white with red base plus '51' on doors at each
side. Red hubs, silver bumpers and white interior. Price
£2.75. Issued 177mm. DC/P. Same basic casting as No.
266 below.

£95   £20   £10

No. 266 ERF Fire Tender
Red with removable extending ladder with wheels. Price
£2.99. Issued 1976. Deleted 1980. 223mm. DC/P.

£80   £20   £10

No. 271 Ford Transit Fire Appliance
Redesign of No. 286. Red with automatic hose and
rewind system. Price £2.25. Issued 1975. Deleted 1977.
129mm. DC/P.

£80   £20   £10

No. 276 Airport Fire Tender
Red with 'Airport Fire Control' on sides. Also appeared
with the 'Fire Brigade' transfers of No. 259. Bell, flashing
roof lights and rotating roof extinguisher with foam.
Price 10/6. Issued August 1962. Deleted 1970. 120mm.
DC/P/RT/TP. Mint boxed is rare.

£60   £30   £15

No. 282 Land Rover Fire Appliance
Red with plastic Speediwheels and 'Fire Service' on sides.
Price £1.25. Issued 1973. Deleted 1978. 119mm.

£65   £20   £10

No. 282 Land Rover Fire Appliance
Dark red with 'Danske Redingskorp'. Issued in Denmark
1974. Deleted 1978. 119mm.

£150   £50   £25

No. 285 Merryweather Marquis Fire Tender
First issue in metallic red is worth double the second issue
in red. Silver trim, wheels etc. Operating water pump and
extending ladder with twin bells. Hose. Price 14/11. First
issue 1964. Second issue 1974. Deleted 1980. 177mm.
DC/P.

£75   £40   £20

No. 285 Merryweather Marquis Fire Engine
Red. Made for Danish market. Issued 1974. Deleted 1978.
177mm. DC/P.

£175   £60   £30

No. 286 Ford Transit Fire Appliance
Red with yellow ladder and twin bells on roof. Automatic
hose rewind with opening doors at side and rear. 'Fire
Services' and badge on sides. Silver wheels and bumpers
etc. The reissued version has second grille and one piece
rear door. Price 9/11. Issued 1962. Reissued as No. 271 in
1975. Deleted 1980. 122mm.   £95   £30   £15

No. 286 Ford Transit
Red. Made for Danish market. Issued 1974. Deleted 1978.
122mm. DC/P.   £175   £60   £30

No. 384 Convoy Fire Rescue Truck
Red with removable ladder etc. Price £2.75. Issued 1977.
Deleted 1980. 126mm.   £65   £30   £15

No. 555 Fire Engine with Extending Ladder
Red and silver. Renumbered with bell and brown ladder
(worth double). Price 9/6. Issued November 1952. Finally
deleted 1970. 145mm. RT/TP.   £95   £30   £15

No. 954 Fire Station
Red, yellow and brick with clear plastic roof. 'Dinky Toys
Fire Station' on front. Price £1/1/-. Issued November
1961. Deleted 19654. P. Base 252 x 203mm.   £75   £40   £20

No. 955 Fire Engine with Extending Ladder
Red and silver. Metal and then later plastic hubs.
Windows from 1960. Silver or grey hoses (non-working).
Price 7/6. Issued January 1955 as renumbering of 555.
Deleted 1970. 145mm. DC/TP/RT.   £125   £50   £25

No. 956 Turntable Fire Escape with Windows
Red, yellow or blue (worth double). Made in metal and
later in plastic with windows from 1960 (Bedford cab).
All-angle ladder action. Price 13/-. Issued February 1958.
Deleted 1970. 200mm.   £175   £80   £20

No. 956 Berliet Fire Escape
Red and silver. Made for Danish market. Price £1.55.
Issued 1974. Deleted 1978. 200mm. DC/P.   £250   —   —

No. 956A Turntable Fire Escape
The first No. 956 was replaced by this turntable fire
escape with a French Dinky Berliet Cab. Turntable and
escape are the same as those used on the Bedford one.
Price £2.75. Issued 1970. Deleted 1972. 200mm. DC/P.   £175   £80   £20

No. 3276 Mogul Fire Engine
Red and black with large extending ladder and fire hose.
Strong towing hook in front and trailing hook behind.
Extra robust axles and tough working parts, originally
made for the toddlers of the collecting world. This is
definitely a Dinky product and was advertised in their
catalogues. Not very successful. Price £2.25. Issued 1978.
Deleted 1980. 390mm. P.   £75   £25   £15

FRENCH DINKIES

No. 32D   Fire Engine

The French Dinky models have always been widely sought after by collectors from many parts of the world. I hope that the following information will help people who have written to me over the years. I have chosen what I consider to be the best models from a French company that never really liked to associate itself with its English counterpart although it had the greatest respect for Frank Hornby and his team of brilliant experts at the Binns Road factory in Liverpool.

I have read the books *Histoire des Dinky Toys Français* by Jean-Michel Roulet, *French Meccano Trains Hornby-Dinky-Toys Marques Deposées* and *Dinky Toys-ET-Dinky Supertoys Fabriqués-en-France par Meccano Paris* by Jean Masse, but I found no guidelines about prices in the collector's market. My book should prove the ideal guide to the models which are now in the hands of some very fortunate people.

'25' SERIES TRUCKS

This commercial series was roughly equivalent to the English '25' series in the very early era from 1935 to 1949. The castings were almost identical, although very different in many of the details, especially with the French cast bumpers as front parts of the chassis. The major castings on the Fords manufactured between 1949 and 1957 had two chassis lengths and two wheelbase lengths, one short and the other long. The 'short' models had an integral cab and a separate rear body casting, and the 'long' chassis had integral body one piece castings. The very early models had more protruding grilles and lamps and could be recognised by the cast 'tow hooks' at the back end. These were made between 1949 and 1951, while the later models had tinplate tow hooks from 1951 to 1955. The very early models were fitted with all-metal wheels, although some had normal wheels with rubber tyres. The models which followed this series all had rubber tyres fitted. From 1950 to 1955/56 the short chassis versions all had rubber tyres fitted to the wheels. All castings were the same with no variations.

STUDEBAKERS

These models also had two variations. From 1949 to 1950 they had smaller windows with a rather thick centre bonnet strip. From 1951 to 1954 there was a raised rectangular line which indicated a toolbox on each side of the cab directly under the doors. However, on the much earlier type the casting had a larger raised rectangular blob under the right-hand door. The 25K Studebaker model in the early series had no toolbox moulding at either side of the cab, and it was in red and blue and had all-metal wheels. This model is not rare but still a nice item to have in one's French collection. The 25K was a Market Gardens Truck and was always in two colours, mainly red and blue, green and red, red and yellow, or any combination. Grey and black was rare.

The 25M Studebaker Tipping Wagon had a dark green cab with a metallic grey body complete with spare wheel and tow hook. Roulet says it had no spare wheel or tow hook, but I have seen one in a fine collection. Indeed it is one of the nicest in the '25' series.

Another nice model was the 250 Studebaker Milk Wagon. Early models had 'Nestlé' stamped on them and the later models used transfers. There are also models showing no printing whatsoever and these were used to advertise certain local milk firms and private European farmers.

Of all the pick-up trucks produced the 25P Studebaker was one of the best. Both cab types were used. The early models had an extra H shape to strengthen their bodies, like a kind of brace underneath. Later ones were quite flat. The livery was always yellow with a red body. Another nice pick-up with a tilt was the 25Q Studebaker which was the 25P complete with a tin tilt. It had a green cab and tilt with the body showing a prominent red or yellow. Some of the models looked rather brown and this was because of the brown tilt coming from the 25T to the 25P.

The Studebaker 25R Breakdown Truck was actually a 25P model with a red livery and a tinplate crane fixed at the rear with 'Dinky Service' stamped in white on the side. Both cab types were produced.

FORDS

The 25A was a Cattle Truck in light metallic blue or metallic grey. Shades could vary. This model has a short chassis. The 25H Ford Beverage Truck had the long chassis with a cast hook and crane in the following colours: red, brown, blue, grey green and yellow. One or two of these had rubber tyres and a tinplate tailboard.

The 25I Wagon was available in a wide range of colours with a long chassis, and the 25I Covered Wagon, with a tin tilt, became 25J in the colours of brown, gold, blue or red with green, cream or brown tilt.

Adverts and names always mean money and good examples are the 25JB which has printed on the cover 'Société Nationale des Chemins de Fer Français' and the 25JV Covered Wagon with 'Grands Moulins de Paris' which is quite rare as an early cab series in grey livery with black tilt. These models will bring anything from £250 up to £500, but it is worth remembering that there is always the chance of an even higher price being paid for something that is termed as a one-off.

The 25M Ford Tipping Wagon has exactly the same body as the 25M Studebaker Tipping Wagon but only on a much shorter chassis with identical livery. Again it has the spare wheel and tow hook. The 250 Ford Milk Wagon with its short chassis was produced in a limited number in the early part of 1950 with the main production line coming along between 1954 and 1955. This model has a light blue cab with a white body and 'Nestlé' on the side. At a later date this model had the Nestlé transfers with hollow letters.

The 25R Ford Breakdown Truck was introduced in 1954. It has quite a smooth tailboard with 'Dinky Service' again stamped in white. A much later version has chrome wheels showing no stamping on the rear at all.

VANS

Once again I must emphasise the importance of adverts which were the forerunners of the promotional models of today. One outstanding name was the following: the 25B Peugeot D3A which were first issued in 1953 with 'Lampe Mazda' and 'Postes' in grey or blue livery. Then in late 1953 this was superseded by the yellow and green version, and in 1954 was replaced by the green model and given the catalogue number 25BV. At a still later stage it became 560. In the beginning 'Postes' was engraved on the side. Several different decals were used at a later stage. There can also be found a few odd colours on this same casting which were possibly done by artistic collectors, which of course is a common practice now. Both the genuine factory produced models and those designed by an individual have a high price in the collector's market.

The 25C Citroën 1200kg Van is a large corrugated iron type which was typical of the kind that could be seen all over France in the pre- and post-war years. The model itself was identical to its large counterpart in four main liveries of grey, green, red and blue. The first model made in 1954 had no adverts and was metallic grey.

In 1957 the 25C was superseded by the 25CG Citroën 1200kg CH Gervais which was in cream with green, blue and white decals. After being renumbered 561 it was deleted in 1959. Then along came the 25CG Citroën 1200kg Cibie issued in 1959 in a very attractive blue livery with yellow, red and black decals. This model was also renumbered 561 about the middle of 1960 and then finally deleted in 1963.

The 561 Citroën 1200kg Glaces Gervais was the final version, being issued in 1963 and deleted in 1966. Painted in white on the top and blue on the bottom, it made a very attractive two-tone model with decals painted in red and blue. Another very fine model which is extremely rare is the Baroclem Citroën 1200kg. There was a combination of workmanship and skills by both the French Dinky company and the firm of Baroclem itself. It was produced by Dinky and the decals were done in blue and white by Baroclem. It came out in 1964 and was deleted almost at once. I am not sure of the production run, but it must have been small as the last model of this type I saw being sold reached a price of £750.

Apart from the large vans there were some small attractive models, four of which stand out. The first was the Citroën 2cv which was a small mobile corrugated iron garden shed. There was the Paris Fire Service issued in 1958 in red, renumbered 562 in 1959 and finally deleted in 1964. Then there was the 560 PTT issued in 1963 in very attractive yellow livery with blue decals and deleted in 1970. Finally, I must mention the Wegenwacht made specially for the Dutch market between 1965 and 1968 in another attractive yellow livery with jet black decals.

MORE WAGON VARIANTS

Apart from the models which I have listed in this section on French Dinkies, I know the following information makes very good reading for the collector of this much sought after series. The following are facts which I am pleased to say were given to me by a very reliable source. It would be impossible to name everyone who helped me, but I would like to express my grateful thanks at this point.

Petrol tankers remain favourites regardless of what make they happen to be. Models such as the 25U Ford Petrol Tanker, which was made with a later type cab with a one piece casting, have always appealed to collectors. The much earlier models had a support bracket and a hook cast at the rear, underneath the body, while the later ones did not. They were always in red when the Esso sign was on the sides and rear. In 1957 there was another very attractive Esso Tanker, the 32C Tracteur Panhard, which is very much sought after. Some attractive refuse trucks were produced like the 25V Ford Refuse Truck with its short chassis, tipping body and opening tailgate. It had tinplate centre sections at the top of the body, which could slide neatly apart, and a favourite colour was dark green.

I must also mention the 25S and 25T Trailers, which were actually pick-up bodies fitted with tinplate chassis. One was painted red, yellow or green without the tilt, while in the other with the tilt the livery was shown as yellow and brown or red and green. These fine models became part of one of the most valuable diecast series and certainly among the vest investments.

No. 14 Three Wheeled Carrier
Grey or brown. Made in 1935 with smooth hubs and
Dunlop tyres, and from 1939 to 1940 with solid metal
wheels. Reissued 1949 in red with green driver, yellow
with blue driver or grey with yellow driver. Deleted 1952.
Imported into England pre-war dates only. Never
individually boxed.

	MB	MU	GC
With Dunlop tyres	—	£75	£35
With solid metal wheels	—	£55	£25
With 'M' tyres	—	£45	£25

No. 22a Roadster
Red or blue. Silver with red wings or green with yellow
wings. There could be other colours, all highly valued.
Completely different casting from the English No. 22a.
One piece body/wings, and casting with separate
windscreen. Cast dashboard and steering wheel. Cast in
lead with solid metal wheels or with smooth hubs and
Dunlop tyres. Issued 1933. Deleted 1939. | — | £550 | £250 |

No. 22A Maserati Sport 2000
Red with white driver. Silver wheels, grille, lights and
screen. Black tyres. Issued 1958. Deleted 1966. 88mm.
DC/P. | £80 | £15 | £10 |

No. 22b Sports Coupé
Again very different from the English version. Colours
and dates as No. 22a. | — | £550 | £250 |

No. 22c Roadster Sports
Royal blue with yellow wings or cream with red wings.
Details and casting as No. 22a. Issued 1933. Deleted 1939. | — | £550 | £250 |

No. 22d Sports Coupé 2
Colours, details and castings as No. 22a. Issued 1933.
Deleted 1939. | — | £550 | £250 |

1st No. 23a MG Model
Blue and white or silver stripes, orange and white or
green stripes, or cream and greenish blue or red stripes.
Cast in lead always with a driver (compare first English
release). Four exhaust stubs but no exhaust pipe. White
rubber tyres with 'Dunlop' stamped on them. Issued
1934. Deleted 1940. Not individually boxed. | — | £175 | £75 |

2nd No. 23a MG Model
Cast in Zamac always with driver and with six branch
exhaust pipe. White Dunlop tyres. Issued 1935. Deleted
1939. | — | £150 | £50 |

3rd No. 23a MG Model
As above but with solid Zamac wheels. Issued 1939.
Deleted 1940. Reissued 1949 in identical form. Deleted
1958.

	MB	MU	GC
	—	£125	£40

1st No. 23b Renault Record Car
This first model was not really a racing car but rather a
private businessman's invention. Specifically French
casting, never issued in England. There are at least 14
colour schemes which are all very much sought after. The
model is so scarce that a good price will be paid by any
Dinky enthusiast. Issued 1935. Deleted 1940. Reissued
1947. Deleted 1956. 97mm. Not individually boxed.

Pre-war	—	£550	£250
Post-war	—	£100	£65

2nd No. 23b Hotchkiss Racing Car
Identical in every way to the English model, except that
it was marked 'Made in France'. It had French wheels
with smooth hubs and white coloured tyres. Some of the
tyres were coloured and later replaced by solid metal
wheels. Post-war model had ribbed hubs with black 'M'
tyres, also with a range of colour schemes connected with
the car itself. Any colour will bring a good price in this
range. Red with silver flash etc. Issued 1939. Deleted 1940.
Reissued 1946. Deleted 1954. 95mm.

Pre-war	—	£125	£50
Post-war	—	£40	£25

No. 23c Mercedes Racing Car
Silver with red grille and exhaust pipe. Solid metal
wheels on post-war model only. Ribbed hubs and black
'M' tyres. '2' on sides. Issued 1949. Deleted 1956. 92mm.
DC/TP. Not individually boxed.

	—	£150	£50

No. 23c Auto-Union Racing Car
Red or silver, or pale green with red number and silver
radiator and grille. Driver slotted into body. Issued 1950.
Deleted 1954. 100mm. DC/TP.

	—	£125	£50

No. 23H Auto De Course Talbot Lago
Blue with white driver. Blue wheels and large ribbed
racing tyres. Silver grille and exhausts. '6' in orange or
yellow on sides. Issued 1950. Deleted 1966. 83mm.

	£125	£100	£50

No. 23J Auto De Course Ferrari
Red with white driver. Silver wheels, grille and exhausts.
Red exhausts. Black ribbed tyres. '1' on sides. Issued 1950.
Deleted 1966. 102mm.

	£150	£100	£50

No. 23m Thunderbolt Record Car
Imported into France from England. Silver or dark blue.
Driver cast into body. Issued 1938. Deleted 1940. 126mm.
DC/RT/TP. One of the first Dinky models to be
individually boxed.

| | £275 | £175 | £75 |

No. 24a Ambulance
Never issued in France although it had 'Made in France'
marked on the model. Off-white or cream colour with
French wheels and smooth hubs, plus white or coloured
Dunlop tyres. Had the same body style and features as its
English counterpart of the '24' series. Issued 1934.
Deleted 1939. Reissued 1945. Deleted 1952.

| Pre-war | — | £175 | £75 |
| Post-war | — | £75 | £60 |

No. 24A Chrysler New Yorker
Yellow with green interior or red with white interior.
Silver grille, bumpers, screen, lights, radiator and wheels.
White tyres and silver trim. Issued 1950. Deleted 1968.
112mm. DC/P.

| Yellow | £175 | £75 | £35 |
| Red | £145 | £65 | £25 |

No. 24b Limousine
Red with red chassis; yellow with black chassis; yellow
with red chassis; red with grey chassis; and others.
Criss-cross chassis and horizontal bonnet louvres. Issued
1934. Deleted 1939. 98mm. DC/RT. Not individually
boxed.

| | — | £250 | £100 |

No. 24B 403 Peugeot
Blue or grey (worth double). Silver wheels, grille, lights,
radiator and bumpers. White tyres and off-white interior.
Issued 1952. Deleted 1968. 104mm. DC/P.

| | £150 | £75 | £40 |

No. 24c Town Sedan
Never issued in France although had 'Made in France'
marked on the model. Various colours with French white
or coloured tyres marked 'Dunlop'. Same features and
body style as English '24' series. Issued 1934. Deleted
1939. Reissued 1946. Deleted 1952.

| Pre-war | — | £250 | £100 |
| Post-war | — | £125 | £75 |

No. 24C DS19 Citroën
Light or dark green. Also lime green with white roof.
Silver bumpers, grille, wheels etc. White tyres.
Windscreen, windows and headlights. Issued 1952.
Deleted 1968. 112mm. DC/P.

| | £125 | £75 | £45 |

No. 24CP DS19 Citroën
Golden lemon body with white roof. Silver wheels, grille,
bumpers, etc. White tyres. Issued 1953. Deleted 1963.
112mm. Rare.　　　　　　　　　　　　　　　　　£125　　£75　　£45

No. 24d Vogue Saloon
Dark blue; blue with black chassis; green with red chassis;
grey with red chassis; and others. First issued with spare
wheel and later without. Wheel variant issued
concurrently with presence or absence of spare wheel.
Issued 1935. Deleted 1939. Reissued 1947. Deleted 1952.
107mm. DC/RT.
Pre-war　　　　　　　　　　　　　　　　　　　—　　£150　　£80
Post-war　　　　　　　　　　　　　　　　　　—　　£125　　£65

No. 24D Plymouth Belvedere
Green with black roof and side panels. Silver grille,
bumpers, wheels, trim etc. White tyres. Issued 1953.
Deleted 1968. 110mm. DC/P.　　　　　　　　　£100　　£75　　£45

No. 24e Super Streamlined Saloon
Red and dark red with black chassis; green with red
chassis; and others. See comments for No. 24B. Never had
spare wheel. 97mm. DC/RT.
Pre-war　　　　　　　　　　　　　　　　　　　—　　£150　　£75
Post-war　　　　　　　　　　　　　　　　　　—　　£100　　£60

No. 24E Renault Dauphine
Maroon or orange. Silver trim, grille, wheels, bumpers
etc. Black tyres. Issued 1957. Deleted 1968. 92mm. DC/P.　£125　　£75　　£45

No. 24f Sportsman Coupé
Yellow with brown chassis; green with yellow chassis; or
yellow with red chassis. With or without spare wheel.
Issued 1937. Deleted 1939. Reissued 1947. Deleted 1952.
100mm. DC/RT.
Pre-war　　　　　　　　　　　　　　　　　　　—　　£150　　£75
Post-war　　　　　　　　　　　　　　　　　　—　　£125　　£65

No. 24F Peugeot Familiale 403
Pale or medium blue with silver trim, wheels, grille,
bumpers, radiator and lights. Issued 1957. Deleted 1968.
107mm. DC/P.　　　　　　　　　　　　　　　　£125　　£75　　£35

No. 24g Four Seater Sports Tourer
Blue body with brown or black chassis or green with red
chassis. Issued with full spare wheel on the boot or later,
concurrently with introduction of solid metal wheels,
with a simulated spare-wheel cover cast on boot. Open

screen. Issued 1936. Deleted 1939. Reissued 1946. Deleted 1952. 98mm. DC/RT.

	MB	MU	GC
Pre-war	—	£150	£75
Post-war	—	£125	£65

No. 24h Two Seater Sports Tourer
Red body with green chassis; green with blue chassis; or green with red chassis. See comments for No. 24g. 98mm. DC/TP.

Pre-war	—	£125	£65
Post-war	£100	£60	£35

No. 24H Mercedes 190SL
Silver grey with purple or blue roof. Silver wheels, grille, bumpers, lights etc. White tyres. Issued 1957. Deleted 1968. 99mm. DC/P.

	£15	£8	£6

No. 24J Alfa Romeo 1900 Sprint
Red with silver grille, bumpers, headlights and wheels. Black tyres. Issued 1957/58. Deleted 1968. 99mm. DC/P.

	£75	£35	£15

No. 24k Peugeot
Model of the Peugeot 402. Dark blue, grey blue, maroon, white, green or red. Black wheels and black or white tyres. Smooth hubs and Dunlop tyres. Later version with solid metal wheels. Issued 1939. Deleted 1940. Reissued 1948. Deleted 1950. 95mm. DC/TP/RT.

Pre-war	—	£395	£250
Post-war	—	£150	£75

No. 24l Peugeot Taxi
No driver and two-tone finish of various colours with yellow side panels, black roof and wings. Black wheels with black or white tyres. Later version with solid metal wheels. Paris markings. Issued 1939. Deleted 1940. Reissued 1948. Deleted 1950.

Pre-war	—	£395	£250
Post-war	—	£150	£75

No. 24N Citroën IIBL
Grey, blue or black. Later version with boot in place of spare wheel cover. Issued 1949. Reissued 1953.

First version	—	£150	£75
Second version	—	£100	£50

No. 24N Citroën IIBL
Silver-grey body with matching or red wheels, silver headlights and white tyres. Issued 1955. Deleted 1968. 96mm. DC/P.

	£125	£75	£35

No. 24R Peugeot 203
Light or medium grey with white tyres. Silver bumpers,
wheels, grille, trim etc. Issued 1953. Deleted 1968. 100mm.
DC/P.

	MB	MU	GC
No. 24R Peugeot 203	£100	£50	£25

No. 24S Simca 8 Sport
Grey body with black roof and tyres. Yellow or silver
wheels. Silver-grey bumpers, grille etc. Issued 1954.
Deleted 1968. 88mm. DC/P.

| | £60 | £30 | £15 |

No. 24U Simca Aronde
Medium or dark blue. Also off-white or light grey with
green roof. Silver wheels, grille, radiator, bumpers and
lights. White tyres. Issued 1954. Deleted 1968. 95mm.
DC/P.

| Medium or dark blue | £40 | £20 | £15 |
| Off-white or light grey | £50 | £30 | £20 |

No. 24UT Taxi Aronde
Two-tone red with blue roof and red and white taxi sign.
Silver grille and bumpers. Red wheels and white tyres.
Issued 1955. Deleted 1965. 95mm. DC/P.

| | £45 | £20 | £15 |

No. 24XT Taxi Vedette
Royal blue with white, fawn or cream roof. Silver wheels,
bumpers, grille and white tyres. White and red taxi sign
on roof. Issued 1956. Deleted 1966. 105mm. DC/P.

| | £100 | £50 | £35 |

No. 24V Buick Roadmaster
Sky-blue, medium blue or dark blue with yellow, cream
or fawn roof. Silver grille, lights, bumpers and white
tyres. Silver or blue wheels. Issued 1956. Deleted 1968.
112mm. DC/P.

| | £130 | £75 | £35 |

No. 24W Simca Vedette
Dark blue with white tyres, black wheels, silver bumpers
and headlights. Possibly in other colours. Issued 1956/57.
Deleted 1968. 105mm. DC/P.

| | £83 | £45 | £30 |

No. 24Y Studebaker Commander
Bright orange with mustard or fawn roof. Silver trim,
grille, wheels, bumpers, radiator and lights. White tyres.
Issued 1956. Deleted 1968. 109mm. DC/P.

| | £100 | £75 | £35 |

No. 24Z Simca Versailles
Buttercup or dull yellow body with black roof. Silver
wheels, grille, radiator, bumpers, lights etc. White tyres.
Issued 1957. Deleted 1968. 105mm. DC/P.

| | £95 | £55 | £35 |

No. 25a Generic Lorry
This lorry of the 1930s is the same as far as description is
concerned as No. 25d. No advertising.

	MB	MU	GC
	—	£175	£65

No. 25b Citroën Covered Wagon
Comments etc. as for No. 25a. No advertising.

	—	£175	£65

No. 25B Lampe Mazda Peugeot Van
Two-tone lime-green top and yellow lower body. Green
wheels with black tyres, silver grille, lights and bumpers.
'Lampe Mazda' on sides in black on yellow background.
Issued 1954/55. Deleted 1968. DC/P. 90mm. Rare.

	£325	£150	£75

No. 25BV Fourgon Postal Van
Medium, light or dark green with 'Postes' and a middle
line in orange or golden yellow. Matching green wheels
and black tyres. Silver, black or green grille, radiator and
lights. Issued 1954. Deleted 1968. 90mm. DC/P.

	£175	£75	£35

No. 25c Citroën Flat Truck
Red or green. See comments for No. 25a. No advertising.

	—	£250	£125

No. 25CG Camionette Citroën Gervais
Fawn or light mustard van with a decorative design in
blue and green with 'Gervais' in white. Also dark red
body with gold lettering (rare and worth double). Ribbed
sides and roof. Silver wheels, grille, radiator and black
tyres. Issued 1954. Deleted 1968. 90mm. DC/P.

	£125	£75	£35

No. 25d Petrol Tanker
Completely different profile to that of English version; in
fact all the '25' series differ. The French '25' series were
made between 1935 and 1939. Then they reappeared
between 1945/46 and 1950. This is the description for all
tankers. In 1935 they had smooth hubs with white Dunlop
tyres and front bumpers cast on. From 1939 to 1940 they
had solid metal wheels. After the war the models
appeared without livery or with 'Standard', 'Essolube',
'Esso' or 'Mobiloil' advertising. 108mm. RT/DC/TP.

	MB	MU	GC
Pre-war without advertising	—	£250	£100
Pre-war with advertising	—	£350	£175
Post-war without advertising	—	£150	£75
Post-war with advertising	—	£175	£75

No. 25D Fourgonnette Incendie 2cv Citroën
Red ribbed body with red wheels and black tyres, or blue
body with matching blue wheels. Curved roof. Silver
grille, radiator, lights. Shield emblem in green and gold
on doors. Issued 1957. Deleted 1968. 84mm. DC/P

	MB	MU	GC
Red ribbed body	£50	£30	£20
Blue body	£100	£75	£35

No. 25e Tipping Wagon
Blue with green chassis; yellow with blue rear and black
chassis; maroon, yellow or fawn; and others. Comments
and prices as for No. 25d.

No. 25f Citroën Dropside Truck
Green, red or fawn. French version of the Market
Gardeners Wagon (Stake Truck). Comments as for No.
25d. No advertising.   —   £175   £75

No. 25g Trailer
Marked 'Made in France' with tinplate hook. Smooth
hubs with Dunlop tyres (1935/39). Cast metal wheels
(1939/40 and 1946/48). Ribbed hubs and black 'M' tyres
from 1948 to 1952. Made for use with the '25' Ford and
Studebaker series. Otherwise comments and prices as for
No. 25d. 69mm. DC/RT.

No. 25h Fire Engine
Red. Issued in France, marked 'Made in England'.
Identical model to English version. See Fire Engines and
Stations section for comments and prices.

No. 29b Streamlined Bus
Never issued as a French Dinky, although many people
thought it was. This was an import and English models
appeared in France before the war. Details of this model
have already been given in the Buses and Coaches
section.

No. 29d Panhard Paris Autobus
Dark green with off-white roof. The lower part is in
diecast Zamac while the roof and windscreen are tinplate.
Smooth metal hubs and Dunlop tyres from 1939 to 1940;
solid metal wheels from 1940 to 1949; and ribbed metal
hubs and 'M' tyres from 1950 to 1952. Deleted 1960.
Pre-war   —   £295   £150
Post-war   —   £150   £100

No. 29D Panhard Paris Autobus
Two-tone green lower and cream upper. Gold or silver
radiator, bumpers and lights. Green wheels and black
tyres. Issued 1954. Deleted 1968. 143mm. DC.   £95   £50   £30

No. 29F Autocar Chausson
Fine streamlined coach with cream upper and red lower
with red wheels and white tyres. Also blue lower with
matching blue wheels (rare). Silver or yellow ribs. Silver

FRENCH DINKIES	MB	MU	GC

or gold grille, radiator etc. Issued 1955. Deleted 1968.
154mm. DC/P.

Red lower	£100	£65	£30
Blue lower	£115	£75	£30

No. 30a Chrysler Airflow Saloon
Green or cream. Issued pre-war in France with smooth
hubs and Dunlop tyres. Model was assembled in France,
but still marked 'Made in England'. Issued June 1935.
Deleted 1936/37. 103mm. DC/RT.   —   £275   £125

No. 30b Rolls Royce
Very dark green or dark grey with black chassis. Issued
1936 in France. Deleted 1940. 101mm. DC/RT. Very rare.   —   £495   £250

No. 30e Breakdown Car
Dark red, dark green or very dark grey with black chassis.
This French Dinky was totally different to the English
version. It was in fact one of the '25' series trucks. With
the cast metal crane from a French Dinky train set. Issued
1935. Deleted 1939. 120mm.   —   £175   £75

No. 32AB Panhard Articulated SNCF
Blue cab with matching box trailer body with 'Société
Nationale des Chemins de Fer Français' in gold or yellow.
Also green square with white line border and 'SNCF' in
black on sides. Matching blue wheels. Silver grille,
bumpers and lights. Issued 1955. Deleted 1968. 165mm.
DC/P.   £180   £75   £45

No. 32C Panhard Esso Tanker
Red articulated tanker with white lines. 'Esso' in red in
white circle and black wings. Red wheels and black tyres.
Silver radiator grille, bumper and lights. Issued 1955.
Deleted 1968. 178mm. DC/P.   £180   £130   £75

No. 32D Fire Engine
Red with white or silver extending ladder on red winch.
Red wheels and white tyres. Silver grille, radiator and
windscreen. Issued 1954. Deleted 1968. 120mm. DC/P.
Fine model.   £130   £75   £35

No. 32E Berliet Fire Engine
Red with silver or white ladder. Red wheels and white
tyres. Silver grille, radiator and bumpers. Removable
ladder. Hose pipe reels in separate trailer. Issued 1955.
Deleted 1968. 105mm. Overall length (with hose pipe
reels) 118mm. DC/P. Another fine model.   £150   £75   £35

No. 33AN Simca Cargo Removal Van
Yellow ribbed body with off-white or cream roof, matching yellow wheels and black tyres. Silver grille, radiator, bumper and trim. 'Bailly Déménagement Garde Meubles' in thick yellow on black base. Issued 1955. Deleted 1968. 133mm. DC/P.   £70   £30   £25

No. 33B Simca Cargo Tipper Lorry
Lime-green cab and chassis with grey tipper body and tailboard. Matching green wheels and black tyres. Silver grille and radiator. Issued 1955. Deleted 1968. 127mm. DC/P.   £70   £35   £25

No. 33C Simca Cargo Glass Carrier
Yellow cab and chassis with green flat trailer back. Matching yellow wheels and rear framework for mirror glass. 'Miroitier' in red on rear. Silver radiator and grille. Issued 1956. Deleted 1968. 129mm. DC/P.   £120   £80   £30

No. 34A Berliet Tipper Lorry
Blue cab and chassis with matching wheels and black tyres. Mustard or yellow tipper body with silver grille and radiator. Issued 1956. Deleted 1968. 128mm. DC/P.   £70   £40   £30

No. 34B Berliet Container Lorry
Red cab and chassis with matching red wheels and black tyres. Grey rear with black box container. Silver grille and radiator. Issued 1956. Deleted 1968. 125mm. DC/P.   £140   £100   £55

No. 35A Citroën Breakdown Van
All-red body and cab with matching wheels. Silver grille, bumper and radiator. Spare wheel and black crane with silver hook on rear. Matching red wheels and black tyres. 'Dinky Service' in gold on sides. Issued 1956. Deleted 1958. 125mm. DC/P.   £80   £40   £25

No. 36A Willeme Articulated with Log Trailer
Orange cab and chassis with yellow or orange trailer carrying log load. Yellow wheels and black tyres. Silver grille, radiator and bumpers. Spare wheel at rear of cab. Issued 1955. Deleted 1968. 235mm. DC/P.   £150   £80   £55

No. 36B Willeme Articulated with Tarpaulined Trailer
Red cab and chassis with matching red wheels. Orange and red trailer body with green tarpaulin cover. Silver bumper, grille and radiator. Grey tyres and spare wheel. Issued 1958. Deleted 1969. 267mm. DC/P.   £120   £60   £35

No. 38A Camion Unic Multibenne Marrel
The first issue (1957) had an all-grey cab with matching
bucket and wheels, with orange or dark fawn bucket
holder. The second issue (1958) had a grey cab with
yellow mudguards and matching bucket holder body
with yellow wheels. Issued 1957. Deleted 1968. 132mm.
DC/P. Fully extended 197mm.

	MB	MU	GC
First issue	£175	£100	£55
Second issue	£135	£75	£45

No. 39A Articulated Car Transporter
Exceptional car transporter in silver-blue livery with
matching wheels and black tyres. Silver bumper, grille,
radiator and trim. 'Dinky Toys Service Livraison' in
black. Issued 1957. Deleted 1968. 325mm. DC/P.

	£275	£125	£75

No. 45D Esso Petrol Pumps Set
Blue and white plus red and white pumps on grey stand
with red and white Esso sign and 'Esso' in oval advert.
Issued early 1950s. Deleted 1968.

	£75	—	—

No. 50 Salev Crane
Red and silver-grey with matching crane and wheels
with black tyres. Blue driver. Two levers control the
movement of the crane. Issued 1957. Deleted 1968. 89mm
long. 156mm long with crane horizontal. DC/P.

	£95	£45	£15

No. 60A Mystère IVA (Marcel Dassault)
First of a compact aeroplane super toy series in silver with
orange, blue and yellow decals. Issued 1955. Deleted
1968. 68mm long. Wing span 59mm. DC/P.

	£45	£25	£15

No. 60B Vautour (Sud Aviation)
Silver body with blue, orange and yellow decals on
wings. Issued 1955. Deleted 1968. 92mm long. Wing span
80mm. DC/P.

	£45	£25	£15

No. 60C Lockheed Super G Constellation
Silver, blue and white with Air France decals in black.
Issued 1957. Deleted 1968. 181mm long. Wing span
197mm. DC/P.

	£120	£55	£30

No. 60D Sikorsky S58 Helicopter
Silver, blue and white with black blades with orange tips.
Issued 1956. Deleted 1968. 80mm long. Rotor span 87mm.
DC/P.

	£45	£25	£15

No. 60E Vickers Viscount
Silver, blue and white with black decals and lettering on
wings. Issued 1957. Deleted 1968. 132mm long. Wing
span 150mm. DC/P.   £35   £15   £10

No. 60F Caravelle Air France Airliner
Silver, black and yellow with authentic Air France decals.
Issued 1957/58. Deleted 1968. Approx. 181mm long.
Wing span 197mm. DC/P.   £175   £95   £35

No. 70 Four Wheeled Covered Trailer
Red trailer body and chassis with matching wheels and
smooth black tyres. Green canopy and silver tow bar.
Removable cover. The trailer fixes on to lorries equipped
with hooks. Issued 1957. Deleted 1968. Length 111mm.
DC/P.   £30   £15   £10

No. 80A Panhard Armoured Reconnaissance Car
French military green. Revolving gun turret. Black tyres
and displaying army decals. Issued 1958. Deleted 1968.
103mm. DC/P.   £50   £25   £10

No. 80B Jeep Hotchkiss Willys
Military green with black tyres and spare wheel on rear.
Issued 1958. Deleted 1968. Length 66mm. DC/P.   £45   £20   £10

No. 80C AMX 13-Tonne Tank
Military green with revolving gun turret and rubber
tracks. Army decals. Issued 1958. Deleted 1968. 108mm.
DC/P.   £45   £25   £10

**No. 80D Berliet Cross-Country Military Lorry
(Removable Cover)**
Military green with large ribbed black wheels and spare
wheel. Issued September 1958. Deleted 1968. 144mm.
DC/P.   £125   £65   £35

No. 80E 155 ABS Howitzer
Military green. Adjustable gun. Issued 1958. Deleted
1968. 146mm. DC/P.   £45   £20   £10

No. 90A Richier Steam Roller
Golden yellow with red and grey wheels. Driver in dark
uniform. Issued 1957/58. Deleted 1968. 96mm. DC/T.   £95   £55   £25

No. 151a Medium Tank
Green with French Army squadron markings. Rotating
turret and aerial. Chains. Issued in France 1938. Deleted
1940. 92mm. DC/TP.   £135   £75   £35

FRENCH DINKIES	MB	MU	GC

No. 152a Light Tank
Matt green with aerial and rotating turret and French
Army squadron markings. Chains. Imported into France
1938. Deleted 1940. 68mm. DC.

	£75	£45	£24

No. 161 Anti-Aircraft Unit
Matt green with French squadron markings. Issued in
France 1939. Deleted 1940. 115mm. DC/TP/RT.

	£75	£55	£25

No. 162 Anti-Tank Gun
Matt green with French squadron markings. Made and
issued in France 1939. Deleted 1940. 78mm. DC/RT.

	£45	£25	£10

No. 268 Renault Dauphine
Red with silver wheels, bumpers, lights and grille. Issued
1958. Deleted 1968. 92mm. DC/P.

	£125	£75	£35

No. 514 Alfa Romeo Giulia 1600
White. Silver wheels, bumpers, grille and lights. Issued
1961. Deleted 1963. 102mm.

	£95	£55	£25

No. 520 Fiat 600D
Cream with red interior. Silver wheels, grille, lights and
bumpers. Black tyres. Issued 1958. Deleted 1960. 71mm.

	£115	£75	£35

No. 529 Vespa 2cv
Mid- or dark blue. Black roof, silver wheels, bumpers,
grille and lights. Issued 1957. Deleted 1965. 88mm.

	£65	£25	£10

No. 531 Fiat Grande Vue
Cream with grey roof. Gold or silver wheels and black
tyres. Silver grille, bumpers and lights. Issued 1960.
Deleted 1964. 91mm.

	£125	£75	£35

No. 532 Lincoln Premier
Blue body although shades vary. Silver roof, wheels,
bumpers and lights. White wall tyres. Issued 1957.
Deleted 1965. 112mm.

	£250	£100	£50

No. 533 Mercedes Benz
Metallic blue or red body. Silver wheels, grille, bumpers
and lights. White or fawn interior. Black tyres. Issued
1954. Deleted 1978. 147mm.

	£95	£45	£15

No. 536 Renault 16
Light blue. Silver wheels, grille, bumper and lights. Black
tyres. Issued 1957. Deleted 1965. 92mm.

	£65	£35	£15

No. 539 Citroën ID19 Estate
Fawn with white roof. Red interior. Silver bumpers, grille
and lights. White wall tyres. Issued 1957. Deleted 1965.
112mm.

£75 £65 £25

No. 542 Simca Aronde Taxi
Dark blue or black with white interior. Red roof with taxi
sign in red and grey. Silver wheels, bumpers, grille and
lights. White wall tyres. Issued 1957. Deleted 1963. 95mm.

£125 £75 £35

No. 543 Renault Floride
Metallic fawn, light brown or purple (worth treble).
Silver wheels, grille and bumpers. White wall tyres.
Issued 1957. Deleted 1965. 92mm.

£85 £35 £15

No. 546 Austin Healey 100
White body with red interior and blue driver. Silver
wheels, grille and bumpers. Black tyres. Watch for colour
variants which could be worth more. Issued 1957.
Deleted 1960. 85mm.

£175 £100 £45

No. 547 Panhard PL17
Purple. Silver wheels, grille, bumpers and lights. Black
tyres. Issued 1957. Deleted 1968. 100mm.

£125 £75 £35

No. 548 Fiat 1800 Estate
Cream with dark brown roof and red interior. Silver
wheels, grille, bumpers and lights. White wall tyres.
Issued 1957. Deleted 1965.

£65 £35 £15

No. 533 Peugeot 404
White or grey with red interior. Silver wheels, bumpers,
grille and lights. White wall tyres. Issued 1957. Deleted
1960. 100mm.

£65 £35 £15

No. 561 Citroën Cibie Van
Blue or bluish green with yellow wheels and black tyres.
Silver grille and bumpers. 'Cibie' in red on yellow
background on sides. Issued 1952. Deleted 1968. 90mm.

£175 £95 £55

No. 575 Panhard SNCF Articulated Lorry
Dark blue with matching mudguards etc. Decals and
lettering in gold, white and blue on sides. Issued 1963.
Deleted 1968. 220mm.

£180 £95 £65

No. 811 Caravan
Golden yellow with red lines and white roof. Issued 1960.
Deleted 1968. 118mm.

£45 £25 £10

FRENCH DINKIES	MB	MU	GC

No. 814 AML Panhard Armoured Car
French military colours. Issued 1960. Deleted 1968.
80mm.

	£95	£55	£25

No. 815 EBR Panhard Tank
French military colours. Issued 1960. Deleted 1968.
132mm.

	£85	£45	£15

No. 817 AMX 13-Tonne Tank
French military colours. Issued 1960. Deleted 1968.
134mm.

	£95	£55	£25

No. 820 Renault Army Ambulance
Military green with large red cross on white background
on roof and sides. Issued 1960. Deleted 1968. 110mm.

	£95	£55	£25

No. 821 Mercedes Unimog Army Truck
French military green with fawn cover. Issued 1962.
Deleted 1964. 118mm.

	£95	£45	£25

No. 822 Half Track M3
French military green with decals. Issued 1962. Deleted
1964. 122mm.

	£95	£45	£25

No. 884 Brockway Bridge Layer
French military green. Issued 1962. Deleted 1964. 181mm.
Rare.

	£255	£125	£55

No. 886 Richier Road Level Machine
Yellow body with red wheels. Black tyres and blue driver.
Issued 1960. Deleted 1964. 122mm.

	£145	£75	£35

No. 893 Articulated Pipe Carrier
Light fawn body with matching wheels and black tyres.
Black pipe load. Issued 1963. Deleted 1965. 132mm.

	£155	£75	£45

No. 899 Turntable Fire Escape
Red body with matching wheels. White tyres. Silver grille
and extending ladder. Issued 1964. Deleted 1967. 121mm.

	£275	£125	£55

No. 972 Coles Crane Lorry
Orange, yellow and black with two drivers in blue.
Yellow wheels and black tyres. Silver grille and bumpers.
Two levers control the crane which pivots on a lorry.
Issued 1958. Deleted 1968. Lorry 163mm long overall.
240mm long with crane lowered. DC/P.

	£165	£100	£50

No. 1411 Alpine Renault A310
Red. Metal wheels. Black tyres. Silver grille. White
interior. Issued 1965. Deleted 1968. 89mm.

	£75	£35	£15

No. 1421 Opel GT 1900
One of the early Super Speedy wheels models 'Super Rapide'. Blue. Silver wheels, bumpers, lights and grille. Silver luggage carrier on rear. Red interior. Issued 1965. Deleted 1968. 92mm. £75 £35 £15

No. 1453 Renault 6
Red or rose pink. Silver wheels, bumpers, lights and grille. Silver trim with white interior. Black tyres. Issued 1964. Deleted 1967. 86mm. £65 £25 £10

GIFT SETS

No. 10 Railway Miniatures Set
Station master, mechanic, controller, greaser and lamp lighter. Issued 1956. Deleted 1968. £65 — —

No. 11 Travellers Miniatures Set
Campers, skier, lady traveller and porter with luggage. Issued 1956. Deleted 1968. £65 — —

No. 24/58 Gift Box Tourisme 1958
Unique French Dinky set consisting of five cars. Issued 1958. Deleted 1968. £350 — —

No. 40 Road Signs Set
Six road signs in yellow box. Issued 1955. Deleted 1968. £65 — —

No. 41 Road Signs Set
Six more road signs in special box. Issued 1955. Deleted 1968. £65 — —

No. 49D Service Station
Set of Esso pumps with station flag in red, white and blue livery on grey stand. Issued 1955. Deleted 1968. 90mm long x 92mm high. £50 — —

No. 60 Air Gift Box Set
Vickers Viscount Mystère IVA, SO4050 Vautour and Sikorsky S58. Issued 1958. Deleted 1968. £50 — —

No. 64 French Factory Aeroplanes Set
Contains Nos. 61a Dewoitine, 64a Amiot 370, 64b Bloch 200, 64c Potez 63 and 64d Potez 662. Issued 1937(?). Deleted 1940(?). £2200 — —

FRENCH DINKIES	MB	MU	GC

Meccano Set (Box) No. 0
Makes 30 Meccano models. Instruction booklet. Box 0A
transforms box 0 into box 1. Issued 1952. Deleted 1968. £75 — —

Meccano Set (Box) No. 1
Makes 62 Meccano models. Instruction booklet. Box 1A
transforms box 1 into box 2. Issued 1952. Deleted 1968. £95 — —

Meccano Set (Box) No. 2
Makes 84 Meccano models. Instruction booklet. Box 2A
transforms box 2 into box 3. Issued 1953. Deleted 1968. £275 — —

Meccano Set (Box) No. 3
Makes 84 Meccano models, although contents are
different from Set No. 2. Larger models can be made.
Instruction booklet. Box 3A transforms box 3 into box 4.
Issued 1953. Deleted 1968. £295 — —

Meccano Set (Box) No. 4
Makes 94 large Meccano models. Instruction booklet. Box
4A transforms box 4 into box 5. Issued 1954. Deleted 1968. £310 — —

Meccano Set (Box) No. 5
Makes 105 super models. Instruction booklet. Box 5A
transforms box 5 into box 6. Issued 1954. Deleted 1968. £350 — —

Meccano Set (Box) No. 6
Makes 115 models of a large size and super quality.
Instruction booklet. Box 6A transforms box 6 into box 7.
Issued 1954. Deleted 1968. £295 — —

Meccano Set (Box) No. 7
Even larger set to make 136 models. Instruction booklet.
Box 7A transforms box 7 into box 8. Strong box container.
Issued 1955. Deleted 1968. £350 — —

Meccano Set (Box) No. 8
Makes 157 models. Instruction booklet. Box 8A
transforms box 8 into box 9. Issued 1955. Deleted 1968. £375 — —

Meccano Set (Box) No. 9
With this fine set one could make a large bulldozer or a
hydraulic press. In a new three-tier box beautifully
illustrated on cover. Altogether one could build 177
models. Instruction booklet. Box 9A transforms box 9 into
box 10. Issued 1955. Deleted 1968. £400 — —

FRENCH DINKIES	MB	MU	GC

Meccano Set (Box) No. 10
As a result of the growing demand for more parts and
even bigger sets after a nationwide poll in model shops
in France, Germany, Holland and Italy, the firm decided
to excel itself and put out a large Meccano set in a wooden
case with handles both inside and out. The trays were a
treasure to behold and any person owning such a set is
very lucky indeed. This set enables collectors to build
over 200 models. Instruction booklet. Issued 1956.
Deleted 1966. £450 — —

RAILWAYS

Apart from cars and Meccano, the French Dinky company made marvellous
train sets and fine coaches, wagons and buildings to go with them. I give a list
of good investments from catalogues and leaflets.

The mechanical Hornby trains are extremely well made and are guaranteed a
long life. They are particularly successful due to their excellent presentation and
the remarkable performance of their locomotives. And don't forget that the track
can be added to with more straight or curved rails, points or crossings. Each train
has a rail operated by a lever which enables the train to stop automatically.

BUFFER
Buffer No. 1
Sprung stoppers. Can be adapted for use on all electric
and mechanical Hornby rails. Place for standard lighting.
Issued 1955. Deleted 1968. £25 £10 £5

CARRIAGES
Mixed Passenger/Baggage Car
Sliding doors. Issued 1956. Deleted 1968. 25cm long. £55 £35 £15

Pullman Saloon Car
Issued 1958. Deleted 1968. 25cm long. £55 £35 £15

Restaurant Car
Issued 1958. Deleted 1968. 25cm long. £55 £35 £15

CONTROL PANEL
Control Panel
Supplies current for the running of five accessories. Book
with instructions for the wiring of the transformer. Issued
1955. Deleted 1968. £25 £10 £5

EXPRESS TRAINS
Express Train 1
Locomotive, tender and car. The curved rails of the track
form a circle of 60cm in diameter. Train 33cm long. Issued
1953. Deleted 1968. £55 — —

Express Train 2
Same composition as Express Train 1 but with two cars
instead of one. Train 45cm long.

	MB	MU	GC
	£65	—	—

Express Train 3
As well as the locomotive, tender, and two cars, this set
contains an attractively decorated metal siding. In
addition, the rail track is more important than that of
Express Trains 1 and 2, consisting of 6 curved and 2
straight sections of rail to form an oval of 86 x 60cm.
Issued 1955. Deleted 1968.

	£75	—	—

FOOTBRIDGE
Metallic Footbridge
Equipped with two semaphores. Can span two tracks.
Issued 1954. Deleted 1968.

	£45	£25	£10

LEVEL CROSSINGS
Level Crossing No. 1
With signalman's box. In two separate parts, allowing the
passage of one or more tracks. Working barriers. Place for
standard lighting. Issued 1956. Deleted 1968.

	£45	£25	£10

Level Crossing M
In two separate parts. Working barrier. Place for standard
lighting. Issued 1955. Deleted 1968.

	£25	£15	£10

LOADING BAY
Loading Bay
Equipped with a working crane which pivots. Issued
1955. Deleted 1968. 58cm long x 14cm wide x 55cm high.

	£65	£45	£15

POINTS
Electric Points
Radio controlled points. Issued 1955. Deleted 1968.

	£35	£15	£10

SIGNAL
Round Signal
Lever for red signal. Place for standard electric lighting.
Issued 1955. Deleted 1968.

	£25	£15	£10

SIGNAL BOXES
Automatic Signal Box
Red and green lights. Can be used on any electric Hornby
track. Controls the arrival and departure of trains.
Instruction booklet and wiring instructions. Issued 1954.
Deleted 1968.

	£50	£30	£15

Signal Box
Can be dismantled. Plexiglass cabin. Issued 1957. Deleted
1968. 29cm long x 28cm wide x 15cm high.

	£35	£15	£10

STATIONS
Station No. 20
Can be dismantled. Crossing over the track to interior of
the station. Issued 1957. Deleted 1968. 43cm long x 29cm
wide x 17cm high.

£75 £45 £25

Station No. 21
Can be dismantled. Plexiglass. Crossing over two tracks
to the station interior. Issued 1957. Deleted 1968. 52cm
long x 28cm wide x 22cm high.

£95 £55 £25

TRAIN SETS
Electric Autorail Train Set
Bugatti type with two cars. Same motor as the O.BB
locomotive, two lights and automatic coupling. Issued
1957. Deleted 1968.

£195 — —

Mechanical Autorail Train Set
Two Bugatti-type autorail cars with automatic coupling
devices, allowing the coupling of Hornby wagons. Same
engine as 'M' series. Curved rail sections forming a circle
of 60cm in diameter. Possible to buy the autorails
separately. Issued 1955. Deleted 1968. Locomotive 42cm
long.

£125 — —

'M' SERIES
This robust train consists of a locomotive, the movement
of which is protected from dust and shocks. The wagons
come with automatic coupling devices and standard
railway track. This layout can be completed with straight
or curved rails, points and crossings. Each track has an
automatic stopping lever. Guarantee leaflet.

Train Set M5
An electric BB-M type locomotive with 2 passenger cars
with opening windows. Six curved and 2 straight rail
sections form an oval of 86 x 60cm. Locomotive can be
bought separately. Issued 1955. Deleted 1968.

£135 — —

Train Set M6
An electric BB-M type locomotive with two tip cart
wagons. Same track as M5. Issued 1956. Deleted 1968.

£135 — —

Train Set M7
Same train and track as M5, plus station, siding, signal
box and two signals. All the accessories are in finely
decorated metal. Issued 1956. Deleted 1968.

£150 — —

FRENCH DINKIES | MB | MU | GC

MO Train Set
An electric BB-M type locomotive with 2 passenger cars
with slit windows. Six curved and 2 straight rail sections
form an oval of 86 x 60cm. Locomotive can be bought
separately. Issued 1955. Deleted 1968.

£135 — —

ELECTRIC SERIES 0–20 VOLTS — 32MM GAUGE
It is possible to change the direction of the locomotives or
autorails of the 'O' series. Each train has an O
transformer, 12 curved rail sections forming a circle of
120cm in diameter, and 2 pamphlets containing a
guarantee and explanations on how the Hornby trains
work.

OB-BM Train Set Le Bourguignon
O.BB locomotive, refrigeration car with sliding doors and
wagon with detachable tarpaulin. Issued 1956. Deleted
1968.

£150 — —

Train Set OV-AM Le Breton
O.VA steam locomotive with tender, refrigeration car
with sliding doors and wagon with opening doors. Issued
1956. Deleted 1968.

£175 — —

Train Set OB-BV Le Mistral
O.BB locomotive, passenger car with bogies and mixed
car (passengers and baggage) with bogies and opening
doors. Issued 1956. Deleted 1968.

£150 — —

'T' SERIES – NOVELTY (TOTAL SECURITY)
These two remote control trains are equipped with a new
locomotive and transformer ensuring total safety. The
transformer can be connected to currents of either 110 or
220 volts and controls from a distance the speed and
direction of the T-BB locomotive. This locomotive is
equipped with special tyres and has exceptional track
and traction holding which allows the train to start
smoothly with its 20 wagons and bogies. Each train in the
Hornby 'ST' series comes with 2 brochures containing a
guarantee and instructions on the use of the radio
controlled train. All the parts which go with these trains
can be bought separately.

£225 — —

TB-BV Train Set Le Drapeau
This is an exceptional set in the authentic livery of Le
Drapeau. T-BB locomotive, pullman car, restaurant car,
ST transformer and 12 curved rail sections forming a
circle of 120cm in diameter. Issued 1956. Deleted 1968.

£155 — —

TB-BM Train Set Le Provençal
T-BB locomotive, car, low sided car, ST transformer and 12 curved rail sections forming a circle of 120cm in diameter. Issued 1958. Deleted 1968. £135 — —

T-BB Locomotive
The locomotive could be purchased separately from the sets. Motor with permanent magnet. Rubber tyres (four wheels). New hinged pantographs. Stoppers, automatic coupling, headlights. Issued 1958. Deleted 1968. £125 £75 £35

TRANSFORMERS
O Transformer
Three speed, hand controlled. 20v debit. Supplied with plug to light up the accessories, which are able to function when the train is stationary. Fused for safety. Issued 1955. Deleted 1968. £55 — —

ST Transformer
Power up to 40v. It is protected on the circuit by a self righting system. There was a special price for the speed control (introduced in 1958) which allows separate control of the speed and direction of the two locomotives on the same track or on two different tracks, as well as the possibility of a wide range of manoeuvres. A single hand control with a potentiometric rheostat reverser controls the speed and direction of the locomotives. Issued 1958. Deleted 1968. £55 — —

TUNNEL
Tunnel
Can be dismantled. Issued 1955. Deleted 1968. 29cm long x 28cm wide x 19cm high. £35 £15 £10

WAGONS
Arbel Wagon
For transporting coal and ore. Arbel decals on sides. Issued 1957. Deleted 1968. 23.5cm. £55 £35 £15

Azur Tanker Wagon
Azur decals on side. Issued 1958. Deleted 1968. 23.5cm. £65 £35 £15

Cattle Wagon No. 2
Opening doors. Issued 1956. Deleted 1968. 23.5cm. £55 £35 £15

Crane Wagon No. 1
Function crane with pivot. Issued 1954. Deleted 1958. 15.5cm. £35 £15 £10

Double Bolt Wagon
Issued 1952. Deleted 1968. 15.5cm. £55 £35 £15

FRENCH DINKIES	MB	MU	GC
Esso Tanker Wagon Aluminium paintwork. Issued 1954. Deleted 1968. 15.5cm.	£65	£35	£15
IS Wagon Two sliding doors. Issued 1956. Deleted 1968. 18cm.	£55	£35	£15
Low Sided Wagon Ideal for transporting Dinky Toys. Issued 1957. Deleted 1968. 23.5cm.	£55	£35	£15
Novelty Covered Wagon Two sliding doors. Issued 1967. Deleted 1968. 23.5cm.	£55	£35	£15
Passenger Wagon Issued 1957. Deleted 1968. 25cm.	£65	£45	£25
Primagaz Tanker Wagon White paintwork. 'Primagaz le Butane Français' decals on sides. Issued 1955. Deleted 1968. 15.5cm.	£65	£35	£10
Relief Wagon with Crane Working crane with pivot. Two sliding doors. Issued 1958. Deleted 1968. 23.5cm.	£55	£35	£15
Stef Refrigerated Wagon Two sliding doors. Issued 1953. Deleted 1968. 18cm.	£50	£25	£10
Tarpaulin Wagon Hoops and tarpaulin are removable. Issued 1953. Deleted 1968. 15.5cm.	£45	£25	£10
Timber Wagon For transporting tree trunks. Issued 1957. Deleted 1968. 23.5cm.	£65	£35	£15
Tip Cart Wagon with Look-Out Seat Issued 1954. Deleted 1968. 15.5cm.	£35	£15	£10
Tip Wagon Tips two ways. Issued 1955. Deleted 1968. 15.5cm.	£45	£25	£15

GARAGES, PUMPS, TYRES AND SPECIAL TELEPHONE BOXES

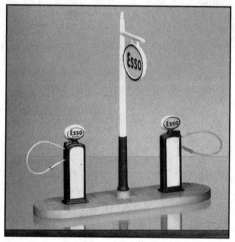

No. 781   Esso Petrol Pump Station

MODEL	MB	MU	GC

No. 12c Telephone Box
Cream with silver windows. Red from 1946 to 1954 when
it was renumbered 750. Boxes of six. Price 4d. Post-war
price 10d. Issued 1936. Deleted 1940.

Pre-war	—	£45	£10
Post-war	—	£25	£7

No. 42a Police Box
Very dark blue police colours (much darker than the
post-war variety) with 'Police' on sides. Never had
individual boxes but sold single and unwrapped or in a
set with Nos. 42B, 42C and 42D. Should anybody find a
set for any Dinky models of the pre-war period they

should write to me for a separate valuation. Price 6d.
Issued August 1936. Deleted 1940. DC.

	MB	MU	GC
Single	—	£45	£10
Set	£125	—	—

No. 42A Police Box
Blue police colours with 'Police' on sides. Not individually boxed but sold in boxes of six at 5/-. Issued 1948. Renumbered 751 in 1954/55. Deleted 1960. 66mm high. DC.

Single	—	£35	£10
Box of six	£75	—	—

No. 43a RAC Box
Blue with RAC badge on sides. Never had individual box but sold single and unwrapped or in a set with Nos. 43B, 43C and 43D. Price 6d. Issued October 1935. Deleted 1940. 81mm high. TP.

Single	—	£55	£15
Set	£175	—	—

No 44a AA Box
Black and yellow with AA badge and three signposts on top. Not individually boxed. Price 8d. Issued October 1935. Deleted 1940. 81mm high. TP.

Single	—	£55	£15
Set	£175	—	—

No. 45 Garage
Opening double doors. Price 1/6. Issued December 1935. Deleted 1940. TP.

	£175	£100	£50

No. 48 Garage and Service Station
Pink or maroon with 'Filling and Service Station...Petrol, Oil, Air, Tyres and Spares'. Price 1/6. Issued June 1935. Deleted 1940. TP. Garage 145mm x 45mm. 97mm high.

	£175	£100	£50

No. 49 Set of Petrol and Oil Pumps
Price 1/6. Issued June 1935. Deleted 1940.

	£200	—	—

No. 49 Set of Petrol and Oil Pumps
Price 5/-. Issued 1948. Deleted 1953. DC.

	£125	—	—

No. 49a Bowser Petrol Pump
Green with rubber pipe. Not individually boxed but boxed only with No. 49. Price 4d. Issued 1935. Deleted 1940. 46mm high.

	—	£35	£10

No. 49A Bowser Petrol Pump
Green with plastic pipe. Not individually boxed. Price 1/-. Issued 1948. Deleted 1953. 46mm.

	—	£20	£5

ROADSIDE SERVICES	MB	MU	GC

No. 49b Wayne Petrol Pump
Blue with rubber pip. Not individually boxed. Price 4d.
Issued June 1935. Deleted 1940. 39mm. DC.   — £35 £10

No. 49B Petrol Pump
Blue with plastic hose. Not individually boxed. Price 1/-.
Issued 1948. Deleted 1953. 39mm. DC.   — £20 £5

No. 49c Theo Petrol Pump
Royal blue with rubber pipe. Not individually boxed.
Price 4d. Issued June 1935. Deleted 1940. 58mm. DC.   — £35 £10

No. 49C Petrol Pump
Brown with plastic hose. Not individually boxed. Price
1/-. Issued 1948. Deleted 1953. 53mm. DC.   — £20 £5

No. 49d Shell Petrol Pump
Red with white top to pump. Rubber pipe. Not
individually boxed. Price 4d. Issued June 1935. Deleted
1940. 58mm. DC.   — £35 £10

No. 49D Shell Petrol Pump
Red with plastic hose. Not individually boxed. Price 1/-.
Issued 1948. Deleted 1953. 53mm. DC.   — £20 £5

No. 49e Pratts Oil Bin
Yellow with 'Pratts Motor Oil'. Front hinges to show
three red oil dispensers. Not individually boxed. Price 3d.
Issued June 1935. Deleted 1940. 32mm. DC.   — £35 £10

No. 49E Oil Bin
Post-war casting identical to pre-war. Post-war version
had no transfer as Pratts no longer existed; only Shell
survived the war. Not individually boxed. Price 10d.
Issued 1948. Deleted 1953. 32mm. DC/TP.   — £20 £5

No. 502 Garage
Light blue and grey. Automatic opening doors. Imported
French Dinky Toy. Price 8/7. Issued September 1961.
Deleted 1963. 272mm. P.   £30 £15 £5

No. 750 Telephone Box
Post Office red. The casting is the same as No. 12C. Sold
in boxes of six. Price 10d. Issued 1954. Deleted 1962.
58mm high. DC.
Single   — £15 £5
Box of six   £100 — —

No. 751 Police Box
Blue. Renumbering of No. 42A. Price 1/9. Issued 1954.
Deleted 1960. 66mm high. Sold in boxes of six.

	MB	MU	GC
Single	—	£15	£5
Box of six	£100	—	—

No. 781 Esso Petrol Pump Station
Brown with cream and red etc. or pale grey base (rare and
worth double). Plastic hoses. Price 4/11. Issued July 1955.
Deleted 1966. 114mm long.   £25 £10 £5

No. 782 Shell Petrol Station
Brown or grey base with four red and yellow pumps
which are metal, while sign is plastic. Plastic kiosk and
plastic hoses on pumps. Price 7/6. Issued November
1960. Deleted 1971. 203mm. DC/P.   £35 £15 £10

No. 783 BP Petrol Station
Grey, green and yellow. BP plastic sign and kiosk. Price
7/6. Issued November 1960. Deleted 1971. 203mm.
DC/P.   £35 £15 £10

No. 785 Service Station
Yellow and black with garage opening door. Price
£1/7/6. Issued June 1960. Deleted 1964. 335mm x 185mm.
P.   £35 £15 £10

No. 786 Tyre Rack and Tyres
Green with 21 tyres of various sizes. Four white and the
rest black. Dunlop trade mark tyres. Not individually
boxed. Price 2/11. Issued June 1960. Deleted 1967. 52mm.
DC/RT.   — £20 £5

SETS OF TYRES IN BOXES OF 12

Prices are for mint boxed in good condition. Tyres are in demand owing to the
increasing number of collectors and the fact that Dinky no longer makes any
models, tyres, parts etc. Any original parts, such as tyres, are often worth more
than many collector dealers tell customers. No model is worth a high price unless
it is in good condition and complete with correct tyres etc.

It should be noted that only genuine Dinky products are priced in this section.
In no way are prices quoted for mock-up tyres or imitation items.

No. 097 Rubber Wheels
Issued for the '35' series and motor cycles respectively. In
boxes of 12. Price 1/6. Issued late 1940. Stopped through
war. Reissued 1948/49. Deleted 1962. 13/32in.   £10 — —

	MB	MU	GC
No. 097 Rubber Wheels Price 1/6. Issued 1948. Deleted 1962. 7/16in.	£10	—	—
No. 020 Black Tyres Rubber. Price 2/-. Issued 1962. Deleted 1977. 16mm.	£5	—	—
No. 080 Black Tyres Rubber. Price 5/-. Issued 1962. Deleted 1976. 38mm.	£10	—	—
No. 081 White Tyres Price 1/6. Issued 1962. Deleted 1976. 14mm.	£5	—	—
No. 082 Black Tyres Price 2/-. Issued 1962. Deleted 1976. 20mm.	£5	—	—
No. 083 Grey Tyres Price 2/-. Issued 1963. Deleted 1969. 20mm.	£20	—	—
No. 084 Black Tyres Price 1/6. Issued 1963. Deleted 1976. 18mm.	£10	—	—
No. 085 White Tyres Price 1/6. Issued 1963. Deleted 1976. 15mm.	£10	—	—
No. 086 Black Tyres Price 2/-. Issued 1963. Deleted 1976. 16mm.	£10	—	—
No. 087 Black Tyres Price 4/6. Issued 1963. Deleted 1976. 35mm.	£15	—	—
No. 088 Black Tyres Price 2/-. Issued 1963. Deleted 1976. 25mm.	£10	—	—
No. 089 Black Tyres Price 2/-. Issued 1963. Deleted 1976. 19mm.	£10	—	—
No. 090 Black Tyres Price 1/6. Issued 1964. Deleted 1976. 14mm.	£10	—	—
No. 091 Black Tyres Price 1/6. Issued 1964. Deleted 1976. 13mm.	£10	—	—
No. 092 Black Tyres Price 2/-. Issued 1964. Deleted 1976. 15mm.	£10	—	—
No. 093 Black Tyres Price 3/6. Issued 1964. Deleted 1976. 27mm.	£15	—	—
No. 094 Black Tyres Price 2/-. Issued 1963. Deleted 1976. 20mm.	£10	—	—

	MB	MU	GC
No. 095 Black Tyres Price 1/6. Issued 1963. Deleted 1976. 18mm.	£10	—	—
No. 096 Black Tyres Price 2/-. Issued 1963. Deleted 1976. 24mm.	£15	—	—
No. 097 Black Tyres Price 3/6. Issued 1964. Deleted 1976. 32mm.	£15	—	—
No. 098 Black Tyres Price 2/-. Issued 1963. Deleted 1976. 17mm.	£10	—	—
No. 099 Black Tyres Price 2/-. Issued 1963. Deleted 1976. 20mm.	£15	—	—
No. 6677 Engraved Tyres Price 1/3. Issued 1963. Deleted 1968. 24mm.	£25	—	—
No. 10253 Engraved Tyres (Black) Price 1/3. Issued 1963. Deleted 1966. 32mm.	£25	—	—
No. 13978 Engraved Tyres Price 2/6. Issued 1962. Deleted 1965. 32mm.	£15	—	—
No. 14094 Engraved Tyres (Black) Price 1/3. Issued 1963. Deleted 1966. 25mm.	£25	—	—
No. 14095 Engraved Tyres (White) Price 1/3. Issued 1963. Deleted 1966. 13mm.	£10	—	—
No. 60036 Engraved Tyres (Black) Price 1/3. Issued 1963. Deleted 1966. 13mm.	£15	—	—
No. 030 Set of Tracks (Black) For No. 104. Price 2/-. Issued 1964. Deleted 1976.	£15	—	—
No. 031 Set of Tracks For Nos. 619, 622, 690, 694 and 984. Price 30p. Issued 1975. Deleted 1979.	£10	—	—
No. 032 Set of Tracks For Nos. 353 and 977. Price 45p. Issued 1965. Deleted 1979.	£7	—	—
No. 033 Set of Tracks For Nos. 654 and 683. Price 45p. Issued 1965. Deleted 1979.	£7	—	—

GARDEN TOOLS

No. 381   Garden Roller,   No. 382   Wheelbarrow and No. 384   Grasscutter

Many of the following models never had individual boxes and were sold in boxes of 6 (or sometimes 12). Therefore many of the items are priced as in mint unboxed and good condition, although prices are also given for mint boxes of six.

MODEL	MB	MU	GC
No. 105A Garden Roller Green and red. Price 1/-. Issued June 1948. Renumbered 381 in 1954. Deleted 1958. 66mm. DC.			
Single	—	£8	£5
Box of six	£125	—	—
No. 105B Wheelbarrow Brown with red interior. Metal wheel. Price 1/2. Issued June 1949. Renumbered 382 in 1954. Deleted 1958. 82mm. DC.			
Single	—	£8	£5
Box of six	£125	—	—
No. 105C Four Wheeled Hand Truck Green or blue. Four wheels with front swivel and extended handle. Price 1/11. Issued June 1949. Renumbered 383 in 1954. Deleted 1958. 126mm.			
Single	—	£8	£5
Box of six	£125	—	—

	MB	MU	GC

No. 105E Grass Cutter
Red, green or yellow. Rotating wheels and blade. Price
1/8. Issued November 1949. Renumbered 384 in 1954.
Deleted 1958. 73mm. DC.

	MB	MU	GC
Single	—	£8	£5
Box of six	£250	—	—

No. 381 Garden Roller
Red and green or brown and yellow (very rare and worth
at least double). Price 1/-. Issued July 1954. Deleted 1958.
67mm. DC.

	MB	MU	GC
Single	—	£15	£8
Box of six	£150	—	—

No. 382 Wheelbarrow
Brown with red interior. Also black and green with red
interior (worth at least double). Metal wheels.
Renumbering of 105B. Price 1/3. Issued June 1954.
Deleted 1958. 82mm. DC.

	MB	MU	GC
Single	—	£15	£8
Box of six	£150	—	—

No. 383 Four Wheeled Hand Truck
Blue, green or brown (worth double). Renumbering of
105C. Price 2/-. Issued 1954. Deleted 1958. 128mm. DC.

	MB	MU	GC
Single	—	£15	£8
Box of six	£150	—	—

No. 384 Grasscutter
Red, green or yellow. Rotating wheels and blade.
Renumbering of 105E. Price 1/4. Issued 1954. Deleted
1958. 73mm. DC.

	MB	MU	GC
Single	—	£15	£8
Box of six	£150	—	—

No. 385 Sack Truck
Blue with black wheels. Price 1/-. Issued 1954. Deleted
1960. 63mm. DC.

	MB	MU	GC
Single	—	£15	£8
Box of six	£150	—	—

No. 386 Lawn Mower
Green or red. Full working blades. First model in this
range to have individual box. Renumbering of 751. Price
5/6. Issued 1954. Deleted 1958. 140mm. DC.

	MB	MU	GC
	£75	£30	£15

No. 751 Lawn Mower
Green and red with full working blades. Price 5/-. Issued
June 1949. Renumbered 386 in 1954. Deleted 1978.
140mm. DC.

	MB	MU	GC
	£75	£30	£15

GIFT SETS

No. 239   Motorway Services Set

Ever since the first diecast models were made, people have been interested in collecting sets as a means of making sure that they did not miss any particular number as they were manufactured. I have set out the full list of all the sets made by the Dinky firm from the beginning.

I have given the prices as mint boxed only since once the box is lost the models become individual items. The very first sets had plain boxes, and later the name of the firm was added, plus the drawings or photographs of the particular models in question.

MODEL	MB	MU	GC
1st Set '22' Series Contains Nos. 22a Sports Car; 22b Sports Coupé; 22c Motor Truck; 22d Delivery Van; 22e Farm Tractor; and 22f Army Tank. Price 3/11. Advertised in the December 1933 *Meccano Magazine* but officially did not appear until 1934. Deleted 1940.	£3000	—	—
2nd Set '24' Series Contains Nos. 24a Ambulance; 24b Limousine; 24c Town Sedan; 24d Vogue Saloon; 241 Super Streamlined Saloon; 24f Sportsman Coupé; 24g Four Seater Sports Tourer; and 24h Two Seater Sports Tourer. Fitted with rubber tyres and silver plated radiators. Price 6/6. Issued 1934. Deleted 1940.	£3000	—	—
3rd Set '25' Series Contains Nos. 25a Wagon; 25b Covered Wagon; 25c Flat Truck; 25d Petrol Tank Wagon; 25e Tipping Wagon; and 25f Market Gardener's Van. Square-type vans with no rear wheel covers. Price 4/6. Issued 1934. Deleted 1940.	£3000	—	—

GIFT SETS	MB	MU	GC

4th Set '28/1' Series
Contains Nos. 28a Hornby Trains Van; 28b Pickford's Removal Van; 28c Manchester Guardian Van; 28d Oxo Van; 28f Palethorpe's Sausages Van; and 28l Ensign Cameras Van. Square-type vans with no rear wheel covers. Price 4/6, later reduced to 3/-. Issued August/October 1934. Deleted 1940. £3000 — —

5th Set '28/2' Series
Contains Nos. 28g Kodak Cameras Van; 28h Sharps Toffees Van; 28l Crawfords Biscuits Van; 28m Wakefield's Oil Van; 28n Marsh and Baxter's Sausages Van; and 22o Meccano Van. Price 3/-. Issued September/November 1934. Deleted 1940. £3000 — —

6th Set '30' Series
Contains Nos. 30a Chrysler Airflow Saloon; 30b Rolls Royce; 30c Daimler; 30d Vauxhall; 30e Bedford Breakdown Van; and 30f Ambulance. Fitted with rubber tyres and silver plated radiators. Price 4/6. Issued August 1935. Deleted 1940. £2500 — —

7th Set '28/1' Revised Set
Contains Nos. 28a Hornby Trains Van; 28b Pickford's Removal Van; 28c Manchester Guardian Van; 28e Firestone Tyres Van; 28f Palethorpe's Sausages Van; and 28n Atco Lawn Mowers Van. Price 4/6. Issued 1935. Deleted 1940. £2650 — —

8th Set '28/2' Revised Set
Contains Nos. 28d Oxo Van; 28g Kodak Cameras Van; 28h Dunlop Van; 28k Marsh and Baxter's Sausages Van; and 28p Crawfords Biscuits Van. Price 4/6. Issued 1935. Deleted 1940. £2600 — —

9th Set '33' Series
Contains Nos. 33a Mechanical Horse; 33b Flat Truck; 33c Open Wagon; 33d Box Van; 33l Dust Wagon; and 33f Petrol Tank Trailer. Price 3/6. Issued 1935. Deleted 1940. £2500 — —

10th Set Petrol Pumps Set
Contains Nos. 49a Bowser Pump; Wayne Pump; Theo Pump; Shell Pump; and one Pratt's Oil Bin fitted with thin rubber hose pipes and a metal nozzle which hooked onto the pump body. Price 1/6. Issued 1935. Deleted 1940. £1250 — —

11th Set '43' Series RAC Set
Contains Nos. 43a RAC Hut; 43b RAC Motor Cycle Patrol; 43c RAC Guide Directing Traffic; and 43d RAC Guide Saluting. Price 2/3. Issued 1935. Deleted 1940. £1000 — —

12th Set '44' Series AA Set
Contains Nos. 44a AA Hut; 44b AA Motor Cycle Patrol;
44c AA Guide Directing Traffic; 44d AA Guide Saluting.
Price 2/3. Issued 1935. Deleted 1940. — £2000 — —

13th Set '28/3' Series
Contains Nos. 28r Swan's Van; 28s Fry's Van; 28t Ovaltine
Van; 28w Osram Van; 28x Hovis Van; and 28y
Exide/Drydex Van. Price 4/6. Issued 1936. Deleted 1940. £2000 — —

14th Set '42' Series Police Set
Contains Nos. 42a Police Box; 42b Motor Cycle Patrol; 42c
Point Duty Policeman in white coat; and 42d Point Duty
Policeman. Price 1/11. Issued 1936. Deleted 1940. £600 — —

15th Set '280' Series
Contains Nos. 280a Viyella Van; 280b Lyon's Van; 280c
Shredded Wheat Van; 280d Bisto Van; 280e Ekco Van; and
280f Mackintosh's Van. Price 4/6. Issued 1937. Deleted
1940. £4000 — —

**16th Set '151' Series Royal Tank Corps Medium Tank
Set**
Contains Nos. 151a 12-Ton, 90hp Medium Tank; 151b
3-Ton Transport Wagon; 151c Cooker Trailer with Jack
Stand; 151d Water Tank Trailer; and 151d Driver. Price
3/6. Issued 1938. Deleted 1940. £850 — —

17th Set '152' Series Royal Tank Corps Light Tank Set
Contains No. 152a Light Tank; 152b Reconnaissance Car;
152c Austin 7 Car; and 150d Driver. Price 2/6. Issued
1938. Deleted 1940. £850 — —

18th Set '150' Series Royal Tank Corps Personnel Set
Contains Nos. 150a Officer; 150b Private in sitting
position; 150c Private in standing position; and 150e
NCO. Price 10d. Issued 1938. Deleted 1940. £250 — —

19th Set '12' Series Postal Set
Contains Nos. 12a Pillar Box GPO; 12b Pillar Box Airmail;
12c Telephone Call Box; 12d Telegraph Messenger; 12e
Postman; and 34b Royal Mail Van. Price 2/3. Issued 1938.
Deleted 1940. £1000 — —

20th Set '37' Series Cyclist Set
Contains Nos. 37a Civilian Motor Cyclist; 37b Police
Motor Cyclist; and 37c Royal Corps of Signals Despatch
Rider. This set had an intricate casting with driver cast in
and solid white rubber wheels. Price 1/6. Issued 1938.
Deleted 1940. £350 — —

21st Set '36' Series Motor Vehicle Set

Contains Nos. 36a Armstrong Siddeley Limousine with driver and footman; 36b Two Seater Bentley Sports Coupé with driver and passenger; 36c Humber Vogue Saloon with driver and footman; 36d Streamlined Rover Saloon with driver and passenger; 36e Two Seater British Salmson Sports Car with driver; and 36e Four Seater British Salmson Sports model with driver. A very unusual set comprising cars, drivers and passengers etc. Fitted with detachable rubber tyres and silver plated radiators. Price 5/6. Issued 1938. Deleted 1940.

| | £4750 | — | — |

22nd Set '161' Series Mobile Anti-Aircraft Unit Set

Contains Nos. 161a Lorry with searchlight and 161b Anti-Aircraft Gun on mobile platform. Price 3/-. Issued 1939. Deleted 1940.

| | £300 | — | — |

23rd Set '162' Series Field Gun Set

Contains Nos. 162a Light Dragon Motor and Tractor; 162b Trailer; and 162c Gun. Price 2/-. Issued 1939. Deleted 1940.

| | £400 | — | — |

24th Set '38' Series Sports Car Set

Contains Nos. 38a Frazer Nash BMW Sports Car; 38b Sunbeam Talbot Sports Car; 38c Lagonda Sports Car; 38d Alvis Sports Tourer; 38e Triumph Dolomite Sports Coupé; and 38f SS Jaguar Sports Car. All fitted with detachable rubber tyres. Price 5/-. Issued 1939. Deleted 1940.

| | £6000 | — | — |

25th Set '39' Series Sedans and Coupés Set

Contains Nos. 39a Packard Super 8 Touring Sedan Car; 39b Oldsmobile 6 Sedan Car; 39c Lincoln Zephyr Coupé; 39d Buick Viceroy Saloon Car; 39e Chrysler Royal Sedan; and 39f Studebaker State Commander Saloon Car. All fitted with detachable rubber tyres. Price 5/-. Issued 1939. Deleted 1940.

| | £6000 | — | — |

26th Set '160' Series Royal Artillery Personnel Set

Contains Nos. 160a NCO; 160b Gunner sitting; two figures; 160c Gun Layer; and 160d Standing Gunner. These models were intended for use on the guns of the '161' and '162' series sets. Price 10d. Issued 1939. Deleted 1940.

| | £75 | — | — |

27th Set '156' Series Mechanised Army Set

Special combined set in a special box consisting of the four army '151', '152', '161' and '162' series sets. Price 12/6. Issued 1939. Deleted 1940.

| | £1500 | — | — |

28th Set '23' Series Racing Car Set
Contains Nos. 23F Alfa Romeo; 23G Cooper Bristol
Racing Car; 23H Ferrari Racing Car; 232J HWM; 23K
Talbot Lago; and 23N Maserati. Price 12/6. Issued 1953.
Deleted 1966.   £4500   —   —

No. 1 Military Set
Contains Nos. 621 3-Ton Army Wagon; 641 1-Ton Army
Cargo Truck; 674 Austin Champ; and 676 Armoured
Personnel Carrier. Price 12/6. Issued March 1955.
Deleted 1968.   £2500   —   —

No. 695 Howitzer and Tractor Set
Contains Nos. 689 and 693. Price 13/11. Issued 1962.
Deleted 1966.   £250   —   —

No. 697 25-Pounder Field Gun Set
Contains Nos. 688 Field Artillery Tractor and Driver; 687
Trailer; and 686 Gun. Price 10/9. Issued 1957. Deleted
1972.   £250   —   —

No. 698 Tank Transporter Set
Contains Nos. 660 Tank Transporter carrying 651 Tank.
Price £1/1/11. Issued 1957. Deleted 1964.   £450   —   —

No. 699 Military Vehicles Set
Contains Nos. 621, 641, 674 and 676. Green. Price 17/6.
Issued March 1955. Deleted 1964.   £350   —   —

No. 1 Farmyard Equipment Set
Contains Nos. 27A, 27B, 27C, 27G and 27H. Price 17/3.
Issued December 1952. Deleted 1954. Renumbered 398.
Deleted 1976.   £350   —   —

No. 2 Commercial Vehicles Set
Contains Nos. 27D, 25M, 30N, 30P and 30S. Price 17/9.
Issued December 1952. Deleted 1966.   £750   —   —

No. 3 Passenger Cars Set
Contains Nos. 27F, 30H, 40E, 40G, 40H and 140B. Price
15/-. Issued November 1952. Deleted 1976.   £750   —   —

No. 4 Racing Cars Set
Contains Nos. 23F, 23G, 23H, 23J and 23N. Price 12/6.
Issued October 1953. Deleted 1971. Renumbered 249 in
1954. Deleted 1960.   £750   —   —

No. 118 Tow-Away Glider Set
Contains Nos. 135 Triumph 2000 in metallic green with
white roof and red interior. 'Southdown Gliding Club' in

red. Glider set is also in blue (worth double). Price 15/3.
Issued 1965. Deleted 1966. 289mm long overall. £150 — —

No. 121 Goodwood Racing Set
Contains Nos. 112, 113, 120 and 182 plus figures. Price
£1/2/11. Issued 1963. Deleted 1966. £400 — —

No. 122 Touring Set
Contains Nos. 188, 193, 195, 270, 295 and 796. Price
£1/5/11. Issued 1963. Deleted 1965. £300 — —

No. 123 Mayfair Set
Contains Nos. 142, 150, 186, 194, 198 and 199 plus four
civilians from No. 009 set. Price £1/15/11. Issued 1963.
Deleted 1965. £500 — —

No. 124 Holiday Set
Contains Nos. 952, 137, 142 and 796. Price £1/15/11.
Issued 1964. Deleted 1967. £300 — —

No. 125 Fun Ahoy Set
Contains Nos. 130 in pale blue and 796. Price 9/11. Issued
July 1964. Deleted 1969. £150 — —

No. 126 Motor Show Set
Contains Nos. 171, 133, 127 and 151. Price £1/1/-. Issued
1965/66. Deleted 1969. £300 — —

No. 149 Sports Models Set
Contains Nos. 107, 108, 110 and 111. Price 15/-. Issued
September 1958. Deleted 1961. £750 — —

No. 201 Racing Car Set
Contains No. 240 Cooper Racing Car and BRM Racer.
Price 9/6. Issued 1965/66. Deleted 1969. £200 — —

No. 237 Dinky Way Set
Contains 4 Dinky diecast vehicles (AA Bedford Service
Van; Triumph TR7; Police Mini; and Dumper Truck), 20ft
of scale model roads and 2 traffic signs. Price £4.55. Issued
1978. Deleted 1980. £350 — —

No. 245 Superfast Set
Contains Nos. 131 Jaguar E Type; 153 Aston Martin; and
188 Jensen FF. Price £1/18/11. Issued 1969. Deleted 1973. £350 — —

No. 246 International Set
Contains Nos. 187 De Tomaso 5000; 215 Ford; and 216
Dino Ferrari. Price £1/12/6. Issued 1969. Deleted 1973. £250 — —

No. 249 Racing Cars Set
Contains Nos. 231, 232, 233, 234 and 235. Renumbering of
No. 4 gift set. Price 12/6. Issued 1956. Deleted 1960.   £550   —   —

No. 249A Racing Cars Set
Contains Nos. 230, 231, 233 and 234. Talbot Lago replaced
the HWM which was deleted 1960. Price 14/11. Issued
1960. Deleted 1964.   £400   —   —

No. 297 Police Vehicles Set
Contains Nos. 250, 254, 255 and 287. No. 254 Ford Zodiac
Police Car replaced by No. 254 Police Range Rover. Price
14/6. Issued 1967. Replaced by No. 294 gift set in 1967.
No. 294 deleted 1970.
No. 297   £300   —   —
No. 294   £150   —   —

No. 298 Emergency Services Set
Contains Nos. 258, 263, 276 and 277 plus figures in plastic.
Price £1/16/11. Issued 1963. Deleted 1966.   £300   —   —

No. 299 Police Crash Squad Set
Contains Nos. 244 Plymouth Police Car; 732 Bell Police
Helicopter; and some bollards and signs. US models.
Price £2.75. Issued 1978. Deleted 1980.   £200   —   —

No. 299 Post Office Services Set
Contains Nos. 260, 261 and 750 plus messenger and
postman. Price 9/11. Issued 1957. Deleted 1960.   £550   —   —

No. 299 Motorway Services Set
Contains Nos. 257, 263, 269, 276 and 434. Price £2/13/11.
Issued 1963. Deleted 1967.   £500   —   —

No. 300 London Scene Set
Contains London taxi and London Routemaster bus.
Price £2.99. Issued 1978. Deleted 1980.   £250   —   —

No. 302 Emergency Squad Set
Contains paramedic truck, Cadillac ambulance and two
figures. Price £2.99. Issued 1978. Deleted 1980.   £350   —   —

No. 303 Special Commando Squad Set
Contains army truck, armoured car and army helicopter.
Price £2.25. Issued 1978. Deleted 1980.   £200   —   —

No. 304 Fire Rescue Set
Contains Nos. 384 Convoy Fire Rescue Truck; 282 Land
Rover Fire Appliance; and 195 Range Rover Fire Chief's
Car. Price £2.55. Issued 1978. Deleted 1980.   £300   —   —

No. 307 New Avengers Set
Not officially released because of industrial problems. However, some sets did become available in the very early part of 1978. Contains Purdey's TR7 car and Steed's Special Leyland Jaguar, featuring a novel fly-off assailant. Price £3.75. Issued and deleted 1978. DC/TP/P. Very rare and much sought after. £750 — —

No. 309 Star Trek Set
Contains USS Enterprise and Klingon Battle Cruiser. Price £3.75. Issued 1978. Deleted 1980. £750 — —

No. 387 Farm Equipment Set
Contains Nos. 300, 320, 321 and 324. Renumbering of No. 1 gift set. Price £1/1/-. Issued 1954. Deleted 1968. £200 — —

No. 399 Convoy Set
Contains Nos. 380, 381 and 382. Colour liveries varied a great deal in this set. Price £4.50. Issued 1978. Deleted 1980. £150 — —

No. 784 Dinky Goods Train Set
Contains blue engine, fawn trailer and red tanker wagon. Price £2.25. Issued 1972. Deleted 1975. Engine 115mm; trailer 92mm; and tanker wagon 92mm. £100 — —

No. 900 Building Site Set
Contains Nos. 437, 960, 962 and 965. Price £2/17/11. Issued 1963. Deleted 1970. £200 — —

No. 957 Fire Services Set
Contains Nos. 257, 955 and 956. Price £1/3/6. Issued 1959. Deleted 1966. £300 — —

No. 990 Car Transporter Set
Contains No. 982 Transporter and cars Nos. 154, 156, 161 and 162. Price £1/8/11. Issued 1955. Deleted 1960. £750 — —

No. 23 Series Racing Car Set
Contains Nos. 23C Mercedes Benz Racing Car; 23D Auto-Union Racing Car; and 23E Speed of the Wind Racing Car. Fitted with driver and detachable racing tyres. Price 1/11. Issued 1934. Deleted 1940. £1000 — —

No. 47 Road Signs Set
Contains Nos. 47E, 47F, 47G, 47H, 47K, 47M, 47N, 47P, 47Q, 47R, 47S and 37T. Price 1/6. Issued 1935. Deleted 1940. £50 — —

No. 50 Ships of the British Navy Set
Contains Nos. 50A Battle Cruiser Hood; 50B Battleship
Nelson (2 models); 50C Cruiser Effingham; 50D Cruiser
York; 50E Cruiser Delhi; 50F Destroyer Broke Class (3);
50G Submarine K Class; 50H Destroyer Amazon Class
(3); and 50K Submarine X Class. Price 3/6. Issued 1935.
Deleted 1940.   £200   —   —

No. 51 Famous Liners Set
Contains Nos. 51B Europa Star; 51C Rex; 51D Empress of
Britain; 51E Strathaird; 51F Queen of Bermuda; and 51G
Britannic. Price 3/6. Issued 1934. Deleted 1940. DC.   £200   —   —

No. 60 Aeroplanes Set
Contains Nos. 60A Imperial Airways Liner; 60B DH
Leopard Moth; 60C Percival Gull Plane; 60D Low Wing
Monoplane; 60E General Monospar Plane; and 60F
Cierva Autogiro. Price 3/-. Issued 1935. Deleted 1940.   £1000   —   —

No. 61 RAF Aeroplanes Set
Contains Nos. 60h Singapore Flying Boat; 60n Fairey
Battle Bombers (2 models); and 60p Gloster Gladiator
Biplanes (2). Issued 1937. Deleted 1940.   £350   —   —

No. 68 Camouflaged Aeroplanes Set
Contains Nos. 60s Fairey Battle Bombers (2 models); 60t
Armstrong Whitworth Whitley Bomber; 62d Bristol
Blenheim Bombers (2); 62e Vickers Supermarine Spitfire
Fighters (3); 62h Hawker Hurricane Fighters (3); 68a
Armstrong Whitworth Ensign Liners; and 68b Frobisher
Liner. Issued 1938. Deleted 1940.   £3000   —   —

No. 1 Station Staff Set
Contains Nos. 1A Stationmaster; 1B Guard; 1C Ticket
Collector; 1D Driver; 1E Porter with bags; and 1F Porter.
Price 1/6. Issued 1935. Deleted 1940.   £50   —   —

No. 2 Farmyard Animals Set
Contains Nos. 2A Horses (2 models); 2B Cows (2); 2C
Pigs; and 3D Sheep. Price 1/6. Issued 1934. Deleted 1940. £40   —   —

No. 3 Passengers Set
Contains Nos. 3A Woman and Child; 3B Businessman;
3C Male Hiker; 3D Female Hiker; 3E Newsboy; and 3F
Woman. Price 1/6. Issued 1935. Deleted 1940.   £40   —   —

No. 4 Engineering Staff Set
Contains Nos. 4A, 4B (2 models), 4C and 4E. Price 1/6.
Issued 1935. Deleted 1940.   £40   —   —

GIFT SETS	MB	MU	GC

No. 5 Train and Hotel Staff Set
Contains Nos. 5A Pullman Car Conductor; Pullman Car
No. B Waiters (2 models); and 5C Hotel Porters (2). Price
1/3. Issued 1935. Deleted 1940.

£40 — —

No. 6 Shepherd Set
Contains Nos. 6a Shepherd; 6d Sheepdog and 2d Sheep
(four models). Price 1/-. Issued 1934. Deleted 1940.

£50 — —

No. 16 Silver Jubilee Set
Price 1/6. Issued 1935. Deleted 1940.

£150 — —

No. 17 Diecast Passenger Train Set
Contains Nos. 17A Locomotive; 17B Tender; 20A Coach;
and 20B Guard's Van. Price 2/3. Issued 1935/36. Deleted
1940.

£150 — —

No. 18 Diecast Goods Train Set
Contains Nos. 21A Tank Locomotive and 21B Wagons
(three models). Price 1/9. Issued 1935. Deleted 1940.

£50 — —

No. 19 Diecast Mixed Goods Set
Contains Nos. 21A Tank Locomotive; 21B Wagon; 21D
Petrol Tanker; and 21E Lumber Wagon. Price 1/11.
Issued 1935. Deleted 1940.

£200 — —

No. 20 Diecast Passenger Train Set
Contains Nos. 21A Tank Locomotive; 20A Coaches (two
models); and 20B Guard's Van. Price 2/6. Issued 1935.
Deleted 1940.

£300 — —

No. 33R Mechanical Horse and Trailer Set
Contains Nos. 33RA Railway Mechanical Horse and
33RD Trailer with detachable rubber tyres. LMSR, LNER,
GWR or SR livery. 'Express Parcels Traffic' on sides. Price
1/6. Issued 1935. Deleted 1940.

£300 — —

No. 35 Small Cars Set
Contains Nos. 35A Saloon Car; 35B Racer; and 35C MG
Sports Model. Price 9d. Issued 1934/35. Deleted 1940.

£200 — —

LORRIES, TRUCKS AND COMMERCIAL VEHICLES

No. 504   Mobilgas Foden 14 Ton Tanker

All commercials are much sought after, especially what are called 'The Big Wheelers'. Anyone having the rare early pre-war models is indeed fortunate. Most of the early models had no individual boxes, and therefore I give only prices for mint unboxed and good condition in such instances.

MODEL	MB	MU	GC
No. 14A Electric Truck			
Grey, pale blue or dark blue. Price 3/3. Issued July 1948. Deleted 1954. Renumbered 400 in 1954, when a box was provided. 85mm. DC/TP/RT.			
Grey	—	£50	£25
Pale blue	—	£35	£10
Dark blue	—	£50	£15
No. 14C Coventry Climax Fork-Lift Truck			
Green and orange or brown and green. Fork raised by handle. Price 5/9. Issued November 1949. Deleted 1954. Renumbered 401 in 1954. 108mm. DC/RT/SW/D. Box in brown or blue cardboard.	£50	£25	£10

No. 22c Motor Truck
Blue and fawn or blue and red. Metal wheels and tinplate
radiator without headlights. Price 8d. Issued December
1933. Deleted 1935. 84mm. DC/TP.

	MB	MU	GC
	—	£250	£150

No. 22c Motor Truck
Red, green or blue with rear window in cab. Price 6d.
Issued May 1935. Deleted 1940. 84mm. DC/RT.

	—	£10	£7

No. 22s Small Searchlight Lorry
Grey, dark blue or dark grey. Price 1/-. Issued 1935/39.
Deleted 1940. 84mm. DC/RT.

	—	£295	£75

No. 25a Wagon
Red with black chassis. Open chassis, tinplate radiator
and as Type 1 with no lights. Price 9d. Issued April 1934.
Deleted 1938. 108mm. DC/RT/TP.

	—	£125	£30

No. 25a Wagon
Blue, red or grey with black chassis. Some Type 2s had
coloured chassis (pre-war only). This model had open
chassis and diecast radiator and is classed as Type 2 with
lights. Price 9d. Issued 1938. Deleted 1940. 105mm.
DC/RT/TP. Type 2 came out briefly post-war with
thicker axles.

Pre-war with black chassis	—	£95	£30
Pre-war with coloured chassis	—	£65	£30
Post-war	—	£65	£30

No. 25a/2 Wagon
Orange with pale green chassis or blue with orange
chassis. Otherwise as above.

Orange	—	£95	£45
Blue	—	£125	£45

No. 25A Wagon
Grey, blue or green with black chassis, diecast radiator
and lights as Type 3. Price 9d. Issued 1946. Deleted 1947.
105mm. DC/RT.

	—	£55	£15

No. 25A Wagon
Grey, red or red and cream. Black moulded chassis,
diecast radiator, and lights and bumpers as Type 4. Price
9d. Issued 1947. Deleted 1950. 110mm. DC/RT.

	—	£55	£15

No. 25b Covered Wagon
Blue or cream, or blue and cream with canvas top and
black chassis. It makes little difference what adverts
appear on this model as none are common. The only
adverts I have seen are for 'Meccano' and 'Carter
Paterson'. Both are for Type 2 and are listed later on. I
have not seen adverts on Type 1, which is the model with
open chassis, tinplate radiator and no lights. Price 9d.
Issued April 1934. Deleted 1938. 108mm. DC/TP/RT.

	MB	MU	GC
	—	£75	£40

No. 25b Covered Wagon
Grey body with grey canvas and black chassis. Open
chassis and diecast radiator with lights as Type 2. No
publicity. Price 9d. Issued 1938. Deleted 1940. 105mm.
DC/RT/TP. Type 2 came out briefly post-war.

	MB	MU	GC
Pre-war	—	£95	£30
Post-war	—	£50	£20

No. 25b Carter Paterson Covered Wagon
There are two 'Carter Paterson' transfers.
   The first is green or grey. Red band with 'Carter
Paterson' in white. Also 'Express Carrier London'. Open
chassis and diecast radiator with no lights as Type 2. Price
9d. Issued 1939. Deleted 1940. 105mm. DC/TP/RT. Came
out briefly post-war with thicker axles.
   The second is green with cream canopy and 'Carter
Paterson, Express Carriers, London, Brighton and
Seaside'. Otherwise as first transfer.

	MB	MU	GC
First transfer pre-war	£1000	£250	£75
First transfer post-war	£450	£150	£50
Second transfer pre-war	£1750	£450	£95
Second transfer post-war	£750	£250	£75

No. 25B Covered Wagon
Green with black plain chassis or pale grey with dark grey
canvas. Diecast radiator and lights as Type 3. No
publicity. Price 9d. Issued 1946. Deleted 1947. 105mm.
DC/TP/RT.

	MB	MU	GC
	—	£65	£25

No. 25B Covered Wagon
Yellow with blue hubs and blue canvas, or cream body
with red hubs and red canvas. Black moulded chassis,
diecast radiator, lights and bumpers as Type 4. No
publicity. Price 9d. Issued 1947. Deleted 1950. 110mm.
DC/TP/RT.

	MB	MU	GC
	—	£55	£25

No. 25c Flat Truck
Grey, blue, black or red. Black open chassis, tinplate
radiator and no lights as Type 1. Price 9d. Issued April
1934. Deleted 1938. 105mm. DC/TP/RT.

	MB	MU	GC
	—	£150	£50

No. 25c Flat Truck
Open chassis, diecast radiator and lights as Type 2. Price
9d. Issued 1938. Deleted 1940. Reissued 1946. Deleted
1950. Post-war model had thicker axles and different
wheels.

Pre-war	—	£75	£35
Post-war	—	£45	£15

No. 25C Flat Truck
Green with black plain chassis, diecast radiator and lights
as Type 3. Price 9d. Issued 1946. Deleted 1947. 105mm.
DC/RT. — £35 £10

No. 25C Flat Truck
Orange with black moulded chassis or green with black
chassis. Diecast radiator with lights and bumpers as Type
4. Price 9d. Issued 1947. Deleted 1950. 110mm. DC/RT. — £35 £10

No. 25d Petrol Tank Wagon
Red or pale green with black open chassis, tinplate
radiator and no lights as Type 1. Price 9d. Issued April
1934. Deleted 1938. 108mm. DC/RT/TP. — £75 £35

No. 25d Shell BP Tank Wagon
Red with 'BP' in yellow on sides. Black open chassis,
tinplate radiator and no lights as Type 1. Price 9d. Issued
1936. Deleted 1938. 108mm. DC/RT/TP. — £350 £150

No. 25d Tank Wagon
Red or dark green with 'Petrol' in black or white on sides.
Black open chassis, diecast radiator and lights as Type 2.
Price 6d. Issued 1938. Deleted 1940. 104mm. DC/RT.
Came out briefly post-war with thicker axles.

Pre-war	—	£75	£35
Post-war	—	£55	£25

No. 25d Texaco Petrol Wagon
Red with 'Texaco Petroleum Products' and white star on
sides. Black open chassis, diecast radiator and lights as
Type 2. Price 9d. Issued 1936. Deleted 1940. 107mm.
DC/RT. — £550 £100

No. 25d Shell BP Tank Wagon
Red with 'Shell BP' in yellow on sides. Black open chassis,
diecast radiator and lights as Type 2. Price 9d. Issued
1939. Deleted 1940. 107mm. DC/RT. — £350 £150

No. 25d Power Tank Wagon
Green with 'Power' in gold on sides. Black open chassis,
diecast radiator and lights as Type 2. Price 9d. Issued
1939. Deleted 1940. 107mm. DC/RT. — £350 £150

No. 25d Tanker Wagon
Mid-green with 'Pratts' in gold. Tinplate radiator and no
headlights as Type 1. Price 9d. Issued April 1934. Deleted
1936. 108mm. DC/RT/TP. Very rare.

	—	£750	£250

No. 25d Esso Tank Wagon
Green with 'Esso' in gold on sides. Black open chassis,
diecast radiator and lights as Type 2. Price 9d. Issued
1939. Deleted 1940. 107mm. DC/RT. Also came out
briefly post-war.

Pre-war	—	£350	£150
Post-war	—	£250	£100

No. 25d Mobil Oil Tank Wagon
Red with 'Mobil Oil' in blue with white band along sides.
Black open chassis, diecast radiator and lights as Type 2.
Price 9d. Issued 1939. Deleted 1940. 107mm. DC/RT. Also
came out briefly post-war.

Pre-war	—	£350	£150
Post-war	—	£250	£100

No. 25d Castrol Tank Wagon
Green with 'Wakefield Castrol Motor Oil' in red and
black on sides. Black open chassis, diecast radiator and
lights as Type 2. Price 9d. Issued 1939. Deleted 1940.
107mm. DC/RT. Also came out post-war.

Pre-war	—	£350	£150
Post-war	—	£250	£100

No. 25d Redline Glico Petrol Wagon
Dark blue with 'Redline Glico' in gold with red band on
sides. Black open chassis, diecast radiator and lights as
Type 2. Price 9d. Issued 1939. Deleted 1940. 107mm.
DC/RT.

	—	£500	£100

No. 25d Pool Petrol Wagon
Grey with front wings which are sometimes white and
with 'Pool' in white on sides. Black open chassis, diecast
radiator and lights as Type 2. Price 9d. Issued January
1940. Deleted October 1940. DC/RT.

	—	£500	£100

No. 25D Petrol Tank Wagon
Green or red body with 'Petrol' in black or white on sides.
Black plain chassis, diecast radiator and lights as Type 3.
Price 9d. Issued 1946. Deleted 1947. 110mm. DC/RT.

	—	£100	£30

No. 25D Petrol Tank Wagon
Dark green or orange and light green (rarer) with 'Petrol'
on sides. This model was Type 4. Price 9d. Issued 1948.
Deleted 1950. 110mm. DC/RT.

Dark green	—	£100	£30
Orange and light green	—	£150	£35

No. 25e Tipping Wagon
Maroon and yellow with black opening chassis, tinplate
radiator and no lights as Type 1. Price 9d. Issued April
1934. Deleted 1938. 108mm. DC/RT/TP.　　　　　　— 　£550 　£250

No. 25e Tipping Wagon
Fawn or brown with opening chassis, diecast radiator
and lights as Type 2. Price 9d. Issued 1938. Deleted 1940.
105mm. DC/RT. Also briefly came out post-war in grey
or fawn.

Pre-war	—	£550	£250
Post-war	—	£60	£25

No. 25E Tipping Wagon
Grey, yellow, green or beige with black plain chassis,
diecast radiator and lights as Type 3. Price 9d. Issued
1946. Deleted 1947. 105mm. DC/RT.　　　　　　— 　£50 　£20

No. 25E Tipping Wagon
Brown or blue and pink with black moulded chassis,
diecast radiator, lights and bumper as Type 4. Price 2/3.
Issued 1947. Deleted 1950. 110mm. DC/RT.　　　　— 　£50 　£20

No. 25f Market Gardener's Van
Yellow with green, military green or black open chassis.
Diecast radiator and lights as Type 2. Price 9d. Issued
1938. Deleted 1940. 105mm. DC/RT. Type 2 trucks also
came out briefly 1946 until they were replaced by Type 3,
where the only difference was axle thickness.

Pre-war	—	£450	£140
Post-war with thicker axles	—	£250	£100

No. 25F Market Gardener's Van
Green with black plain chassis, diecast radiator and lights
as Type 3. Price 9d. Issued 1946. Deleted 1947. 110mm.
DC/RT.　　　　　　　　　　　　　　　　— 　£70 　£30

No. 25F Market Gardener's Van
Yellow with black moulded chassis, diecast radiator,
lights and bumper as Type 4. Price 9d. Issued 1947.
Deleted 1950. 110mm. DC/RT.　　　　　　　— 　£60 　£20

	MB	MU	GC

No. 25g Trailer
Blue, green or dark green with swivelling front axle and tinplate tow bar. Price 7d. Issued June 1935. Deleted 1940. 69mm. DC/TP/RT. — £50 £7

No. 25G Trailer
Grey, blue or green to match Nos. 25c Type 2 or 25C Type 3; green or orange to match No. 25C Type 4; and green or red to match No. 30R Fordson Thames Flat Truck. The rear hook was cast integrally at first with tinplate draw-bar, then came the wire draw-bar from 1948 and finally the tinplate hook at rear from 1950. Price 7d. Issued 1947. Renumbered 429 in 1954. Deleted 1960. 69mm. DC/RT. Only No. 429 has an individual box as all the others came in boxes of six.

	MB	MU	GC
Tinplate draw-bar	—	£35	£15
Wire draw-bar	—	£25	£10

No. 25M Bedford End Tipper
Orange, dark green or cream with red chassis and cream rear. Handle tips at rear and tailboard hinges. Price 5/9. Issued March 1948. Renumbered 410 in 1954. Deleted 1960. 98mm. DC/TP/RT. Boxed.

	MB	MU	GC
Orange	£275	£100	£45
Dark green	£375	£150	£100
Cream	£250	£75	£35

No. 25R Forward Control Lorry
Red, green or grey; also cream and orange or brown with green wheels. Price 2/6. Issued May 1948. Renumbered 420 in 1954. Deleted 1961. 107mm. DC/TP/RT. — £55 £25

No. 25s Six Wheeled Wagon
Brown with grey tinplate canopy. Holes in seats for driver and passenger. Price 1/-. Issued 1937. Deleted 1940. 101mm. DC/RT/TP. — £250 £50

No. 25S Six Wheeled Wagon
Green or blue; also brown with grey tinplate canopy. Later models have no holes in seats for driver and passenger. Price 1/-. Issued 1946. Deleted 1948. 101mm. DC/TP/RT. — £150 £35

No. 25T Flat Truck and Trailer
Brown, grey or blue. Matching truck (No. 25C) and trailer (No. 25G). Type 2 was in fawn and Type 3 in grey or green; the only difference between Types 3 and 4 is that

the latter came in a box. Price 3/6. Issued 1946. Deleted
1951. Overall length 179mm. DC/RT.

	MB	MU	GC
Type 2	—	£150	£75
Type 3	—	£150	£75
Type 4	£350	£150	£75

No. 25V Bedford Refuse Wagon
Fawn and green with tipping body, opening side and rear
doors. Price 5/6. Issued October 1948. Renumbered 252
in 1954. Deleted 1960. 107mm. DC/TP/RT. Boxed.

	£75	£45	£25

No. 25W Bedford Truck
Green or brown (rare and worth double). Price 5/6.
Issued February 1949. Renumbered 411 in 1954. Deleted
1960. 104mm. DC/TP/RT. Boxed.

	£95	£45	£25

No. 25X Breakdown Lorry
Colours are very important on this model. Orange and
green with dark grey cab and dark blue rear; with dark
brown cab and light green rear; with light fawn cab and
dark blue rear; with dark brown cab and light green rear;
and with light brown cab and light green rear. 'Dinky
Service' on sides. Price 5/6. Issued September 1950.
Renumbered 430 in 1954. Deleted 1960. 123mm.
DC/TP/RT. Boxed.

	MB	MU	GC
With dark grey cab and dark blue rear	£150	£50	£25
With dark brown cab and light green rear	£150	£50	£25
With light fawn cab and dark blue rear	£195	£75	£45
With light brown cab and light green rear	£150	£50	£25

No. 30J Austin Wagon
Blue or brown. Price 2/4. Issued June 1950. Renumbered
412 in 1954. Deleted 1960. 104mm. DC/RT/TP. Only
boxed as No. 412.

	—	£75	£35

No. 30M Rear Tipping Wagon
Orange with green rear, maroon with green rear or dark
blue with grey rear. Handle works tipping action and
tailboard hinges. Price 2/11. Issued August 1950.
Renumbered 414 in 1954. Deleted 1960. 99mm.
DC/RT/TP.

	—	£75	£35

No. 30P Petrol Tanker
Red or green with 'Petrol' on sides and Studebaker cab.
Price 2/6. Issued 1950. Deleted 1952. 112mm.
DC/TP/RT.

	—	£150	£45

No. 30P Petrol Tanker
Red with 'Mobilgas' in white. Price 3/4. Issued 1952.
Renumbered 440 in 1954. 112mm. DC/TP/RT.

    —   £150   £45

No. 30PA Petrol Tanker
Green with 'Castrol' in red on white on sides. Price 2/6.
Issued 1952. Renumbered 441 in 1954. 112mm.
DC/TP/RT.

    —   £150   £45

No. 30PB Petrol Tanker
Red with 'Esso Motor Oil Petrol'. Price 3/4. Issued
August 1952. Renumbered 442 in 1954. 112mm.
DC/RT/TP.

    —   £150   £45

No. 30R Fordson Thames Flat Truck
Red, dark green or light green. Price 2/5. Issued February
1951. Renumbered 422 in 1954. 112mm. DC/TP/RT.
Red or dark green
Light green

	MB	MU	GC
Red or dark green	—	£150	£45
Light green	—	£100	£35

No. 30S Austin Covered Wagon
Maroon and fawn; blue and light blue; or maroon with
red rear (very rare and worth double). Price 2/10. Issued
September 1950. Renumbered 413 in 1954. 104mm.
DC/RT/TP.

    —   £150   £45

No. 30W Electric Articulated Lorry
Maroon with 'British Railways' on front. Trailer states
'30W Hindle Smart Helics'. Price 4/6. Issued February
1953. Renumbered 421 in 1954. 135mm. DC/RT/TP.

  £195   £75   £35

No. 33a Mechanical Horse
Various colours, most common being grey. Price 6d.
Issued June 1935. Deleted 1940. 65mm. DC/RT. Only
boxed when in '33' series set with five trailers, commonly
in red. Three wheels.

    —   £180   £75

No. 33b Flat Truck Trailer
Grey or green. Price 6d. Issued June 1935. Deleted 1940.
64mm. DC/RT. Only boxed when in '33' series set.

    —   £100   £25

No. 33b Open Truck Trailer
Grey, green, yellow or red. Price 6d. Issued June 1935.
Deleted 1940. 64mm. DC/RT. Only boxed when in '33'
series set.

    —   £100   £25

No. 33d Box Van Trailer
Grey or green. Price 8d. Issued June 1935. Deleted 1940.
70mm. DC/RT/TP. Only boxed when in '33' series set.

    —   £150   £75

COMMERCIAL VEHICLES	MB	MU	GC

No. 33e Refuse Wagon Trailer
Most common colours are dark blue or yellow. Also grey
or green. Part diecast on lower part and pale blue tinplate
upper part. Price 8d. Issued June 1935. Deleted 1940.
64mm. DC/RT/TP. Only boxed when in '22' series set.

	MB	MU	GC
	—	£150	£75

No. 33E Refuse Wagon Trailer
Much scarcer than pre-war model. Grey or red and blue
(worth at least treble). Price 9d. Issued 1946. Deleted early
1947. 61mm. DC/RT/TP.

	—	£75	£25

No. 33f Petrol Tank Trailer
Green with red tank; red with green tank; red with red
tank; or green with green tank (worth double). Price 8d.
Issued June 1935. Deleted 1940. 61mm. DC/TP/RT. Only
boxed when in '33' series set.

	—	£150	£50

No. 33f Esso Petrol Tank Trailer
Green with red tank and green tug. 'Esso' in gold on sides.
Price 1/6. Issued 1937. Deleted 1940. 61mm. DC/RT/TP.

Trailer only	—	£250	£100
With matching tug	—	£350	£150

No. 33f Castrol Petrol Tank Trailer
Red with green tank and red tug. 'Wakefield Castrol
Motor Oil' in red and black on sides. Price 1/6. Issued
1937. Deleted 1940. 61mm. DC/RT/TP.

Trailer only	—	£250	£100
With matching tug	—	£350	£150

No. 33W Mechanical Horse and Open Wagon
Colours are very important on this model. Grey cab and
rear; brown cab and rear; dark green cab and rear; yellow
cab and rear; red cab and fawn rear; dark green cab and
maroon rear; and blue cab and cream rear. Price 2/6.
Issued October 1947. Renumbered 415 in 1954. Deleted
1959. 102mm. DC/RT/TP.

Grey cab and rear	—	£125	£35
Brown cab and rear	—	£125	£35
Dark green cab and rear	—	£150	£45
Yellow cab and rear	—	£150	£45
Red cab and fawn rear	—	£150	£45
Dark green cab and maroon rear	—	£175	£55
Blue cab and cream rear	—	£250	£75

No. 60y Thompson Aircraft Tender
Red with 'Shell Aviation Services' in gold on sides. Three
wheels and driver cast in. Price 8d. Issued 1938. Deleted
1940. 84mm. DC/TP/RW. Box extremely rare.

	£1750	£500	£100

No. 107A Sack Truck
Blue. Price 9d. Issued June 1949. Renumbered 385 in 1954.
65mm. DC. Sold in boxes of six.

£450 — —

No. 151b Six Wheeled Transport Wagon
Green with six wheels and one spare. Holes in seat for
passengers at rear. Price 1/1. Issued February 1938.
Deleted 1940. 100mm. DC/TP/RT.

— £450 £100

No. 151B Six Wheeled Transport Wagon
Green with six wheels and one spare. Holes in seat for
driver and passenger. Also holes in rear plus tinplate
cover over rear. Price 3/6. Issued 1946. Deleted 1948.
99mm. DC/TP/RT. Military model.

— £350 £75

No. 151c Cooker Trailer with Stand
Green. Price 7d. Issued February 1938. Deleted 1940.
60mm. DC/RT. Military model.

— £95 £25

No. 151C Cooker Trailer with Stand
Green. Price 1/-. Issued 1946. Deleted 1948. 60mm.
DC/RT. Military model.

— £65 £15

No. 151d Water Tank Trailer
Green. Price 4d. Issued February 1938. Deleted 1940.
52mm. DC/RT. Military model.

— £95 £25

No. 151D Water Tank Trailer
Green. Post-war models in this series are scarce and have
much thicker axles. Price 1/-. Issued 1946. Deleted 1948.
52mm. DC/RT. Military model.

— £65 £15

No. 252 Refuse Wagon with Bedford Chassis
Fawn and green or cream and green (worth double).
Tipping body with side and rear opening doors. Price
6/4. Issued March 1954. Deleted 1964. 107mm.
DC/TP/RT. Boxed.

£150 £80 £45

No. 252 Refuse Wagon with Bedford Chassis
Fawn and green. Also in pale grey with orange cab; black
with green shutters; green with black shutters. The
orange, grey and green model also made with silver
rather than black radiator grille. Windows. Price 5/6.
Issued 1960. Deleted 1965. 107mm. DC/RT/TP.

	MB	MU	GC
Fawn and green	£250	£100	£50
Pale grey and orange	£350	£150	£75
Green and black	£250	£100	£50
Orange, grey and green	£120	£75	£45

No. 267 Emergency Paramedic Truck

Red with silver trim bumpers and wheels etc. From the
TV series Emergency. Price £2.25. Issued 1978. Deleted
1980. 119mm. DC/P.

	MB	MU	GC
	£100	£60	£35

No. 321 Guy 2-Ton Lorry

Two-tone blue with front as Type 2. Renumbering of 511
and 911. Price 5/9. Issued 1956. Deleted 1958. 132mm.
DC/TP/RT.

	MB	MU	GC
	£100	£50	£25

No. 340 Land Rover

From 1955 to 1964, green with cream seats or orange with
dark green seats and with all metal parts except tyres.
From 1964 to 1968, orange with dark green seats and red
plastic wheels. From 1968 to 1971, red with red or yellow
seats, red plastic wheels and black plastic steering wheel
in completely new casting with body and seats much
shallower, while body was minutely narrower with front
bumper reinforced. Renumbering of 27D with tinplate
screen, spare wheel and driver. Price 4/5. 90mm.
DC/TP/RT/P.

	MB	MU	GC
1955/64 version in green	£100	£50	£25
1955/64 version in orange	£75	£35	£20
1964/68 version	£50	£25	£15
1968/71 version	£50	£25	£15

No. 341 Land Rover Trailer

Various matching trailers: orange with red wheels or
green with cream wheels and grey tyres; orange with red
plastic wheels with grey or black tyres; red with red or
yellow plastic wheels. Renumbering of 27M. Price 2/-.
Issued 1955. Deleted 1971. 79mm. DC/RT/TP.

	MB	MU	GC
Orange with red wheels	£55	£25	£15
Green with cream wheels	£75	£35	£20
Orange with plastic wheels	£55	£30	£15
Red with red or yellow plastic wheels	£45	£30	£15

No. 380 Convoy Skip Truck

Lemon cab and chassis with white cab interior, orange
skip, black bumper and silver wheels. Price £1.45. Issued
1978. Deleted 1980. 112mm. D/P.

	MB	MU	GC
	£75	£50	£25

No. 383 Convoy NCL Truck

All-lemon with orange flash and 'National Carriers' and
'Medallion Guaranteed Deliveries' on sides. Black
bumper and silver hubs. Price £1.45. Issued 1978. Deleted
1980. 110mm. DC/P.

	MB	MU	GC
	£65	£40	£20

No. 384 Convoy Fire Rescue Truck
Red and orange with 'Rescue' on yellow plastic board on
sides. Price £1.25. Issued 1977. Deleted 1980. 126mm.
DC/P.

	MB	MU	GC
	£75	£40	£20

No. 385 Convoy Mail Truck
Red with white cab interior, Royal Mail transfers and
motifs. Price £1.25. Issued 1978. Deleted 1980. 110mm.
DC/P.

	£75	£45	£25

No. 385 Sack Truck
Blue or red (worth double). Renumbering of 107A. Price
9d. Issued 1954. Deleted 1958. 65mm. DC. Sold in boxes
of six.

	£75	—	—

No. 386 Avis Convoy Truck
Red with black chassis and 'Avis' on side. Price £1.25.
Issued 1977/78. Deleted 1980. 110mm. DC/P.

	£75	£45	£25

No. 387 Pickfords Convoy Truck
Dark blue with red cab and chassis. 'Pickfords' in white
and wide red flash on sides. Price £1.35. Issued 1978.
Deleted 1980. 110mm. DC/P.

	£65	£40	£15

No. 400 BEV Electric Truck
Blue. Renumbering of 14A. Price 2/9. Issued 1954.
Deleted 1960. 85mm. DC/TP/RT.

	£50	£30	£20

No. 401 Coventry Climax Fork-Lift Truck
Orange, black and green with grey tyres. Driver cast in.
Renumbering of 14C. Price 6/7. Issued 1954. Deleted
1964. 108mm. DC/TP/RT.

	£55	£30	£10

No. 402 Coca-Cola Bedford Lorry
Red with white roof and crate load. 'Coca-Cola' and
designs on sides, front etc. Price 15/6. Issued 1966.
Deleted 1969. 121mm. DC/RT/P.

	£200	£100	£50

No. 404 Conveyancer Fork-Lift Truck
Red and yellow with red pallet in plastic (stamped 973)
and black forks with blue plastic driver and yellow plastic
safety frame. Then from 1977 the body colour was yellow
and orange with other details identical. 'Conveyancer' on
front and sides. Price 12/11. Issued 1969. Deleted 1980.
97mm. DC/P.

	MB	MU	GC
Red and yellow	£50	£30	£15
Yellow and orange	£40	£30	£10

No. 405 Universal Jeep
Green or red. From 1966 red with red plastic wheels.
Tinplate screen with spare wheel on right side of body at
rear. Price 3/2. Issued 1955. Deleted 1969. 83mm.
DC/LHD/SW/TP/RT.

	MB	MU	GC
Early version	£75	£40	£20
Later version	£50	£30	£15

No. 406 Commer Articulated Lorry
Mentioned by Gibson but no details given. Export only
model, being No. 424 without plastic accessories. There
are two colours: the first is a yellow cab with grey rear
and blue plastic wheels, windows and interior; the
second is a dark green cab with black rear and green
plastic wheels etc. (much rarer and worth treble). Price
9/11. Issued 1963. Deleted 1966. DC/TP/RT. Boxes very
rare.   £200   £100   £50

No. 408 Big Bedford Lorry
Blue cab with yellow wheels, grey tyres and yellow
trailer. Price 9/11. Issued 1963. Deleted 1966. 165mm.
DC/RT.   £350   £150   £75

No. 409 Bedford Articulated Lorry
Yellow or orange cab with matching trailer, red wheels
and black tyres. Silver or black grille, bumper, radiator
and lights. Price 6/9. Issued 1954. Deleted 1960. 165mm.
DC/RT.   £150   £75   £45

No. 410 Bedford End Tipper
Red cab and chassis. Black wheels and mudguards and
cream or fawn end tipper with hinged tail board. Also
red wheels. Price 5/4. Issued 1954. Deleted 1960. 98mm.
DC/RT/TP.

	MB	MU	GC
With black wheels	£250	£75	£50
With red wheels	£350	£100	£75

No. 411 Bedford Truck
Green. Renumbering of 25W. Price 3/8. Issued 1954.
Deleted 1960. 104mm. DC/TP/RT.   £100   £50   £30

No. 412 Austin Wagon
Blue and maroon. Also yellow with blue wheels.
Renumbering of 30J. Price 2/9. Issued 1954. Deleted 1960.
104mm. DC/TP/RT.   £100   £50   £30

No. 413 Austin Covered Wagon
Blue with blue canvas; maroon with cream canvas; or
blue with cream canvas (worth double). Price 3/5. Issued
1954. Deleted 1960. 104mm. DC/TP/RT.   £150   £75   £40

No. 413 Austin Covered Wagon
Red body and chassis. Off-white cover on rear and
matching lorry wheels. Silver or black grille, radiator and
bumpers. Also red bumpers. Price 3/5. Issued 1954.
Deleted 1960. 104mm. DC/RT/TP.

	MB	MU	GC
	£150	£50	£30

No. 414 Dodge Rear Tipping Wagon
Red and green, blue and grey, orange and green or
maroon and green. Tipping body and hinged tailboard.
Renumbering of 30M. Price 3/5. Issued 1954. Deleted
1964. 99mm. DC/RT/TP.

	MB	MU	GC
Red and green	£75	£45	£20
Blue and grey	£75	£30	£20
Orange and green	£150	£75	£35
Maroon and green	£100	£50	£25

No. 415 Mechanical Horse and Open Wagon
Three wheeled tractor and two wheeled trailer. Blue
horse with cream trailer. Also with red cab and beige rear.
Some models have rounded rather than crimped axle
ends, as do the blue and cream models. Renumbering of
33W, but No. 415 has coloured rather than black hubs.
Price 2/10. Issued 1954 or later. Deleted 1959. 102mm.
DC/RT. Box very rare.

	MB	MU	GC
	£75	£45	£25

No. 417 Leyland Comet Lorry
Blue and yellow, red and yellow or green and yellow. Four
wheels and one spare. Renumbering of 531 and 931.
Price 3/3. Issued 1956. Deleted 1959. 144mm.
DC/TP/RT.

	MB	MU	GC
Blue and yellow	£200	£75	£40
Red and yellow	£125	£75	£50
Green and yellow	£175	£55	£35

No. 418 Leyland Comet with Hinged Tailboard
Green and orange. Renumbering of 532 and 932. Price
5/6. Issued 1956. Deleted 1959. 142mm. DC/TP/RT.

	MB	MU	GC
	£150	£75	£45

No. 418 Leyland Comet with Hinged Tailboard
Sky blue with dark blue cab and chassis. Yellow wheels,
grey tyres and silver bumpers. Issued 1956. Deleted 1960.
Price 6/3. 142mm. DC/TP/RT.

	MB	MU	GC
	£200	£80	£50

No. 419 Leyland Comet Lorry
Yellow with 'Portland Cement' and 'Ferrocrete' on sides.
Four wheels and one spare. Renumbering of 533 and 933.
Price 5/6. Issued 1956. Deleted 1959. 142mm.
DC/TP/RT.

	MB	MU	GC
	£200	£100	£50

No. 420 Leyland Forward Control Lorry
Green with red wheels and grey interior, or red with
cream wheels and grey interior. Price 2/5. Issued October
1954. Deleted 1961. 107mm. DC/TP/RT.

	MB	MU	GC
Green	£200	£100	£50
Red	£150	£75	£35

No. 421 Hindle Smart Electric Lorry
Maroon with 'British Railways' on front trailer.
Renumbering of 30W. Price 3/11. Issued 1955. Deleted
1959. 135mm. DC/TP/RT.

	£200	£150	£50

No. 422 Thames Flat Truck
Green, dark green or red. Renumbering of 30R. Price 2/3.
Issued March 1954. Deleted 1960. 112mm. DC/TP/RT.

	MB	MU	GC
Green or dark green	£150	£85	£50
Red	£100	£75	£50

No. 424 Commer Convertible Truck
Yellow cab, grey rear, blue wheels and grey plastic stake
sides or blue plastic canvas top as No. 406. Casting is same
as No. 430 at rear, but cab has seats and windows added.
Four wheels and one spare plus two wheels. Price 9/11.
Issued May 1963. Deleted 1966. 171mm. DC/TP/RT/P.

	£150	£65	£35

No. 425 Bedford TK Coal Wagon
Red and grey with six bags of coal and set of scales. Red
cab with red or grey rear and grey or silver chassis. On
door is blue and yellow sign with 'Approved Coal
Merchants' in white. Silver petrol tank, bumpers etc.
Price 9/3. Issued 1964. Deleted 1969. 118mm.
DC/RT/TP.

	£100	£50	£25

No. 428 Large Trailer
Red, grey or blue. Red model has silver wheels. Made to
be used with Dinky Toys Nos. 251, 300, 301, 340, 408, 409,
431 and 432 as well as Supertoys Nos. 905, 934, 961 and
962. All models fitted with towing hooks. Price 3/10.
Issued 1955. Deleted 1964. 105mm. DC/TP/RT.

	MB	MU	GC
Red	£45	£15	£8
Grey	£50	£25	£10
Blue	£75	£35	£20

No. 429 Trailer
Green or red with front wheel swivel and tow-bar. Price
1/10. Issued 1955. Deleted 1963. 69mm. DC/T.

	£50	£20	£10

No. 430 Breakdown Lorry
Replaced No. 25X. Green and orange with 'Dinky Service' on sides and grey tow-hook. Working crane in silver finish. Price 5/9. Issued 1962. Deleted 1964. 123mm. DC/TP/RT.

	MB	MU	GC
	£100	£50	£25

No. 430 Commer Breakdown Lorry
Red and grey with windows. Part plastic. Price 5/9. Issued 1962. Deleted 1964. 123mm. DC/TP/RT.

	£100	£50	£20

No. 431 4-Ton Guy Warrior Lorry
Green and fawn. Completely new casting, with four wheels and one spare. Price 4/9. Issued 1958. Deleted 1964. 136mm. DC/TP/RT.

	£100	£75	£35

No. 432 Guy Flat Truck
Blue and red. Type 2 front with four wheels and one space. Renumbering of 512 and 912. Price 5/3. Issued 1956. Deleted 1958. 132mm. DC/RT/TP.

	£150	£75	£40

No. 432 Guy Warrior Flat Truck
Red and green. Price 5/3. Issued 1958. Deleted 1964. 136mm. DC/TP/RT.

	£600	£200	£75

No. 433 Guy Flat Truck with Tailboard
Red and black. Also two shades of green with blue cab and orange rear. Type 2 front. Price 5/6. Issued 1955. Deleted 1958. 132mm. DC/RT/TP.

	MB	MU	GC
Red and black	£200	£100	£50
Two shades of green	£275	£150	£75

No. 434 Bedford TK Crash Truck
White with green flash. Also 'Top Rank' version with red cab, pale grey rear. Also rare red and cream. Also with red cab and white body with the words 'Auto Services'. With the words 'Top Rank Motorway Services' with operating winch and four wheels. Price 7/11. 'Top Rank' made between 1964/65, and the red cab/pale grey rear made 1966/73. 122mm. DC/TP/RT/P.

	MB	MU	GC
Top Rank model	£100	£75	£25
Red and cream	£175	£100	£50
Red and grey	£100	£50	£20

No. 435 Bedford TK Tipper
Light grey, blue and orange and a yellow version with black cab roof which was made between 1966 and 1971. Six wheels, tipping rear and three let-down flaps. Price 7/11. Issued 1964. Deleted 1971. 120mm. DC/RT/TP.

	MB	MU	GC
Light grey, blue and orange	£100	£70	£35
Yellow, black and grey	£100	£45	£20

	MB	MU	GC
No. 436 Atlas Copco Compressor Lorry Yellow or mustard with 'Atlas Copco' on sides. Sides open to show compressor. Price 6/9. Issued February 1963. Deleted 1969.			
Yellow	£100	£60	£30
Mustard	£200	£100	£50
No. 437 Muir Hill 2WL Loader Red until 1969, then yellow from 1970 to 1978. 'Taylor Woodrow' on rear. Working shovel. Price 9/11. Issued February 1962. Deleted 1978. 117mm. DC/RT/P.	£75	£35	£20
No. 438 Bedford D800 Tipper Truck Red cab, green tipper and white interior with silver chassis, bumpers etc. Replaced by No. 440 in 1977, with a casting as per No. 438, but doors do not open. Price 9/11. Issued 1970. Deleted 1978. 132mm. DC/P.			
No. 438 with red cab and yellow rear	£100	£50	£20
No. 440 with red cab and orange rear	£50	£25	£15
No. 439 Ford 800 Snow Plough Tipper Blue, red and yellow with red stripe. Also blue cab, pale grey rear and yellow plough. Main casting is same as No. 438 and plough as No. 958, nearly 10 years later. Price 10/6. Issued 1971. Deleted 1977. 194mm. DC/P.	£150	£75	£35
No. 440 Mobilgas Petrol Tanker Renumbering of No. 30P with two different transfers: the first version is the same as No. 30P with white letters directly into red body, while the second has 'Mobilgas' in blue on white background. Price 2/10. Issued January 1956. Deleted 1961. 112mm. DC/TP/RT.			
First version	£200	£100	£50
Second version	£120	£50	£35
No. 441 Castrol Petrol Tanker Green. Renumbering of 30PA. Price 2/10. Issued August 1954. Deleted 1960. 112mm. DC/TP/RT.	£200	£120	£60
No. 442 Esso Petrol Tanker Red with 'Esso Motor Oil Petrol'. Renumbering of 30PB. Price 2/8. Issued August 1954. Deleted 1960. 112mm. DC/TP/RT.	£200	£120	£75
No. 442 Land Rover Breakdown Truck White with black crane. Opening red bonnet and doors with 'Motorway Rescue' on them. Price £1.75. Issued 1973. Deleted 1980. 121mm. DC/P.	£100	£50	£30

No. 442 Land Rover Breakdown Crane
White, orange and black with orange panels on doors and
bonnet. Silver trim and full working crane at rear.
All-plastic Speediwheels from 1976. Price £1.35. Issued
1973. Deleted 1978. 121mm. DC/P.

£60	£30	£15

No. 443 National Benzole Petrol Tanker
Yellow with 'National Benzole Mixture' on sides. Price
2/-. Issued January 1957. Deleted 1958. 112mm.
DC/TP/RT.

£400	£150	£75

No. 448 Chevrolet El Camino Pick-Up and Trailers
Green and white with open-type red trailers. One trailer
open and one closed. Both have two wheels plus door
trailer. With 'Acme Trailer Hire'. Price 10/6. Issued June
1963. Deleted 1968. 224mm. DC/TP/RT/P.

£175	£100	£50

No. 448 Chevrolet Pick-Up Truck and Trailers
Turquoise, white and orange with matching silver-blue
wheels. Bumper bar, headlights and red interior for cab,
and silver mudguards. Acme badge on square box trailer
at rear. Price 8/11. Issued 1963. Deleted 1968. Overall
length approx. 224mm. DC/TP/RT/P.

£100	£50	£25

No. 449 Chevrolet El Camino Pick-Up
Green, turquoise and white or red and gold. Price 4/11.
Issued August 1961. Deleted 1969. 111mm.
DC/TP/RT/LHD/SS/FTS/S/W.

	MB	MU	GC
Green, turquoise and white	£85	£50	£20
Red and gold	£175	£100	£50

No. 449 Johnston Road Sweeper
First introduced in 1971 in orange and metallic green as
No. 451 with opening cab doors. Replaced in 1977 by No.
449 with revised casting, when doors did not open, but
produced in same colour scheme. From 1978 in lemon or
yellow with black fittings and silver bumpers etc. Finally
deleted in 1980. Price 15/11. 142mm. DC/P.

	MB	MU	GC
No. 451 orange and metallic green	£160	£80	£40
No. 449 orange and metallic green	£80	£50	£20
No. 449 lemon or yellow	£70	£30	£15

No. 501 Foden Diesel Eight Wheeled Wagon
One of the most sought after series in the Dinky range.
Very popular but also very expensive at time of issue. As
far as collecting is concerned, the Fodens were largely
ignored until about 1976 but are now much prized and
fairly expensive. First version above could be called No.
501/2. Remarks about first and second cabs for Guy
trucks apply here. Model was renumbered 901 in 1954.

Colours are red and fawn, and two-tone blue. Price 7/6.
Issued October 1952. Renumbered in 1954. Deleted 1957.
188mm. DC/TP/RT.

	MB	MU	GC
Red and fawn	£800	£200	£100
Two-tone blue	£600	£150	£75

No. 501 Foden Diesel Eight Wheeled Wagon
Early version had a one colour body and cab. Colours
known are brown, dark blue and grey (identified as
501/1A). Later on model came in several colours: red and
fawn, red and brown, brown and red or fawn and brown;
also dark blue and light blue (identified as 501/1B). All
colours are highly priced. Cab as Type 1, eight wheels,
one spare and hook. Price 10/-. Issued October 1947.
Deleted 1952. 188mm. DC/TP/RT.

No. 501/1A	£400	£200	£80
No. 501/1B	£300	£135	£75

No. 502 Foden Flat Truck
Orange and green. Also dark blue cab and chassis with
orange rear. Cab as Type 2, eight wheels and one spare.
Price 7/-. Issued 1956. Renumbered 902 in 1959. Deleted
1962. 188mm. DC/RT/TP.

Orange and green	£400	£125	£75
Dark blue	£300	£150	£75

No. 502 Foden Flat Truck
Red and blue. Also dark green, although further colours
exist. This early version identified as No. 502/1A. Later
version has blue cab and chassis with red rear or orange
cab and chassis with green rear (identified as No.
502/1B). Eight wheels and one spare. Price 10/-. Issued
October 1947. Deleted 1952. 188mm. DC/TP/RT.

No. 502/1A	£400	£130	£85
No. 502/1B	£300	£150	£75

No. 503 Foden Flat Truck with Tailboard
Early version as No. 503/1A in grey or brown, and later
as No. 503/1B in dark blue and orange rear. Also red and
black or red and green with Type 1 cab. Price 10/-. Issued
October 1947. Deleted 1952. 188mm. DC/TP/RT.

No. 503/1A	£400	£130	£85
No. 503/1B	£350	£130	£85

No. 503 Foden Flat Truck with Tailboard
Blue and orange. Type 2 cab. Price 7/-. Issued 1952.
Deleted 1955. Renumbered 903 in 1955. 188mm.
DC/TP/RT.

	£300	£150	£75

No. 504 Foden 14-Ton Tanker
Red and fawn or two-tone blue. Type 1 cab with eight
wheels (identified as No. 504/1A). Type 2 cab without
advertising is in red and fawn (identified as No. 504/1B).
Price 9/6. Issued December 1948. Deleted 1952. 188mm.
DC/RT/TP.

	MB	MU	GC
No. 504/1A	£500	£250	£125
No. 504/1B	£350	£150	£75

No. 504 Mobilgas Foden 14-Ton Tanker
Red with 'Mobilgas' and motif in white on sides. Price
8/3. Issued 1953. Renumbered 941 in 1954. 188mm.
DC/TP/RT.

	£500	£150	£75

No. 505 Foden Flat Truck with Chains
Green or red and grey (rarer). Type 1 cab. Price 11/6.
Issued January 1952. Deleted September 1952. 188mm.
DC/TP/RT. Very scarce because of short production run.

Green	£300	£175	£85
Red and grey	£400	£190	£85

No. 505 Foden Flat Truck with Chains
Green or maroon. Type 2 cab with eight wheels and one
spare. Price 11/6. Issued September 1952. Renumbered
905 in 1955. 188mm. DC/RT/TP.

	£350	£200	£85

No. 511 Guy 4-Ton Lorry
Early versions have body and cab in one colour, brown
or grey, while later versions were in two-tone blue or red
and fawn. Type 1 front with four wheels and one spare.
Price 7/-. Issued October 1947. Renumbered 911 in 1954.
132mm. DC/RT/TP.

Brown or grey	£400	£175	£100
Two-tone blue or red and fawn	£300	£150	£75

No. 512 Guy Flat Truck
Early versions yellow or maroon. Later versions dark
blue and red or dark blue and orange. Type 1 front with
four wheels and one spare. Price 7/-. Issued October 1947.
Renumbered 912 in 1954. 132mm. DC/RT/TP.

Yellow or maroon	£300	£150	£75
Dark blue and red	£200	£100	£50
Dark blue and orange	£125	£75	£35

No. 513 Guy Flat Truck with Tailboard
Early versions yellow, brown or dark blue (rare). Later
versions two-tone green, blue and orange or two-tone red
and black. Type 1 front with four wheels and one spare.

Price 7/-. Issued October 1947. Deleted 1954. 132mm.
DC/TP/RT.

Yellow or brown	£200	£85	£50
Dark blue	£400	£175	£85
Two-tone green or blue and orange	£175	£125	£75
Two-tone red and black	£100	£65	£35

No. 521 Bedford Articulated Lorry
Red or yellow with black wings. Four black wheels, one
spare and two wheels. Price 7/6. Issued April 1948.
Renumbered 921 in 1954. 166mm. DC/RT/TP.

	£85	£50	£25

No. 522 Big Bedford Lorry
Blue and yellow, red and yellow or red and brown. Price
5/-. Issued June 1949. Renumbered 931 in 1954. 144mm.
DC/TP/RT.

Blue and yellow	£300	£150	£75
Red and yellow or red and brown	£100	£50	£25

No. 531 Leyland Comet Lorry
Blue and yellow, red and yellow or red and brown. Price
5/-. Issued June 1949. Renumbered 931 in 1954. 144mm.
DC/TP/RT.

	£100	£50	£25

No. 532 Leyland Comet with Hinged Tailboard
Green and orange, two-tone blue or two-tone green (rare
and worth double). Price 7/9. Issued January 1952.
Renumbered 932 in 1954. 142mm. DC/TP/RT.

	£130	£80	£50

No. 533 Leyland Cement Wagon
Yellow with 'Ferrocrete' and 'Portland Cement' on sides.
Four wheels and one spare. Price 6/-. Issued February
1953. Renumbered 973 in 1954. 142mm. DC/TP/RT.

	£85	£45	£25

No. 551 Trailer
Red, green or grey. Four wheels with front axle swivel.
Price 3/5. Issued May 1948. Renumbered 951 in July 1954.
105mm. DC/TP/RT.

Red or green	£50	£25	£10
Grey	£35	£20	£10

No. 563 Renault Pick-Up Truck
Orange with green removable canvas hood. Four wheels
and one spare. French Dinky imported into England.
Price 6/5. Issued in France 1960. Introduced in England
1962. Deleted 1967. 96mm. DC/TP/RT/P.

	£65	£45	£20

No. 579 Simca Glaziers Lorry
Another French Dinky. Yellow and green. Also grey and
green and the model often has '33C' on the box, which
was the original French number from 1956 to 1959. Mirror
and pane of glass. 'Saint-Gobain' and 'Miroitier' on sides.
Price 8/8. Issued in France 1956. Deleted 1965. Issued in
England 1962. Deleted 1965. 128mm. DC/RT/TP/P.   £150   £85   £50

No. 581 Horsebox
Maroon with 'British Railways' and 'Express Horsebox
Hire Service' on sides. Side and rear opening doors. Price
15/11. Issued April 1953. Renumbered 981 in 1954.
175mm. DC/RT.   £150   £85   £45

No. 581 Berliet Truck with Container
Another French Dinky. Red and grey with six wheels and
one spare with detachable container. Often has '34B' on
box. Price 9/-. Issued in France 1956. Deleted 1971. Issued
in England 1962. Deleted 1966. 130mm. DC/RT.   £135   £85   £45

No. 582 Pullmore Car Transporter
Blue and grey. On a Bedford tractor with 'Dinky Toys
Delivery Service' on sides. Rear folds down. Price 14/6.
Issued May 1953. Renumbered 982 in 1954. 250mm.
DC/TP/RT.   £175   £120   £55

No. 591 AEC Tanker
Red and yellow. AEC Monarch Thompson Tanker with
'Shell Chemicals Ltd' on sides. Price 8/8. Issued
September 1952. Renumbered 991 in 1954. 151mm.
DC/TP/RT.   £550   £250   £100

No. 618 AEC Articulated Transporter with Helicopter
Military colours. Price £2.25. Issued 1976. Deleted 1980.
318mm. DC/P.   £300   £200   £100

No. 642 RAF Pressure Refueller
RAF blue. Price 7/9. Issued May 1957. Deleted 1962.
142mm including hook. DC/TP/RT. Also a military
model.   £120   £60   £30

No. 893 Unic Pipe Line Transporter
Sandy or grey with 10 wheels, 2 spares and 6 removable
pipe lengths. Price 13/-. Issued in France 1959. Deleted
1970. Imported from France 1962. Deleted 1966.   £160   £125   £60

No. 894 Unic/Boillot Car Transporter
Grey or dark blue (worth double) with lowering ramp, 6
x 2 wheels and one spare. 'Dinky Toys Service Liaison'
on sides. Price £1/15/-. Imported from France. 325mm.
DC/TP/RT/P.   £260   £120   £65

No. 901 Foden Diesel Eight Wheeled Wagon
Red and grey or two shades of blue. Type 2 cab with six
wheels and one spare. Price 7/9. Renumbered of 501.
Issued January 1955. Deleted 1957. 188mm. DC/TP/RT.

	MB	MU	GC
Red and grey	£175	£125	£65
Two shades of blue	£120	£85	£45

No. 902 Foden Flat Truck
Orange and green or blue and orange. Type 2 cab with
eight wheels and one spare. Price 7/3. Renumbering of
502/2. Issued 1955. Deleted 1960. 188mm. DC/RT/TP.

Orange and green	£550	£120	£85
Blue and orange	£450	£150	£65

No. 903 Foden Flat Truck with Tailboard
Blue and orange. Type 2 cab with eight wheels and one
spare. Price 7/3. Renumbering of 503. Issued January
1955. Deleted 1960. 188mm. DC/TP/RT.   £175   £85   £50

No. 905 Foden Flat Truck with Chains
Maroon, green or red and grey. Type 2 cab with eight
wheels and one spare. Price 9/6. Renumbering of 505.
Issued January 1955. Deleted 1964. 188mm. DC/TP/RT.

Maroon or green	£175	£85	£50
Red and grey	£200	£125	£65

No. 908 Mighty Antar with Transformer
Yellow and grey. The transformer is a French Dinky from
No. 898 Berliet Transformer Carrier. 5 x 2 wheels and one
spare. Price £1/1/-. Issued October 1962. Deleted 1964.
295mm. DC/RT/P. Quite rare.   £750   £250   £150

No. 911 Guy 4-Ton Lorry
Two-tone blue with Type 2 front. Price 5/6. Renumbering
of 911. Issued January 1954. Renumbered 431 in 1956.
132mm. DC/TP/RT.   £175   £85   £55

No. 912 Guy Flat Truck
Blue and orange with Type 2 front. Price 5/6.
Renumbering of 512. Issued 1954. Renumbered 432 in
1956. 132mm. DC/RT/TP.   £200   £120   £65

No. 913 Guy Flat Truck with Tailboard
Blue and orange or two-tone green with Type 2 front.
Price 5/11. Renumbering of 513. Issued 1954.
Renumbered 433 in 1956. 132mm. DC/TP/RT.

Blue and orange	£185	£125	£65
Two-tone green	£200	£90	£50

No. 914 AEC Articulated Lorry
Red and green or red and green with green or grey
canopy. 'British Road Services' on sides. Price 7/11.
Issued 1965. Deleted 1971. 210mm. DC/RT/P.

| | £160 | £120 | £65 |

No. 915 AEC Vehicle with Flat Trailer
Red cab and white rear with 'Truck Hire Company' in
white on cab doors. Price £1.25. Issued 1973. Deleted 1975.
210mm. DC/P.

| | £130 | £110 | £60 |

No. 917 Mercedes Truck and Trailer
Blue, yellow and white with silver bumpers, grille etc.
Opening cab doors and red interior of cab. Detachable
canopies on special box bodies. Price £2/2/6. Issued 1967.
Replaced by No. 940 in 1977. 397mm. DC/P.

| | £100 | £50 | £30 |

No. 917 Mercedes Truck and Trailer
Black cab and red interior with orange box trailers and
lift-off white covers. White wheels and white top on cab
roof. Price £2/2/6. Issued 1967. Replaced by No. 940 in
1977. 397mm. DC/P.

| | £185 | £135 | £85 |

No. 921 Bedford Articulated Lorry
Yellow with 4 x 2 wheels. Price 5/11. Renumbering of 521.
Issued 1954. Renumbered 409 in 1956. 166mm.
DC/TP/RT.

| | £160 | £120 | £65 |

No. 922 Big Bedford Lorry
Maroon and fawn or blue and yellow with four wheels
and one spare. Price 8/9. Renumbering of 522. Issued
1954. Renumbered 408 in 1956. 156mm. DC/TP/RT.

Maroon and fawn	£200	£120	£60
Blue and yellow	£165	£85	£45

No. 924 Aveling Barford Centaur Dump Truck
Yellow, black and red. Price £1.45. Issued 1972. Deleted
1977. 180mm. DC/P.

| | £80 | £60 | £30 |

No. 925 Leyland Dump Truck
Tilting white cab with blue roof, red or orange dumper
body and silver chassis. Price 6/11. Issued 1965. Deleted
1970. 192mm. DC/RT.

| | £190 | £120 | £65 |

No. 931 Leyland Comet Lorry
Blue and yellow or red and yellow. Price 5/3.
Renumbering of 531. Issued January 1955. Renumbered
417 in 1956. 144mm. DC/TP/RT.

Blue and yellow	£100	£60	£30
Red and yellow	£80	£50	£20

No. 932 Leyland Comet with Hinged Tailboard
Two-tone blue or green and orange. Price 6/-.
Renumbering of 532. Issued January 1955. Renumbered
418 in 1956. 142mm. DC/TP/RT.

	MB	MU	GC
Two-tone blue	£100	£70	£30
Green and orange	£75	£55	£25

No. 932 Leyland Comet Truck with Hinged Tailboard
Green and orange. Colours are darker than previous No.
932. Price 6/-. Issued 1954. Deleted 1956. 142mm.
DC/TP/RT.

	MB	MU	GC
	£100	£60	£30

No. 933 Leyland Cement Wagon
Yellow. Price 5/6. Renumbering of 533. Issued 1954.
Renumbered 419 in 1956. 142mm. DC/RT/TP.

	MB	MU	GC
	£250	£85	£45

No. 934 Leyland Octopus Wagon
Yellow, green and red with eight wheels and one spare.
Price 8/9. Issued April 1956. Deleted 1964. 194mm.
DC/RT/TP.

	MB	MU	GC
	£450	£120	£85

No. 935 Leyland Octopus Flat Truck with Chains
Blue and grey with eight wheels and one spare. Price
10/9. Issued and deleted 1963. 192mm. DC/TP/RT.

	MB	MU	GC
	£750	£300	£120

No. 936 Leyland Eight Wheeled Chassis
Red and silver or red, white and grey with 'Another
Leyland on Test'. Twelve wheels and 3 movable yellow
5-ton weights. Price 14/11. Issued September 1964.
Deleted 1970. 197mm. SW/D/DC/RT/P.

	MB	MU	GC
	£120	£60	£45

No. 940 Mercedes Benz Truck
White with grey canopy, red plastic wheels and red
chassis. This is No. 917 minus the trailer and recast. Cab
doors do not open. Price £2.76. Issued 1977. Deleted 1980.
200mm. DC/P.

	MB	MU	GC
	£100	£60	£25

No. 941 Mobilgas Foden Tanker
Red with Type 2 casting. Price 10/6. Renumbering of 504.
Issued January 1955. Deleted 1957. 188mm. DC/TP/RT.

	MB	MU	GC
	£550	£300	£120

No. 942 Regent Foden Tanker
Red, blue and white with Type 2 casting. Eight wheels
and one spare. Price 10/6. Issued June 1955. Deleted 1957.
188mm. DC/RT/TP.

	MB	MU	GC
	£750	£250	£100

No. 943 Esso Leyland Octopus Tanker
Red with 'Esso Petroleum Company' on sides. Eight
wheels and one spare. Issued 1958. Deleted 1961. 192mm.
DC/TP/RT.

	MB	MU	GC
	£550	£150	£75

No. 944 Shell BP 4000-Gallon Tanker
Yellow and white with 'Shell BP' and badges on sides etc.
Plastic tank, eight wheels and one spare. Price 10/6.
Issued July 1963. Deleted 1964. 192mm. DC/TP/RT/P.

£295 £150 £100

No. 945 Oil Tanker, Promotional Lucas Special
Manufactured by Dinky for the Lucas Oil Company as a
promotional sales gimmick in 1978, using the old casting
of No. 945, and deleted the same year. Green with black
trailer cab chassis, black cab interior and 'Lucas Oil
Company' in white. Grey opening tops. Price £4.95.
266mm. DC/P.

£900 £400 £250

No. 945 Esso Fuel Tanker
White with red and blue markings and 'Esso' on sides.
Opening tops. Price 19/11. issued 1966. Deleted 1977.
266mm. DC/RT/TP.

£100 £50 £25

No. 948 McLean Tractor Trailer
Red and grey with opening rear doors. Tractor with 6
wheels and trailer with 8 wheels. Two bogies. 'McLean
Winston Salem' and badge on sides of tractor, and
'McLean Trucking Company' on sides of trailer. Price
16/6. Issued 1961. Deleted 1965/66. Overall length
290mm. DC/RT/P. Well known as a rare and expensive
1960s Dinky Toy.

£250 £100 £75

No. 950 Foden S20 Fuel Tanker
First version (1977) was red cab with black interior on
black chassis, and white plastic tank with black fillers on
red chassis, with red wheels. Second version (1978) had
red cab chassis, silver fillers and cream wheels.
Detachable cab and opening door. Price £5.52. Issued
1977. Deleted 1980. 266mm. DC/P.
First version

£125 £75 £35

Second version

£95 £55 £25

No. 950 Car Transporter Set
Contains Nos. 136 Vauxhall Viva; 138 Hillman Imp; 162
Triumph 1300; 168 Ford Escort; 342 Austin Mini-Moke;
and 974 Hoynor Car Transporter. Cars are standard
except for the Mini-Moke, which has no roof. Price
£3/7/6. Issued 1969. Deleted 1970.

£750 — —

No. 951 Trailer
Grey with four wheels. Price 3/2. Renumbering of 551.
Issued 1954. Renumbered 428 in 1955. 105mm.
DC/TP/RT.

£35 £15 £10

No. 974 Hoynor Car Transporter
Orange and yellow with blue cab, silver hubs etc. Eight wheels plus two. Price £1/9/11. Issued 1968. Deleted 1976. 322mm. DC/P.

	MB	MU	GC
	£125	£75	£35

No. 978 Refuse Wagon
First version (1964) was light grey and green. Second version (1973) was much darker grey and metallic green with silver wheels and black chassis. Third version (1978) had yellow cab; otherwise as second version. 'Refuse Collector' and crest on sides. Forward tipping body. Back with opening rear doors, tip-down foot stands and two buckets. Price 14/11. Issued October 1964. Deleted 1980. 152mm. SW/S/W/DC/RT/TP.

	MB	MU	GC
First version	£90	£40	£20
Second version	£70	£30	£20
Third version	£70	£30	£20

No. 979 Racehorse Transporter Wagon
Light grey and yellow with two plastic horses. 'Newmarket Racehorse Transport Service Ltd' on sides. Price 15/3. Issued October 1961. Deleted 1964. 173mm. DC/RT/P.

	MB	MU	GC
	£350	£175	£75

No. 980 Coles Hydra Truck 150T
Yellow, silver and black with swing-down outriggers, rotating telescopic boom and winding mechanism. Issued 1972 in bright yellow. Issued 1978 in much darker yellow. Finally deleted 1980. Price £3.35. 210mm. DC/P.

	MB	MU	GC
First version	£125	£85	£50
Second version	£80	£70	£30

No. 981 Horsebox
Maroon with 'British Railways' on sides. Price 14/11. Renumbering of 581. Issued January 1955. Replaced by 979 in 1961. Deleted 1964. 175mm. DC/RT.

	MB	MU	GC
	£130	£80	£40

No. 982 Pullmore Car Transporter
First version (1955) was all pale blue with fawn tracks for cars. Second version (1958) had mid-blue cab with pale blue rear and tracks painted differently. Third version (1960) had windows. Price 14/6. Renumbering of 582. Issued 1955. Deleted 1964. 280mm. DC/TP/RT.

	MB	MU	GC
First version	£155	£125	£65
Second version	£130	£80	£40
Third version	£100	£60	£30

No. 983 Dinky Car Carrier and Trailer
Contains Nos. 984 and 985. Red and grey with 'Dinky Toys Delivery Service' on sides. Price £1/18/6. Issued July 1958. Deleted 1963. Overall length 450mm. DC/TP/RT. First-class investment and much sought after.

£300 £150 £65

No. 984 Dinky Car Carrier
Red and grey with 'Dinky Auto Service' in yellow or orange on sides. Rear ramp lowers and upper storey hinges. Worked by a handle. Price £1/2/-. Issued July 1958. Deleted 1963. 240mm. DC/RT/TP.

£120 £50 £40

No. 985 Dinky Trailer
Red and grey with 'Dinky Auto Service' on sides in yellow and orange. Rear ramp lowers and hinges and front wheels swivel. Price 16/-. Issued July 1958. Deleted 1963. 196mm. DC/RT.

£60 £40 £20

No. 989 Car Transporter
Yellow, blue and grey with 'Auto Transporters' on sides. Made for US market. Equivalent price £1/8/11. Issued 1963. Deleted 1969. 240mm. DC/TP/RT. Rare.

£300 £150 £65

No. 991 AEC Shell Chemicals Tanker
Red and yellow with 'Shell Chemicals Ltd' on sides. Price 6/3. Renumbering of 591. Issued January 1955. Deleted 1958. 151mm. DC/RT.

£250 £150 £85

No. 994 Loading Ramp for Pullmore Carrier
Blue. Price 1/6. Issued December 1954. Deleted 1964. 233mm. TP.

£10 £6 £3

No. 3201 Mogul Dump Truck
Orange and black with white wheels. The making of a model such as this brought about the end of Dinky Toys, but at the same time the end of Dinky as a firm meant the rise of investment toys for collectors. Price £2.45. Issued 1977. Deleted 1980. 286mm.

£55 £35 £15

No. 3222 Articulated Tipper
Mustard and black with 'Mogul' in thick black letters on white background. Large thick black plastic tyres and silver hubs on wheels. Plastic/steel toy. Price £2.45. Issued 1976. Deleted 1978. 525mm.

£60 £40 £15

No. 3243 Tractor Digger
Lime, black and white plastic with thick black tyres and plastic hubs. Plastic/steel toy. Price £2.45. Issued 1977. Deleted 1980. 303mm.

£60 £35 £15

No. 3265 Tractor and Trailer
Orange, grey and black with thick tyres and plastic hubs.
Plastic/steel toy. Price £2.45. Issued 1976. Deleted 1980.
463mm.   £60   £40   £15

No. 3294 Breakdown Truck
Medium rich blue, orange and black with 'Mogul'. Silver
hook, blue wheels and thick tyres. Plastic/steel toy. Price
£2.45. Issued 1976. Deleted 1980. 268mm.   £60   £40   £20

No. 3294 Mogul Breakdown Truck
White and blue with blue plastic wheels and red crane.
Plastic/steel toy. Price £2.45. Issued 1977. Deleted 1980.
268mm.   £70   £50   £30

MILITARY VEHICLES
AND ACCESSORIES

No. 623   Army Covered Wagon

MODEL	MB	MU	GC
No. 22f Army Tank			
Green with rotating turret. Rubber treads. Price 1/-. Issued December 1933. Deleted 1940. 87mm. DC. This early example was marked 'Hornby Series'. Mint			
examples are rare owing to metal fatigue.	£250	£150	£75
Grey	£150	£100	£75
Marked 'Dinky Toys' in green	£200	£100	£75
Marked 'Dinky Toys' in grey	£150	£100	£75
No. 27D Land Rover			
Dark green and black. Spare wheel behind driver and screen. Price 3/9. Issued April 1950. Deleted 1960. 90mm. DC/RT/TP. Very rare.	£350	£250	£150
No. 30HM Daimler Military Ambulance			
Green with red crosses on roof, sides and back. Also numbered 253, made for the US market only. Price 3/-. Issued 1951. Deleted 1960. 96mm. DC/TP/RT.	£250	£150	£100
Light or medium grey	£350	£250	£150
No. 30lm Daimler Military Ambulance			
Green with red crosses on roof, sides and back. Special issue. Same model copied later when brought out for the			

	MB	MU	GC
US market post-war. Pre-war model is rare and owing to metal fatigue will only be found in reasonable condition. Price 3/-. Issued 1938. Deleted 1939. 96mm. DC/RT/TP.	£850	£500	£350

No. 37c Royal Corps of Signals Dispatch Rider
Khaki rider on green machine. Also available in battlefront colours. Rider has blue and white armband, which was missing on certain models. Model had white or black wheels, making a vast difference in value. Price 6d. Issued June 1938. Deleted 1940. 46mm. DC/RW.

	MB	MU	GC
	£250	£150	£100
Missing armband and white wheels	£200	£100	£50
Armband and white wheels	£250	£100	£75
Armband and black wheels	£75	£45	£30

No. 150a Royal Tank Corps Officer
Khaki. Price 2d. Issued February 1938. Deleted 1940. Very rare.

	MB	MU	GC
	£20	£10	£5

No. 150b Royal Tank Corps Private (Sitting)
Khaki. Price 1½d. Issued February 1938. Deleted 1940. DC.

	MB	MU	GC
	£10	£5	£2.50

No. 150c Royal Tank Corps Private (Standing)
Khaki. Price 1½d. Issued February 1938. Deleted 1940. DC.

	MB	MU	GC
	£10	£5	£2.50

No. 150d Army Driver
Khaki. Price 1½d. Issued February 1938. Deleted 1940. DC.

	MB	MU	GC
	£10	£5	£2.50

No. 150e Royal Corps NCO
Khaki. Price 1½d. Issued February 1938. Deleted 1940. DC.

	MB	MU	GC
	£10	£5	£2.50

No. 151a Medium Tank
Matt green with white squadron markings. Rotating turret, aerial and chain. Price 1/6. Issued December 1937. Deleted 1940. 92mm. DC/TP.

	MB	MU	GC
	£75	£50	£30

No. 152a Light Army Tank
Matt green with rotating turret and aerial. White squadron markings and chain. Price 1/-. Issued December 1937. Deleted 1940. 68mm. DC.

	MB	MU	GC
	£50	£35	£20

No. 152/A2 Light Army Tank
Military green with rotating turret, aerial, white squadron markings and chain. Price 2/11. Issued 1946. Deleted 1948. 68mm. DC.

	MB	MU	GC
Pre-war green baseplate	£75	£50	£30
Post-war black baseplate	£50	£30	£20

No. 152A Light Army Tank
Black tracks and no squadron markings. Otherwise
details as above.

	MB	MU	GC
	£75	£50	£30

No. 152b Reconnaissance Car
Military green with six wheels. Price 1/-. Issued February
1938. Deleted 1940. 89mm. DC/TP/RT.

Green baseplate	£50	£30	£20
Black baseplate	£30	£15	£10

No. 152/B2 Reconnaissance Car
Green or brown with six wheels. Price 2/11. Issued 1946.
Deleted 1948. 89mm. DC/TP/RT.

Black baseplate and green body	£30	£20	£15
Black baseplate and brown body	£50	£30	£15

No. 153A Jeep
Green. US model with white star on bonnet.
LHD/SW/TP with screen, four wheels and one spare
wheel at rear. Price 2/6. Issued April 1946. Deleted 1948.
69mm. DC/TP/RT.

Flat bonnet	£35	£20	£15
Curved bonnet	£20	£15	£10

No. 160a Royal Artillery NCO
Khaki. Price 2d. Issued August 1939. Deleted 1940. DC.

	£10	£5	£2.50

No. 160b Royal Artillery Gunner (Seated)
Khaki. Price 1½d. Issued August 1939. Deleted 1940. DC.

	£10	£5	£2.50

No. 160c Royal Artillery Gunlayer
Khaki. Price 1½d. Issued August 1939. Deleted 1940. DC.

	£10	£5	£2.50

No. 160d Royal Artillery Gunner (Standing)
Khaki. Price 1½d. Issued August 1939. Deleted 1940. DC.

	£5	£2.50	£1.50

No. 161 Searchlight on Lorry
Green. Price 1/6. Issued March 1939. Deleted 1940.
99mm. DC/RT.

	£75	£60	£40

No. 161a AA Gun on Trailer
Green. Gun elevates, moves etc. Folding sides and holes
in seats for gunners. Tow-bar and hook. Price 1/6. Issued
March 1939. Deleted 1940. 115mm. DC/TP/RT.

	£50	£40	£30

No. 161/B2 AA Gun and Trailer
Green. Gun elevates, moves etc. Folding sides and holes
in seats for gunners. Tow-bar and hook. Price 3/3. Issued
1946. Deleted 1948. 89mm. DC/TP/RT.

	£50	£30	£20

No. 162a Light Dragon Motor Tractor
Green. Green baseplate. Chain. Price 1/3. Issued March
1939. Deleted 1940. 89mm. DC.   £70   £50   £20

No. 162/A2 Light Dragon Motor Tractor
Dark green with chain. Holes in seats for driver etc. Some
models have rubber wheels instead of chains. Price 3/11.
Issued 1946. Deleted 1948.
Chains and black baseplate   £70   £50   £25
Rubber wheels and black baseplate   £75   £50   £30

No. 162b Trailer
Green. Green baseplate. Price 5d. Issued March 1939.
Deleted 1940. 43mm. DC/RT.   £50   £30   £20

No. 162/B2 Trailer
Green. Tow-bar and hook. Black baseplate. Price 11d.
Issued 1946. Deleted 1948. 54mm. DC/RT.   £30   £20   £10

No. 162c 18-Pounder Gun
Green. Green baseplate. Price 5d. Issued March 1939.
Deleted 1940. 78mm. DC/RT.   £50   £30   £20

No. 162/C2 18-Pounder Gun
Green. Rubber tyres and black baseplate. Tow-bar and
hook. Price 2/-. Issued 1946. Deleted 1948. 78mm. DC. £50   £25   £15

No. 170 Ford Fordor US Army Staff Car
Special model made for the American market. Military
green with white US star on nose. Equivalent price 4/6.
Issued 1957. Deleted 1958. 102mm. DC/TP/RT.   £150   £100   £50

No. 281 Army Military Hovercraft
Green. Black base with 'Army'. Gun and Union Jack on
deck. Price 75p. Issued 1973. Deleted 1976. 139mm.
DC/P.   £50   £25   £15

No. 601 Paramoke
Military green or camouflage or battlefront colours. Last
is worth double. Green canopy with black tyres.
Parachute in plain military green or camouflage.
All-action model with plastic Speediwheels from approx.
1974. Price 8/3. Issued 1966. Deleted 1978. 76mm.
DC/P/RT.
Metal wheels and rubber tyres   £60   £30   £20
Plastic Speediwheels   £50   £30   £15

No. 602 Armoured Command Car
White and khaki with driver. Price 55p. Issued 1977.
Deleted 1980. 57mm. DC/P.   £50   £25   £15

No. 602/A Armoured Command Car
Green with US star and radar scanner. Price 75p. Issued
1975. Deleted 1978. 160mm. DC/P.

| | £50 | £25 | £15 |

No. 603 Army Private (Seated)
Khaki with peg attached to underbody to fix model to
seat of vehicle. Price 3d. Issued 1950. Deleted 1968. 20mm
high.

| | £3 | £1.50 | 25p |

No. 603/A Set of Army Personnel
Green. Set of six in box. Price 1/11. Issued 1950. Deleted
1969/70.

| | £40 | £20 | £10 |

No. 604 Army Personnel (Drivers)
Khaki with new green and yellow boxes. Packed in
numbers of six personnel per box. Issued 1960. Deleted
1973.

| | £40 | £20 | £10 |

No. 604/A Land Rover Bomb Disposal Unit
Rare two-tone green with orange panels on sides.
Blue-green roof light. 'Explosive Disposal' in red on front
headboard. New 1/42nd scale. Price 76p. Issued 1976.
Deleted 1978. 160mm. DC/P.

| | £150 | £50 | £35 |

No. 604/A2 Land Rover Bomb Disposal Unit
Green with orange-red side panels. 'Explosive Disposal'
on headboard. 1/42nd scale. Price 76p. Issued 1976.
Deleted 1979. 160mm. DC/P.

| | £50 | £25 | £15 |

No. 609 105mm Howitzer with Gun Crew
Green. Price 99p. Issued 1976. Deleted 1979. 199mm.
DC/P.

| | £75 | £50 | £20 |

No. 612 Commando Jeep
Two-tone green and black with two guns and driver.
New 1/42nd scale. Price 65p. Issued 1976. Deleted 1979.
105mm. DC/P.

| | £60 | £30 | £20 |

No. 612/A Commando Jeep
Army battlefront camouflage colours. Also plain military
green. Price 65p. Issued 1974. Deleted 1979. 108mm.
DC/P.

| | £50 | £30 | £20 |

No. 615 US Jeep and 105mm Howitzer
Green with authentic US markings and driver. Price
18/11. Issued 1968. Deleted 1978. 199mm. DC/P.

| | £50 | £30 | £20 |

No. 616 AEC Articulated with Chieftain Tank
Green. Price £1/1/-. Issued 1968. Deleted 1978. 318mm.
DC/P/RT.

| | £200 | £100 | £50 |

No. 617 Volkswagen KDF and 50mm Gun
Dark greyish green or German army colour. German
cross on each side. The gun was a Pak anti-tank model.
Price 16/11. Issued 1968/69. Deleted 1978. 159mm.
DC/P.   £75   £35   £20

No. 618 AEC Articulated with Helicopter
Green. Price £1.25. Issued 1976. Deleted 1978. 318mm.
DC/P.   £100   £50   £20

No. 619 Bren Gun
Green. Price 1/11. Issued 1968. Deleted 1972. 35mm. DC. £50   £30   £20

No. 620 Berliet Missile Launcher
Green with full working parts. Price 14/11. Issued 1968.
Deleted 1971. 150mm. DC/P. The French Dinky number
was 816.   £75   £50   £20

No. 621 3-Ton Army Wagon
Green with full squadron markings. Four wheels and one
spare wheel. Price 4/8. Issued June 1954. Deleted 1963.
113mm. DC/TP/RT.   £75   £50   £20

No. 622 Bren Gun Carrier
Green. Price 75p. Issued 1975. Deleted 1978. 125mm.
DC/P. The size was wrongly advertised on some boxes
(159mm).   £50   £30   £15

No. 622/A 10-Ton Army Truck
Green. Six wheels and one spare. Holes for passengers
inside model. Price 6/10. Issued May 1954. Deleted 1963.
137mm. DC/TP/RT. Very rare.   £100   £50   £20

No. 623 Army Covered Wagon
Green with squadron markings etc. Four wheels and one
spare. Price 3/7. Issued March 1954. Deleted 1963.
105mm. DC/TP/RT.   £75   £35   £20

No. 624 Daimler Ambulance
Fine model in US military green. Made specially for
American market with red crosses on roof, sides and
back. Equivalent price 4/6. Issued 1954. Deleted 1960.
96mm. DC/TP/RT.   £250   —   —

No. 625 6-Pounder Tank Gun
Green. Price 35p. Issued 1975. Deleted 1978. 159mm. DC. £50   £20   £10

No. 626 Military Ambulance
Green with red crosses on roof, sides and back. Four wheels, one spare and opening doors at rear. Price 6/11. Issued September 1956. Deleted 1962. 110mm. DC/TP/RT. — £75 — £50 — £20

No. 630 Ferret Armoured Car
Khaki. Price 54p. Issued 1973. Deleted 1978. 80mm. DC/P. — £45 — £20 — £15

No. 641 Army 1-Ton Cargo Truck
Green with squadron markings, four wheels and holes for passengers inside truck. Price 3/9. Issued August 1954. Deleted 1962. 79mm. DC/TP/RT. — £75 — £35 — £20

No. 643 Army Water Tanker
Green with RASC markings, four wheel drive and spare wheel. Austin chassis modified to suit army requirements. Price 4/3. Issued January 1958. Deleted 1964. 89mm. DC/TP/RT. — £50 — £25 — £15

No. 651 Centurion Tank
Green with rotating turret and squadron markings. Price 7/11. Issued 1954. Deleted 1961. 149mm. DC/RT. — £90 — £50 — £20

No. 651/A Centurion Tank
Light or medium green with army markings etc. Price 10/11. Issued 1961. Deleted 1971. 146mm. DC/P/tracks. — £100 — £50 — £25

No. 654 155mm Mobile Gun
Battlefront colours. Price 30p. Issued 1974. Deleted 1976. 151mm. DC/P. — £50 — £25 — £10

No. 654/A 155mm Mobile Gun
Light or medium green. Price 36p. Issued 1976. Deleted 1979. 151mm. DC/P. — £50 — £25 — £10

No. 656 88mm Gun
Battlefront livery and markings. Also in normal military green. 1/35th scale. Price 55p. Issued 1975. Deleted 1979. 218mm. DC/P. — £35 — £15 — £5

No. 660 Tank Transporter
Green with folding ramps at the rear. 6 x 6 wheels and one spare wheel. Price 17/6. Issued June 1956. Deleted 1964. 335mm. DC/RT. — £150 — £50 — £20

No. 660/A Mobile AA Gun with Crew
Light or dark green. Black base. Three crew members. Price 78p. Issued 1978. Deleted 1980. 218mm. DC/P/RT. — £65 — £35 — £20

MILITARY VEHICLES AND ACCESSORIES	MB	MU	GC

No. 661 Recovery Tractor
Green with six wheels and working crane. Price 9/6.
Issued June 1957. Deleted 1964. 134mm. DC/TP/RT.

	£70	£30	£15

No. 662 Static 88mm Gun with Crew
Camouflage or green. Three gun-crew figures. Big gun
which fires plastic shells. 1/35th scale. Price 55p. Issued
1975. Deleted 1978. 185mm. DC/P.

	£50	£20	£10

No. 665 Honest John Missile Launcher
Green with 10 wheels and one spare with elevating ramp.
Firing rocket. Price 17/11. Issued March 1964. Deleted
1969. 188mm. DC/TP/RT/P.

	£200	£75	£50

No. 666 Missile Erector Vehicle with Corporal Missile
Green with working rockets, 4 wheels, one spare and 2
wheels. Price £1/10/11. Issued November 1959. Deleted
1964. 240mm and 90mm. DC/TP/P/RT.

	£250	£75	£35

No. 667 Missile Servicing Platform Vehicle
Green with side supports which fold down. Elevating
platform. Six wheels and one spare. Price 14/3. Issued
April 1960. Deleted 1961. 130mm vehicle only. 197mm.
OA/DC/TP/P/RT. Limited number made and good
investment.

	£100	£50	£30

No. 667/A Armoured Patrol Car
Green. 1/48th scale. Price 99p. Issued 1976. Deleted 1980.
80mm. DC/P.
Battlefield grey.

	£20	£15	£10
	£75	£45	£20

No. 668 Foden Army Truck
Two-tone green with orange panels on cab doors and
white cab interior. 1/42nd scale. Price £1.50. Issued 1976.
Deleted 1978. 197mm. DC/P. Rare.
Normal military green

	£500	—	—
	£95	£30	£15

No. 669 USA Universal Jeep
Green. Specially made for the US market. Equivalent
price 2/9. Issued 1956. Deleted 1958. 83mm. DC/TP/RT.

	£50	£30	£20

No. 670 Armoured Car
Green with rotating turret and squadron markings. Price
2/10. Issued September 1954. Deleted 1964. 73mm.
DC/TP/RT.

	£50	£30	£10

No. 670/A Armoured Car
Green and light green with revolving turret. Squadron
markings and numbers. Price 4/-. Issued 1965. Deleted
1971. 73mm. DC.

	£35	£20	£10

No. 671 Mk 1 Corvette
Grey with black stripes and dark fawn markings. Firing missiles. Price 76p. Issued 1976. Deleted 1979. 260mm. DC/P.

| | £50 | £20 | £15 |

No. 672 OSA Missile Boat
Grey and black with firing missiles. Price 76p. Issued 1976. Deleted 1979. 206mm. DC/P.

| | £50 | £25 | £15 |

No. 673 Scout Car
Green. Holes in seat for driver and passenger. Price 3/2. Issued November 1953. Deleted 1962. 68mm. DC/RT.

| | £50 | £25 | £15 |

No. 674 Austin Champ (Promotional Special)
White with driver and spare wheel. Presented as a souvenir to members of the UN forces in Germany. Price £1. Issued 1965. Deleted 1971. 70mm. DC/P. Rare. Mint boxed only.

| | £750 | — | — |

No. 674 Austin Champ
Green. Four wheels, one spare and holes for driver and passenger. Tinplate windscreen. Price 3/2. Issued 1954. Deleted 1964. 69mm. DC/RT/SW/TP.

| | £50 | £20 | £15 |

No. 674/A Austin Champ
Green or camouflaged with driver and spare wheel on rear. Price 4/-. Issued 1965. Deleted 1971. 70mm. DC/P.

| | £50 | £20 | £15 |

No. 675 Ford Fordor US Army Staff Car
Green. Made specially for the US market. Equivalent price 4/6. Issued 1966. Deleted 1967. 102mm. DC/TP/RT. Rare.

| | £350 | — | — |

No. 675/A 153 Missile Firing Boat
Grey, silver-grey and black. Runs on concealed wheels. Model of the motor patrol boat used in many battles with great success by the Navy. Price 99p. Issued 1976. Deleted 1979. 170mm. DC/P.

| | £50 | £20 | £10 |

No. 676 Armoured Personnel Carrier
Green. Six wheels, rotating turret, squadron markings etc. Price 3/2. Issued February 1955. Deleted 1962. 82mm. DC/RT.

| | £75 | £50 | £25 |

No. 676/A Daimler Armoured Car
Green with squadron markings and numbers. Price 3/11. Issued 1960. Deleted 1966. 72mm. DC/RT.

| | £75 | £35 | £20 |

No. 677 Armoured Command Vehicle
Green with six wheels and squadron markings. Price 5/4. Issued April 1957. Deleted 1962. 134mm. DC/TP/RT.

| | £75 | £35 | £20 |

	MB	MU	GC
No. 678 Air–Sea Rescue Launch Fawn and black with pilot and dinghy. RAF markings and 'Rescue' on each side. Price 79p. Issued 1976. Deleted 1979. 170mm. DC/P.	£75	£50	£25
No. 680 Ferret Armoured Car Medium green with full squadron markings. Price 54p. Issued 1972. Deleted 1979. 80mm. DC/P.	£50	£25	£15
No. 681 DUKW Light green with full squadron markings. Price 54p. Issued 1972. Deleted 1979. 127mm. DC/P.	£75	£45	£25
No. 682 Stalwart Load Carrier Green with six large black wheels and black cab interior. Full squadron markings. Price 90p. Issued 1972. Deleted 1979. 132mm. DC/P.	£75	£35	£25
No. 683 Chieftain Tank Green with full squadron markings and rotating turret. Tracks. Fires plastic shells. Price £1.60. Issued 1972. Deleted 1979. 117mm. DC/P.	£100	£50	£25
No. 683/A Chieftain Tank Camouflaged. Tracks. New 1/50th scale. Price £1.76. Issued 1972. Deleted 1979. 217mm. DC/P.	£100	£50	£20
No. 686 25-Pounder Field Gun Green with tow-bar. Price 2/9. Issued 1957. Deleted 1969. 90mm. DC/RT.	£50	£35	£20
No. 686/A Trailer for 25-Pounder Field Gun Green. Price 1/9. Issued 1957. Deleted 1969. 58mm. DC/R/RT/TP.	£50	£35	£20
No. 686 Convoy Army Truck Military green with black bumper and silver wheels. Model had misprint of number and should be 687; the wrong number on the box makes it more valuable. Price £1.25. Issued 1978. Deleted 1979. 110mm. DC/P.	£75	£40	£20
No. 687 Convoy Army Truck Green with black bumper and removable green canopy and silver wheels. Price £1.25. Issued 1977/78. Deleted 1980. 110mm. D/P.	£65	£35	£20
No. 688 Field Artillery Tractor Green with full squadron markings. Four wheels and one spare. Price 3/5. Issued 1957. Deleted 1969. 81mm. DC/RT/TP.	£65	£35	£25

No. 688/A Field Artillery Tractor
Green with full squadron markings. Spare wheel at rear.
Price 4/-. Issued 1960. Deleted 1969. 79mm. DC/TP/RT. £75 £50 £35

No. 689 Medium Artillery Tractor
Green. Excellent model of a six-wheel drive vehicle used
for towing medium artillery and equipment over rough
and dangerous country. Full squadron markings, driver
and hook. Price 8/9. Issued 1957. Deleted 1962. 140mm.
DC/TP/RT. £100 £50 £25

No. 690 Scorpion Tank
Green with rotating turret and camouflage net. Full
military markings. Four-round rapid firing gun. 1/40th
scale. Price £1.25. Issued 1975. Deleted 1979. 120mm.
DC/P. £75 £40 £20

No. 691 Striker Anti-Tank Vehicle
Camouflaged. Five rockets which fire singly or all
together. New 1/40th scale. Price £1.55p. Issued 1976.
Deleted 1979. 122mm. DC/P. £55 £35 £20

No. 692 5.5 Medium Gun
Green with splitting tow-bar and elevating gun. Price
3/2. Issued September 1955. Deleted 1962. 131mm.
DC/RT. £50 £25 £10

No. 692/A Leopard Tank
Grey or green. Price £1.25. Issued 1976. Deleted 1979.
198mm. DC/P. £75 £50 £20

No. 693 7.2 Howitzer Gun
Green or grey. Elevating gun. Price 3/5. Issued October
1958. Deleted 1963. 130mm. DC/RT. £50 £35 £20

No. 694 Hanomag 7.5cm Tank Destroyer
Dark grey with German markings and '145' on sides.
Large tracks and movable front wheels. Price £1.55.
Issued 1976. Deleted 1979. 171mm. DC/P. £50 £30 £20

No. 694 Hanomag 7.5cm Tank Destroyer
Green or grey. Price £1.55. Issued 1976. Deleted 1979.
171mm. DC/P. £50 £30 £20

No. 696 Leopard Anti-Aircraft Tank
Grey with full military markings and numbers. Price
£1.25. Issued 1976. Deleted 1979. 152mm. DC. £65 £35 £20

No. 697 25-Pounder Field Gun Set
Green. Price 10/6. Issued 1964. Deleted 1971. 174mm.
DC/T/P/RT. £75 £35 £20

MILITARY VEHICLES AND ACCESSORIES	MB	MU	GC

No. 699 Leopard Recovery Tank
Grey with full markings and numbers. Price £1.50. Issued
1976. Deleted 1979. 147mm. DC/P.   £75   £40   £30

No. 739 AGM5 Zero-Sen
Green and black with yellow lines and red circles. Motor
driver propeller. These planes did battle over the Pacific
with great effect. Price £1.25. Issued 1976. Deleted 1979.
184mm. DC/P.   £45   £20   £10

No. 815 Panhard Armoured Car
Green showing the French flag. Four wheels with tyres
and four without. Rotating turret. Price 8/7. Issued July
1962. Deleted 1964. 104mm. DC/RT/TP. Very rare.   £75   £40   £20

No. 817 AMX 13-Ton Tank
Green with rotating turret. Rubber tracks. Price 12/6.
Issued July 1962. Deleted 1964. 107mm. DC/TP.   £90   £50   £20

No. 822 M3 Half-Track
Green with rotating machine gun and rubber tracks. Price
9/11. Issued July 1962. Deleted 1964. 121mm.
DC/TP/RT.   £75   £35   £20

No. 884 Brockway Truck with Bridge
Green with 10 wheels and inflatable pontoons. Price
£1/18/-. Issued September 1962. Deleted 1964. 181mm.
DC/TP.   £100   £50   £35

No. 3284 Army Mogul Wagon
Dark brown and fawn in battlefront livery with driver
and passenger. Price 77p. Issued 1976. Deleted 1978.
236mm. DC/P.   £45   £25   £10

No. 3287 Mogul Army Truck
Dark green with light green cover. US star on bonnet.
Price 77p. Issued 1976. Deleted 1979. 260mm. DC/P.   £45   £20   £10

MODELS FROM TV, SPACE ETC.

No. 967   BBC TV Mobile Control Room

See also some models in the Sports Cars and Saloons section. In addition, should any models or boxes be signed by stars or personalities, they are worth a great deal more.

MODEL	MB	MU	GC
No. 267 Paramedic Truck Red with the figures of De Soto and Gage from the TV series Emergency. Price £2.25. Issued 1978. Deleted 1980. 119mm. DC/P.	£250	£100	£50
No. 281 Pathé News Camera Car Black with 'Pathé News' in white on sides. Red interior, opening bonnet and rear door. Cameraman on roof. Price 9/11. Issued 1968. Deleted 1970. 108mm. DC/P.	£250	£100	£50
No. 351 UFO Interceptor Lime-green, orange, silver and black with red tipped cap firing rocket. From Gerry Anderson's UFO TV programme. Price 14/11. Issued 1971. Deleted 1979. 194mm. P.	£350	£100	£30

No. 352 Ed Straker's Car
Metallic bronze or gold with lemon or off-white interior. Silver hubs. Known as the keyless clockwork motor. Price 7/6. Issued 1971. Deleted 1975. 124mm. DC/P.

	MB	MU	GC
	£250	£100	£50

No. 353 Shado 2 Mobile
All-action model in green, orange and silver with 'Shado' and '2' in white on sides. Twelve wheels and heavy tracks, white interior and firing rocket on roof. Another model from Gerry Anderson's UFO TV programme. Price 17/11. Issued 1971. Deleted 1979. 145mm. DC/P.

	£350	£150	£50

No. 354 The Pink Panther
There is no doubt that this model came to the rescue of a firm which was on the verge of bankruptcy. This same model was rejected by Corgi, and Dinky made it as a gimmick because of the TV series of the same name; it sold by the thousand, not only in England but in America. Pink with the figure of the panther with black markings etc. The model tears along under its own dynamic power. Central gyroscopic road wheel with a pull-through track rod. Price £1.75. Issued 1972. Deleted 1977. 175mm. DC/P.

	MB	MU	GC
Unsigned	£500	£200	£100
Box signed by Peter Sellers	£2000	—	—

No. 355 Lunar Roving Vehicle
Blue and red with thick black plastic wheels and knobby treads with two white spacemen. The front and rear wheels are steered by pivoting a central control column. Model astronauts and simulated solar energy cells. Price 14/11. Issued 1972. Deleted 1975. 114mm. DC/P.

	£250	£100	£50

No. 357 Klingon Battle Cruiser
Blue and silver. From the TV series Star Trek. Price £1.55. Issued 1977. Deleted 1979. 220mm. DC/P.

	£250	£100	£50

No. 358 USS Enterprise
Silver and orange with black lettering. Fires photon torpedoes and doors open for access to shuttlecraft. Taken from the TV series Star Trek. Price £2.25. Issued 1976. Deleted 1979. 234mm. DC/P.

	MB	MU	GC
Unsigned	£500	£200	£90
Signed by Captain Kirk and dated as first flight	£2000	—	—

No. 359 Eagle Transporter
Lime-green, red, white and silver. All-working components, adjustable feet etc. From the TV series Space 1999. Price £2.50. Issued 1975. Deleted 1979. 222mm. DC/P.

	£200	£100	£30

No. 360 Eagle Freighter
All-silver body with red, orange and purple parts.
Adjustable feet. From the TV series Space 1999. Price
£2.50. Issued 1975. Deleted 1979. 222mm. DC/P. £150 £75 £40

No. 361 Galactic War Chariot
Lime-green or yellow-green. Silver rocket attachments,
wheels and six large tyres. Two astronauts in white and
orange or bright yellow. Price £2.50. Issued 1978. Deleted
1980. 126mm. DC/P. £200 £100 £50

No. 362 Trident Star Fighter
Dark brown or chocolate with dark orange and yellow
markings on wings, tail and nose. Rocket which fires by
pressing the centre of the fighter. Price £1.47. Issued 1978.
Deleted 1980. 170mm. DC/P. £100 £50 £20

No. 364 Space Shuttle
Model of the famous American NASA shuttlecraft. White
and dark blue with US flag markings on sides. Price £4.35.
Issued 1978. Deleted 1980. 186mm. DC/P. £350 £200 £100

No. 367 Space Battle Cruiser
White with blue engine and cockpit interior, with
spaceman pilot. With firing rockets and opening clear
plastic hatch, rockets have black tips and holders have
orange or deep red circles around them. Price £3.25.
Issued 1978. Deleted 1980. 187mm. DC/P. £300 £150 £100

No. 370 Dragster Set
Yellow and silver with red stripes, with driver. The
model had the new Speediwheels and proved a great
success; it was also sold as a separate item from the
dragster set. Price 17/11. Issued 1969. Deleted 1976.
113mm. DC/P. £250 £100 £50

No. 370 The Dragster
Yellow, silver, and pink and white striped engine cover.
Large racing wheels. Price 14/11. Issued 1969. Deleted
1975/76. 113mm. DC/P. £150 £75 £40

No. 602 Armoured Command Car
Metallic dark blue or green with black wheels. Model
designed by Gerry Anderson of Thunderbirds TV fame.
Tracer-projector and super-radar scanner powered by its
own clockwork motor. Price £2.95. Issued 1976. Deleted
1978. DC/P. £300 £150 £75

No. 755 Harpoon for Fab 1
These came in packets of six as spare harpoons for No. 100. Being realistic they can only be bought as mint. You would never find six loose harpoons. Price 6d per packet. Issued 1966. Deleted 1977.

	£40	£10	£5

No. 756 Rocket for Fab Car
Spare for No. 100. Issued 1966. Deleted 1977. Price 6d.

	£40	£10	£5

No. 967 BBC TV Mobile Control Room
Green with white flash and 'BBC Television Service' in yellow or gold. Windows. Price 8/3. Issued July 1959. Deleted 1964/65. 151mm. DC/TP/RT/P.

	£250	£150	£75

No. 968 BBC TV Roving Eye Vehicle
Green with white flash to match No. 967 and 'TV Roving Eye' and BBC badge on sides. TV aerial and revolving camera with operator on roof. Price 8/3. Issued May 1959. Deleted 1964. 100mm. DC/RT/TP/P.

	£250	£150	£75

No. 969 BBC TV Extending Mast Vehicle
Green with white flash to go with Nos. 967 and 968. Extending mast with parabolid aerial. Badge on sides. Price 13/6. Issued October 1959. Deleted 1964. 195mm. DC/TP/RT/P.

	£250	£150	£75

No. 987 ABC TV Mobile Control Room
Blue and grey with all authentic markings. Red flash. 'ABC Television' on front and sides with camera and operator on roof. Price 12/6. Issued July 1962. Deleted 1970. 151mm. DC/TP/RT/P.

	£250	£150	£75

No. 988 ABC TV Transmitter Van
Matching blue and grey with red flash. 'ABC' on front and rotating aerial on roof. Price 7/9. Issued May 1962. Deleted 1970. 111mm. DC/TP/RT/P.

	£250	£150	£75

MOTOR CYCLES

Many of these models never had individual boxes as they were packed in either half-dozens or dozens.

MODEL	MB	MU	GC
No. 37a Civilian Motor Cyclist Green or brown rider on black cycle with white wheels. Price 6d. Issued June 1938. Deleted 1940. 46mm. DC/RW.	—	£45	£10
No. 37A Civilian Motor Cyclist Grey or green rider. Cycle with black or white wheels. Many post-war models have white solid rubber wheels and are only distinguishable from pre-war models by the better detailed paint finish. The pre-war models have more details picked out in silver. Price 1/9. Issued 1946. Deleted 1948. 45mm. DC/RW.	—	£35	£10
No. 37b Police Motor Patrolman Blue rider on black cycle with white wheels. Price 6d. Issued June 1938. Deleted 1940. 46mm. DC/RW.	—	£35	£10
No. 37B Police Patrolman Blue rider on black machine with black or white wheels. Price 1/9. Issued 1946. Deleted 1948. 45mm. DC/RW.	—	£25	£10
No. 37e Royal Corps of Signals Rider Khaki rider on green motor cycle. Rider has blue and white armband. White rubber wheels, but black from 1939. Price 6d. Issued June 1938. Deleted 1940/41. Never reissued post-war. 45mm. DC/RW.	—	£45	£10
No. 42b Police Motor Cycle Patrol Very dark blue police livery, much darker than post-war. Dark blue bike and figures with dark green sidecar. White rubber wheels. Price 10d. Issued August 1936. Deleted 1940. 47mm. DC/RW.	—	£45	£10
No. 42B Police Motor Patrol Blue bike with green sidecar and black wheels. Price 1/9. Issued 1948. Deleted 1956. 47mm. DC/RW.	—	£35	£10

No. 43b RAC Patrol Bike
Blue rider with black cycle and blue sidecar. Driver with
white shirt, black tie and red sash painted on. White or
black solid rubber wheels. Price 9d. Issued October 1935.
Deleted 1940. 46mm. DC/RW. — £45 £10

No. 43B RAC Motor Patrol Bike
This model has two or three different shades of blue.
Driver has plain blue uniform and bike has black wheels
and black or blue sidecar. Price 2/6. Issued 1946. Deleted
1950. 45mm. DC/RW. — £35 £10

No. 44b AA Motor Patrol
The pre-war and early post-war AA bikes have a small
'AA' transfer on the sidecar and later ones and No. 270
have larger ones. Driver has shirt and tie with blue
painted sash. White wheels. Price 9d. Issued October
1935. Deleted 1940. DC. — £55 £15

No. 44B AA Motor Cycle Patrol
Black cycle with yellow sidecar with AA badge. Driver
painted plain. Black wheels. Price 2/11. Issued 1946.
Deleted 1949. 45mm. DC/RW. — £45 £10

No. 270 AA Motor Cycle Patrol
This model was a reissue of No. 44B after a gap of 10 years
and was only issued with grey plastic wheels and in an
individual box. The wheels were as those used in the
Hornby Dinky Dublo models Nos. 064, 066 and 073. The
early models were in boxes of six, but later the first
individual boxes were issued. Authentic AA livery with
rider with pink face. Badge on sidecar. Price 2/2. Issued
February 1959. Deleted 1962. £45 £20 £10

No. 271 Touring Secours Motor Cycle Patrol
Yellow with grey plastic wheels and TS badge. This was
identical to No. 270 but made in a special livery for the
Belgian market. Equivalent price 2/6. Issued 1962.
Deleted 1966. 46mm. DC/RW. £125 £60 £30

No. 272 ANWB Patrol Bike
Dark yellow with ANWB badge and markings. Plastic
wheels. Identical to No. 270. Equivalent price 2/6. Issued
for Dutch market 1962. Deleted 1966. 46mm. DC/RT. £125 £60 £30

POLICE, BANKS, FIRE SERVICE AND SECURITY VEHICLES

No. 258   USA Police Car (Dodge Model)

MODEL	MB	MU	GC
No. 243 Volvo Police Car White with brown orange flash. Blue or black edge on each side, opening door at rear, black mudguards and 'Police' roof sign. Price £2.25. Issued 1978. Deleted 1980. 141mm. DC/P.	£75	£50	£25
No. 244 Plymouth Police Car Black and white with light and transfer details on sides and rear. Price £2.25. Issued 1978. Deleted 1980. 161mm. DC/P.	£150	£50	£25
No. 250 Police Mini-Cooper S White with 'Police' sign and dummy light plus aerial on roof, opening doors and bonnet. Silver bumpers etc. Price 8/3. Issued 1968. Deleted 1976. 75mm. DC/P.	£55	£20	£10
No. 251 Pontiac Parisienne USA Police Car Authentic colours, designs etc. White with black roof. Driver. Price 9/6. Issued 1973. Deleted 1975. 132mm. DC/P.	£150	£50	£25

No. 252 RCMP Police Car Pontiac Parisienne
Dark blue and white with two policemen, roof light and
twin aerials. Price 9/6. Issued 1969. Deleted 1975. 132mm.
DC/P.

	£175	£100	£50

No. 254 Police Range Rover
White with orange stripe with black border around each
side. Opening doors at side and rear with 'Police' roof
sign. Blue interior. Silver bumpers, wheels etc. Plastic
Speediwheels from 1976. Price 9/11. Issued 1971. Deleted
1978. 109mm. DC/P.

Early model	£95	£45	£20
Later model	£65	£30	£10

No. 255 Mersey Tunnel Police Van Special
Red with matching wheels and black tyres. Silver
bumper, grille and radiator. 'Mersey Tunnel' in yellow or
gold on sides and 'Police' sign in white with black
background on roof. Issued 1955. Deleted 1960. Price
2/11. 73mm. DC/RT/TP.

	£2500	—	—

No. 255 Ford Zodiac
Authentic police colours. Opening doors, boot and
bonnet. Driver. Price 16/-. Issued 1967. Deleted 1972.
114mm. DC/P.

	£65	£30	£15

No. 255 Police Mini-Clubman
Pale blue with white doors, 'Police' roof sign and 'Police'
on each door. Price £1.25. Issued 1977. Deleted 1980.
82mm. DC/P.

	£65	£30	£15

No. 256 Police Patrol Car
Black. Humber Hawk model with 'Police' sign on roof in
white letters. Driver and passenger. Price 5/3. Issued
December 1960. Deleted 1964. 102mm. DC/RT/TP/P.

	£65	£30	£15

No. 257 Canadian Fire Chief's Car
Red. Nash Rambler model with 'Fire Chief' on sides with
dummy red roof-light. Price 3/5. Issued November 1961.
Deleted 1969. 102mm. DC/TP/RT/P.

	£65	£30	£15

No. 258 USA Police Car
Black with white doors, police badge and wording. Price
4/11. Four models ran in production from October 1960
to July 1969. Cadillac came into production in 1966.
114mm. DC/TP/RT/P.

De Soto model	£125	£50	£25
Dedge model	£125	£50	£25
Ford model	£100	£40	£20
Cadillac model	£100	£40	£20

No. 260 VW Deutsche Bundespost
Yellow. Model of the late VW with opening bonnet, boot
and doors. Issued for sale in Germany only, although a
few were found in shops in England. Price £1.45. Issued
1971. Deleted 1976. 100mm. DC/P.

| | £175 | £50 | £25 |

No. 261 Ford Taunus Polizei Car
White and green with police markings. Released as No.
154 for the German market. 'Polizei' is German for
'police'. Very scarce in England. Equivalent price 7/11.
Issued 1967. Deleted 1978. 110mm. DC/P.

| | £75 | £40 | £20 |

No. 262 VW Swiss Post
Yellow and black with jewelled lights. This model was
used for two versions of the VW Swiss Post. The first
came from a No. 181 casting and was issued in
Switzerland from 1961 to 1966. The second came from a
No. 129 casting with opening boot, bonnet and doors with
jewelled headlights and was issued from 1966 to approx.
1975. There were plastic Speediwheels on the second
version from approx. 1973. Price 7/11. 100mm. DC/P.

First version	£150	£60	£30
Second version with metal wheels	£95	£40	£20
Second version with plastic wheels	£75	£30	£15

No. 264 RCMP Patrol Car
Dark blue with white doors. First model is Ford Fairlane
111mm. Second model is Cadillac 62 113mm. Price 6/6.
First date for models 1962. Finally deleted 1969.
DC/TP/RT/P.

| First model | £130 | £50 | £25 |
| Second model | £115 | £40 | £20 |

No. 264 Police Rover 3500
White with orange stripes edged in blue or black and
'Police' at rear. Same casting as No. 180. Opening boot
and doors. Silver hubs etc. Price £2.50. Issued 1978.
Deleted 1980. 131mm. DC/P.

| | £150 | £50 | £25 |

No. 269 Jaguar Motorway Police Car
White. Two policemen, dummy roof light, aerial and
'Police' on boot. Price 5/6. Issued April 1962. Deleted
June 1966. 95mm. SW/SS/FTS/S/W/DC/TP/RT/P.

| | £100 | £40 | £20 |

No. 269 Ford Transit Accident Unit
White with wide orange flash and 'Police' and 'Accident
Unit' on sides. Opening doors at side and rear. Signs,
cones etc. Silver wheels and bumpers. Price £2.25. Issued
1978. Deleted 1980. 113mm. DC/P.

| | £95 | £40 | £10 |

No. 270 Ford Panda Police Car
Blue and white with opening doors, bonnet and boot.
Ford Escort casting as No. 168. Plastic Speediwheels from
1965. Price 8/11. Issued 1969. Deleted 1977. 97mm. DC/P.

| | £65 | £20 | £10 |

No. 272 Ford Transit Police Accident Unit
White and red. Redesign of No. 287. One piece opening
rear door. Driver's door does not open. Second grille
type. Price £2.35. Issued 1975. Deleted 1978. 129mm.
DC/P.

| | £150 | £75 | £35 |

No. 275 Brinks Armoured Van
Grey with blue chassis. 'Brinks Security since 1895' on
sides. Blue defence guard, gold bars and opening doors.
Price 12/11. Issued 1964. Deleted 1970. 121mm. DC/P.

| | £125 | £50 | £25 |

No. 277 Police Land Rover
Dark or medium blue with white top and part of sides.
'Police' in white on black base on front and sides. Also
blue base and roof light. Opening doors and bonnet. Price
£2.25. Issued 1978. Deleted 1980. 110mm. DC/P.

| | £65 | £20 | £10 |

No. 280 Mobile Midland Bank Van
Light blue, silver and white with opening doors.
'Midland Bank Ltd' on sides and front. Body mounted on
long chassis. Silver grille, bumpers, headlights etc. Hubs
and roof light. Price 9/11. Issued 1966. Deleted 1969.
124mm. DC/P.

| | £150 | £50 | £25 |

No. 287 Police Accident Unit
Orange and cream motorway colours with police
wording, badges etc. Safety cones and barriers, signs etc.
Opening doors at front and rear. Roof light and sign.
Driver and other officer. First grille type. Price 13/11.
Issued 1967. Replaced by No. 272 in 1975/76. Deleted
1978. 122mm. DC/P/RT.

| | £200 | £100 | £50 |

No. 297 Police Vehicle Set
White and pale pink. Opening doors, signs, cones, drivers
etc. This set contained Nos. 250, 255 and 287. Price
£1/17/11. Issued 1967. Changed to No. 294 in 1973.
Deleted 1980. Overall length 300/306mm. DC/P.

| | £250 | £100 | £50 |

ROAD ROLLERS

No. 251   Aveling Barford Roller

MODEL	MB	MU	GC
No. 25P Aveling Barford Roller The first model had no individual box and is a very dark green. Cast in H/D/SW. Price 5/9. Issued 1948. Deleted 1954 when renumbered 251. 110mm. DC/TP. Delivered to shops in boxes of six.	£250	—	—
No. 25P Aveling Barford Roller This model had a box, but the first ones were still a very dark green and are worth double the light green. Price 5/9. Issued 1948. Renumbered 251 in 1954. 110mm. DC/TP.	£75	£40	£20
No. 251 Aveling Barford Roller Green and red, and grey with red rollers. Front roller swivel. Price 4/10. Issued May 1955. Deleted 1963. 110mm. DC/TP/D/S/W.	£65	£40	£10
No. 279 Aveling Barford Roller Orange and green with two base-metal rollers and grey plastic engine cover. Price 9/11. Issued 1965. Deleted 1978. 116mm. DC/P.	£65	£40	£10
No. 279 Aveling Barford Roller Lower body in orange and cab in yellow with black roof, but the cab does not lift off. Silver rollers and grey plastic engine cover. The first bubble packs were introduced in 1971 and some were in boxes (worth double). Price 9/11. Issued 1971. Deleted 1980. 116mm. DC/P.	£65	£30	£15

SHIPS, BOATS AND SIMILAR CRAFT

Information on Dinky ships is very hard to find, but I hope that this section will be of help to collectors of these fine diecast items.

MODEL	MB	MU	GC
No. 50 Gift Set			
Special presentation box of 15 pieces. Contains Nos. 50a, 50b (2), 50c, 50d, 50f (3), 50g, 50h (3) and 50k. Price 3/7. Issued July 1935. Deleted 1940.	£500	—	—
No. 50a Battle Cruiser Hood			
Royal Navy livery. Scale 1in to 150ft. Price 9d. Issued June 1934. Deleted 1940. Only boxed in No. 50 set.	—	£40	£10
No. 50b Battleship Nelson			
Royal Navy livery. Scale 1in to 150ft. Price 6d. Issued June 1934. Deleted 1940. Only boxed in No. 50 set.	—	£40	£10
No. 50c Cruiser Effingham			
Royal Navy livery. Scale 1in to 150ft. Price 4d. Issued June 1934. Deleted 1940. Only boxed in No. 50 set.	—	£50	£15
No. 50d Cruiser York			
Royal Navy livery. Scale 1in to 150ft. Price 4d. Issued June 1934. Deleted 1940. Only boxed in No. 50 set.	—	£50	£15
No. 50e Cruiser Delhi			
Royal Navy livery. Scale 1in to 150ft. Price 4d. Issued June 1934. Deleted 1940. Only boxed in No. 50 set.	—	£50	£15
No. 50f Destroyer Broke Class			
Royal Navy livery. Scale 1in to 150ft. Price 1d. Issued June 1934. Deleted 1940. Only boxed in No. 50 set.	—	£40	£10
No. 50g Submarine K Class			
Royal Navy livery. Scale 1in to 150ft. Price 1d. Issued July 1935. Deleted 1940. Only boxed in No. 50 set.	—	£40	£10

No. 50h Destroyer Amazon Class
Royal Navy livery. Scale 1in to 150ft. Price 1d. Issued 1935. Deleted 1940. Only boxed in No. 50 set.

	MB	MU	GC
	—	£40	£10

No. 50k Submarine X Class
Royal Navy livery. Scale 1in to 150ft. Price 1d. Issued July 1935. Deleted 1940. Only boxed in No. 50 set.

| | — | £50 | £15 |

No. 51 Gift Set
Set of six ships in their authentic liner liveries in special presentation box. Contains Nos. 51b, 51c, 51d, 51e, 51f and 51g. Price 3/6. Issued June 1934. Deleted 1940.

| | £450 | — | — |

No. 51a Liner United States of America
On rollers. Scale 1in to 150ft. Price 1/-. Issued 1936. Deleted 1938. Nice presentation box. Very rare as only a few were released.

| | £95 | £50 | £15 |

No. 51b Liner Europa Star
Authentic livery. Scale 1in to 150ft. Price 1/-. Issued June 1934. Deleted 1940. Only boxed in No. 51 set.

| | — | £95 | £35 |

No. 51c Liner The Rex
Authentic livery. Scale 1in to 150ft. Price 9d. Issued June 1934. Deleted 1940. Only boxed in No. 51 set.

| | — | £95 | £35 |

No. 51d Liner The Empress of Britain
Authentic livery. Scale 1in to 150ft. Price 8d. Issued June 1934. Deleted 1940. Nice presentation box.

| | £95 | £50 | £15 |

No. 51e Liner The Strathaird
Authentic livery. Scale 1in to 150ft. Price 6d. Issued June 1934. Deleted 1940. Only boxed in No. 51 set.

| | — | £55 | £25 |

No. 51f Liner The Queen of Bermuda
Authentic livery. Scale 1in to 150ft. Price 6d. Issued June 1934. Deleted 1940. Only boxed in No. 51 set.

| | — | £40 | £10 |

No. 51g Liner The Britannic
Authentic livery. Scale 1in to 150ft. Price 6d. Issued June 1934. Deleted 1940. Only boxed in No. 51 set.

| | — | £50 | £15 |

No. 52a Liner Cunard White Star
The 'Cunard White Star' title was introduced in June 1934, but by December that year it had gained the name of 'Queen Mary' (No. 52b). Deleted 1940. Reissued 1946. Deleted 1952. The pre-war version has plastic rollers and the post-war brass. There was also a No. 52m pre-war version without rollers in a plain box. Scale 1in to 150ft.

	MB	MU	GC

Price 1/- in fancy presentation box and 9d in plain box.

	MB	MU	GC
No. 52a or 52b pre-war	£50	£30	£15
No. 52A post-war	£25	£15	£5
No. 52m pre-war	£40	£20	£10

No. 52c French Liner Normandie
Made by French Dinky Meccano (France) Ltd. Scale 1in to 150ft. Price 1/6. Issued in France 1935. Imported into England during same period. Deleted 1940. Special presentation box. — £75 £55 £25

No. 53az Battleship Dunkerque
Casts 'steam' from funnel. Made in France. Imported into England. Scale 1in to 150ft. Price 6d. Issued 1937. Deleted 1940. Special presentation box. — £75 £55 £25

No. 281 Military Hovercraft
Black gunner on top of cabin with aerial on one side. Otherwise casting is identical to No. 290. Green and black with white plastic parts and 'Army' and Union Jack on sides. Price £1.76. Issued 1973. Deleted 1976. — £25 £10 £5

No. 290 SRN-6 Hovercraft
Red, white and yellow with black base. All-blue base from 1971. Opening door, propeller and radar scanner which turn as the model is pushed along. Price 17/11. Issued 1970. Deleted 1976. 139mm. DC/P. — £25 £10 £5

No. 671 Mk 1 Corvette
Grey, brown and black with rocket firer. Price £1.58. issued 1976. Deleted 1978. 260mm. — £25 £10 £5

No. 672 OSA Missile Boat
Grey, blue and black with rocket firer. Price £1.58. Issued 1975. Deleted 1978. 206mm. — £25 £10 £5

No. 673 Submarine Chaser
Grey, dark blue and black. Price £1.58. Issued 1977. Deleted 1978. 197mm — £25 £10 £5

No. 673 Coastguard Amphibious Missile Launch
Blue, grey, white and black. Also blue, white and red with 'Coastguard' on sides. Price £2.25. Issued 1977. Deleted 1978. 155mm. — £25 £10 £5

No. 675 Motor Patrol Boat
Grey, cream, black and red. Price £1.55. Issued 1973. Deleted 1978. 170mm. — £25 £10 £5

No. 678 Air Sea Rescue Launch with Dinghy
Mustard, black and blue with orange dinghy and black figure. Transfers and markings on sides. Price £2.25. Issued 1974. Deleted 1977. 170mm.

	MB	MU	GC
No. 678	£25	£10	£5

No. 796 Healey Sports Boat on Trailer
Cream with light green or dark green top and boat interior. the figures are the drivers from Nos. 113 MGB and 125 Triumph Spitfire, only found in the 125 Fun Ahoy Set. Price 2/11. Issued 1960. Deleted 1962. 155mm.

No. 796	£75	£45	£25

No. DH1 Jumping Frog
Green with brown dots and strong clockwork motor. Released at the same time as the pre-war boats and proved a great favourite. Price 3/6. Issued 1939. Deleted 1940. 85mm.

No. DH1	£150	£50	£25

No. H1 Speed Boat Hawk
Red and cream. The clockwork motor enables the boat to travel over 100ft on one winding. Price 2/11. Issued 1937. Deleted 1940. 270mm long, beam 85mm. Special presentation box.

No. H1	£250	£100	£50

No. H1/a Speed Boat Hawk
Blue and white. Otherwise as above.

No. H1/a	£95	£55	£25

No. H1/b Speed Boat Hawk
Green and ivory. Otherwise as No. H1.

No. H1/b	£95	£55	£25

No. H2 Speed Boat Swift
Red and cream. The clockwork motor enables the boat to travel over 300ft on one winding. Price 7/6. Issued 1937. Deleted 1940. 360mm long, beam 85mm.

No. H2	£95	£55	£25

No. H2/a Speed Boat Swift
Blue and white. Otherwise as above.

No. H2/a	£150	£75	£45

No. H2/b Speed Boat Swift
Yellow and white. Otherwise as No. H2.

No. H2/b	£250	£100	£75

No. H3 Speed Boat The Condor Special
One of the best boats ever made. The clockwork motor enables the boat to travel over 500ft on one winding. Price 12/6. Issued 1937. Deleted 1940. 416mm long, beam 85mm.

No. H3	£225	£100	£65

No. H3/a Speed Boat Gannet
Blue and white. Otherwise as above.

No. H3/a	£275	£150	£100

No. H3/b Speed Boat Curlew
Green and ivory. Otherwise as No. H3.   £275   £150   £100

No. H4 Limousine Boat The Venture
Red and cream. The clockwork motor enables the boat to
travel over 500ft on one winding. Price 15/6. Issued 1938.
Deleted 1940. 416mm long, beam 85mm.   £275   £175   £75

No. H4/a Limousine Boat The Venture
Blue and white. Otherwise as above.   £300   £150   £100

No. H4/b Limousine Boat The Venture
Jade and ivory. Otherwise as No. H4.   £350   £150   £100

No. H5 Cabin Cruiser The Viking
Red and cream. The clockwork motor enables the boat to
travel 600ft on one winding. Price 16/6. Issued 1938.
Deleted 1940. 416mm long, beam 85mm.   £350   £150   £100

No. H5/a Cabin Cruiser The Viking
Blue and white. Otherwise as above.   £350   £150   £100

No. H5/b Cabin Cruiser The Viking
Jade and ivory. Otherwise as No. H5.   £450   £250   £150

No. H6 Toy Water Duck Boat
Tinplate model in the shape of a duck. The clockwork
motor enables the boat to travel over 150ft on one
winding. Price 2/6. Issued 1939. Deleted 1940. Approx.
250mm long, beam 85mm. The first few models were in
a special presentation box.
With ordinary box   £175   £100   £50
With special presentation box   £350   £150   £50

No. SB1 Racing Boat Racer I Special
Cream and green. The clockwork motor enables the boat
to travel over 150ft on one winding. Price 4/6. Issued
1938. Deleted 1940. 216mm long, beam 54mm.   £250   £150   £50

No. SB2 Racing Boat Racer II Special
Cream and blue. The clockwork motor enables the boat
to travel over 200ft on one winding. Price 8/6. Issued
1938. Deleted 1940. 324mm long, beam 85mm.   £350   £150   £100

No. SB3 Racing Boat Racer III Special
Red and cream. The clockwork motor enables the boat to
travel over 300ft on one winding. Winner of many awards
at the time of its release. Price 14/6. Issued 1939. Deleted
1940. 432mm long, 98mm. Special gift box.   £1250   £500   £250

No. SB3/a Racing Boat Racer III Special
Green and ivory. Otherwise as above. Rare.

	MB	MU	GC
	£1450	£750	£350

No. SB3/b Racing Boat Racer III Special
Cream and blue. Otherwise as No. SB3. Rare.

	MB	MU	GC
	£1450	£750	£350

SPORTS CARS
AND SALOONS

No. 23G   Cooper Bristol Racing Car

MODEL	MB	MU	GC
No. 22a Sports Car Cream with red wings and interior. Unpainted solid metal wheels. One piece body casting with separate dashboard and windscreen casting. Like all the '22' series, this model was sold individually without a box, although models were packed in half-dozens in plain boxes. They were made from diecast-lead; therefore no metal fatigue was possible, even though metal was often chewed by rats in warehouses and old stone-built shops. Colours do vary and rare colours mean extra money to a collector. Price 6d. Issued December 1933. Deleted 1935. 82mm.	—	£300	£200
No. 22b Sports Coupé Yellow with green wings and roof. Unpainted metal wheels. One piece body. This is a standard colour model. The model is also known in red or cream with green wings, which are more valuable than the normal colours. If any collector wishes to write to me c/o the publishers, I will give a personal valuation. Price 6d. Issued December 1933. Deleted 1935. 82mm.	—	£350	£200
No. 22g Streamlined Tourer Red, cream, pale green or black (rare). Separate wheel and windscreen casting slid into main body casting. Price 6d. Issued May 1935. Deleted 1940. 85mm. DC/RT.	—	£250	£150

No. 22h Streamlined Saloon

1934 Chrysler Airflow. One piece casting with no bumpers. Price 6d. Issued May 1935. Deleted 1940. 85mm. DC/RT.

	MB	MU	GC
	—	£250	£100

No. 23a Racing Sports Car

The first issue of these racing cars represented an MB Magic Midget and were made in lead. There are two distinct colour schemes.

The first type has a cream body with flash on upper surface of body and tail, with circle on nose in orange or green. Cream wheels with white tyres. Some models have matching orange or green tyres. The second type has cream body with orange stripes along body sides, representing the famous George Eyston's 'Humbug'. Cream or coloured tyres.

Price for both types 6d. First type issued April 1934 and deleted 1935, in favour of the second type in similar casting details. Second type deleted 1938. 94mm. DC/RT.

	MB	MU	GC
	—	£250	£150

No. 23a Racing Car or Sports Model

Blue and white or blue and silver. Also yellow with flash and numbers. Six exhausts, pipe and silencer with a raised ridge, round racing number and plated wheels. Price 6d. Issued 1935. Deleted 1938. 94mm. DC/RT.

	MB	MU	GC
	—	£200	£50

No. 23a Racing Car

Red with cream flash, and red or blue with silver or cream flash with driver. Six stem system, pipe and silencer with no ridge. Price 9d. Issued 1938. Deleted 1940. 94mm. DC/RT.

	MB	MU	GC
	—	£100	£50

No. 23A Racing Car

Blue with flash (early post-war), red with silver with red flash. '4' in circle on sides of car. The number is body colour and surrounding circle is flash colour. Black wheels and pinched axles. Later models with silver wheels and turned over axle ends. One of the very early 1950 issues was made of lead and could be the only lead post-war Dinky. Price 2/3. Issued 1946. Renumbered 220 in 1954. Deleted 1955. 94mm.

	MB	MU	GC
Blue	—	£100	£25
Silver or red	—	£70	£25

No. 23b Hotchkiss Racing Car

Blue with white or red flash; yellow with blue or black flash; and yellow with red flash (very rare and worth much more than the other colours). Racing numbers ('5') normally of body colour in circles of flash livery. Price 6d. Issued June 1935. Deleted 1940. 96mm. DC/RT.

	MB	MU	GC
	—	£75	£35

SPORTS CARS AND SALOONS	MB	MU	GC

No. 23B Hotchkiss Racing Car
Red with silver flash or silver with red flash. Number in
body livery, and circle in flash livery. '5' on sides. Price
2/11. Issued 1946. Deleted 1948. 96mm. DC/RT.

	—	£200	£50

No. 23c Mercedes Benz Racing Car
There are two pre-war castings for this model. The first
had no rivets holding the moulded (tinplate) baseplate
on: it was held in place by crimping the body over the
edge at two places on each side. Later, in 1938, the casting
was changed to accommodate rivet pillars inside the
body. The colours for the two variations are the same.
Red, blue, yellow or green (rare and worth double), with
racing numbers of body livery in circles of contrasting
livery. Grille, exhaust pipe and driver picked out in
contrasting or natural livery. 'Mercedes Benz' shows on
model with '2' on sides. Price 8d. Issued May 1936.
Deleted 1940. 92mm. DC/RT/TP.

	—	£250	£50

No. 23C Mercedes Benz Racing Car
Blue or silver. Blue model (worth double) has black
circles around racing numbers, and the silver has red
circles. Moulded tinplate base with driver cast in. Price
1/8. Reissued as large open racing car with 'Mercedes
Benz' in October 1947. Deleted 1950. 92mm. DC/RT/TP.

	—	£75	£25

No. 23d Auto-Union Racing Car
Red or blue with driver slotted into body. Circles are
white or yellow showing various numbers and, like No.
23C, early examples have no rivets holding baseplate on.
Price 7d. Issued May 1936. Deleted 1940. 100mm.
DC/RT/TP.

	—	£100	£50

No. 23D Auto-Union Racing Car
Silver with moulded tinplate baseplate and no driver.
Auto-union red circle with '2' on sides. Price 1/11. Issued
1950. Deleted 1955. 100mm. DC/RT/TP.

	—	£150	£35

No. 23e Speed of the Wind Racer
Blue or yellow with moulded tinplate baseplate,
although early examples had no baseplate rivets. Other
colours were red or green with driver cast into body.
White circles with '1' on sides. Price 8d. Issued May 1936.
Deleted 1940. 104mm. DC/RT/TP.

	—	£150	£50

No. 23e Speed of the Wind Racer Special

Red with silver flash. Driver cast in. Very rare model and although 'Speed of the Wind' was a car used mainly for record-breaking attempts in 1935/36, driven by George Eyston, it did appear on certain race tracks in promotional ideas through the firm of Dinky. The car also made a special appearance through the streets of Liverpool in 1936, from and back to the Meccano factory in Binns Road. A special team of almost 100 men were connected with the show. Special presentation boxes were made and they were autographed by both mechanics and driver. Price 5/-. 104mm.

	MB	MU	GC
No. 23e Speed of the Wind Racer Special	£850	£250	£100

No. 23E Speed of the Wind Racing Car

Silver or red (worth double) with moulded tinplate baseplate and driver cast in. Price 2/11. Issued 1946. Deleted 1949. 104mm.

	£75	£50	£25

No. 23E Speed of the Wind Racer

Silver with plain tinplate baseplate and driver cast in. The model was renumbered when colours of drivers, overalls, exhaust pipes and wheels were slightly altered. 'Speed of the Wind' written on baseplate. Price 2/11. Issued 1949. Renumbered 221 in 1954. Deleted 1954. 104mm. DC/RT/TP.

	£75	£50	£25

No. 23F Alfa Romeo Racing Car

Red with 'Alfa Romeo' and white '8' on tail. Price 3/-. Issued 1952. Renumbered 232 in 1954. Deleted 1962. 100mm. DC/RT/TP.

	£100	£50	£25

No. 23G Cooper Bristol Racing Car

Green. 'Cooper British' or 'Bristol' with white '6' on tail. Price 2/9. Issued February 1953. Renumbered 233 in 1954 with the driver cast in. Deleted 1962. 89mm. DC/TP/RT.

	£75	£45	£25

No. 23G Cooper Bristol Racing Special

White. Otherwise as above. Very rare.

	£750	—	—

No. 23H Ferrari Racing Car

Blue with yellow nose and 'Ferrari' with yellow '5' on tail. Driver cast in. Price 3/-. Issued 1953. Renumbered 234 in 1954. Deleted 1962. 101mm. DC/RT/TP.

	£100	£50	£25

No. 23J HWM Racing Car

Green with driver cast in. 'HWM' with yellow '7' on the tail. Price 2/11. Issued May 1953. Deleted 1960. 99mm. DC/RT/TP.

	£65	£30	£20

No. 23K Talbot Lago Racing Car
Blue with driver cast in. 'Talbot Lago' with yellow '4' on
the tail. Price 2/6. Issued September 1953. Renumbered
230 in 1954. Deleted 1960. 103mm. DC/RT/TP. £100 £50 £25

No. 23m Thunderbolt Speed Car
One of the very first dinky models to be placed officially
in an individual box worth more than many Dinky
models. This explains the difference in original price
between it and No. 23s, which is an identical casting.
Light or dark green, the latter being rare. Driver cast in.
Union Jack flags on tail fin. Price 1/-. Issued 1938. Deleted
1940. 126mm. DC/RT/TP. £500 £150 £50

No. 23N Maserati Racing Car
Red with white flash and driver cast in. 'Maserati' with
white '9' on tail. Price 2/8. Issued June 1953. Renumbered
231 in 1954. Deleted 1962. 94mm. DC/RT/TP. £100 £50 £25

No. 23p Gardner's MG Record Car
Green with driver cast in. 'MG Magnet' and Union Jack
flag on sides, with MG badge on nose. White flashes along
sides. The change to this model on the baseplate was
possibly just pre-war, just as the dropping of the white
flashes along the sides was post-war. Like the
Thunderbolt (No. 23m), this model was issued pre-war
with an individual box, with the scale drawings of the
real car on the box lid. Price 1/-. Issued December 1939.
Deleted 1940. 104mm. DC/RT/TP. £200 £100 £50

No. 23P Gardner's MG Record Car
Green with driver cast in. Union Jack flag on sides, and
MG badge on nose. Price 2/6. Issued 1946. Deleted 1947.
104mm. DC/RT/TP. £70 £35 £20

No. 23s Streamlined Racing Car
Silver with driver cast in. Made with and without flags.
Black grille. There was a brief run of these models in lead
which are worth double, provided that they are in good
condition. Other colours exist and mean extra money so
check with an expert before you sell. Price 1/11. Issued
1938. Deleted 1940. 126mm. DC/RT/TP. £250 £75 £35

No. 23S Streamlined Racing Car
Blue, dark green or silver with red or green details, grille
and exhaust. Price 2/6. Reissued January 1948.
Renumbered 222 in 1954. 126mm. DC/RT/TP.

	MB	MU	GC
Blue	—	£100	£50
Dark green	—	£100	£50
Silver	—	£100	£35

No. 24b Limousine
Colours recorded: maroon with black chassis, maroon with maroon chassis, maroon with grey chassis, cream with royal blue chassis, yellow with brown chassis, light blue with yellow chassis, and yellow with black chassis. Plated or chromed wheels; black or coloured, white or coloured tyres on very early models; black tyres on later. The prices for any of the '24' series are for good unfatigued examples, other prices vary according to condition and the eagerness of the collector. I advise all collectors to consult the very best of experts with regard to these models. It is possible to have either radiator type with or without spare wheel. There are at least 45 variations of the 8 models in this series. No. 24b never had any kind of spare wheel. There are, however, two body castings. The first has three horizontal bonnet louvres of equal length. The second has three louvres of different lengths, the top one being the longest. There are in fact a great number of minor changes to the chassis and radiator throughout the 6 year production run of the '24' series. I do not think that it matters to the value, as all models are very scarce. This is due to metal fatigue. The '24' series never had individual boxes, as they were packed in boxes of eight. Price 6d, with or without badge. Issued April 1934. Deleted 1938. Price 9d. Reissued 1938. Deleted 1940. 98mm.   —   £500   —

No. 24c Town Sedan
Colours recorded: royal blue with royal blue chassis, cream with royal blue chassis, cream with black chassis, light green with cherry red chassis, cherry red with grey chassis, and cream with light green chassis. Wheels and tyres as No. 24b. Criss-cross chassis and radiator with or without badge. Side mounted spare wheel on early models, but this feature was later abandoned. Separate dashboard and windscreen casting. Painted or nickel plated. Price 1/-. Issued 1934. Deleted 1940. 97mm. DC/RT.   —   £500   £250

No. 24c Super Streamlined Saloon
Colours recorded: maroon with black chassis, red with dark red chassis, green with red chassis, red with black chassis, and black with red chassis. Wheels and tyres as No. 24b. Criss-cross chassis, plain radiator, no spare wheel and 'single' side window. Price 9d. Issued April 1934. Deleted 1938. 97mm. DC/RT.   —   £500   £250

No. 24d Vogue Saloon
Colours recorded: cream with royal blue chassis, pink
with cherry red chassis, pink with turquoise chassis,
green with black chassis, medium blue with maroon
chassis, and blue with black chassis. Wheels and tyres as
No. 24b. The spare wheel was never dropped on the
Vogue Saloon, but later models had a very different body
shape with a domed roof. This model was in fact a French
Dinky toy casting, borrowed by the Liverpool Binns Road
Company when its own casting had been remodelled to
make the Humber Vogue Saloon (No. 36c). Price 9d.
Issued April 1934. Deleted 1938. 97mm. DC/RT.   —   £500   £250

No. 24f Sportsman's Coupé
Recorded colours: chocolate with buff chassis, beige with
chocolate chassis, cream with royal blue chassis, yellow
with brown chassis, and brown with chocolate chassis.
Wheels and tyres as No. 24b. This model is entirely
different as regards casting compared with the Bentley
(Nos. 36b and 36B). It has a higher domed roof line and
lower bonnet lines. Plain or badge radiator. Early models
had side mounted spare wheel, but this feature was later
dropped and the hole in the body was filled in. Price 9d.
Issued 1934. Deleted 1940. 100mm. DC/RT.   —   £500   £250

No. 24g Four Seater Sports Tourer
Colours recorded: pale blue with brown chassis, cream
with chocolate chassis, yellow with brown chassis, pale
green with dark green chassis, green with black chassis,
and light blue with black chassis. Wheels and tyres as No.
24b. All No. 24g four seater sports tourers have the rear
mounted spare wheel and tyres. Open or solid screen
radiator with or without badge. Price 1/-. Issued April
1934. Deleted 1938. 98mm. DC/RT.   —   £500   £250

No. 24h Two Seater Sports Tourer
Colours recorded: red with red chassis, green with dark
green chassis, cream with black chassis, red with green
chassis, green with black chassis, and yellow with black
chassis. Wheels and tyres as No. 24b. As with No. 24g,
this model was only issued with a rear mounted spare
wheel and tyres. Open or solid screen, and grille with or
without badge. Price 1/-. Issued April 1934. Deleted 1940.
98mm. DC/RT.   —   £500   £150

No. 24kz Peugeot Special Issue
Colours recorded: dark blue, grey-blue, maroon, white, green and red. Wheels are black with black or white tyres with 'Dunlop' sometimes stamped on side walls. One piece body casting with tinplate bumper and no chassis. A version of this car with a tinplate chassis was made in France during 1948/49, but the model was not imported. Models were purchased by people on holiday or through friends living in France and brought into England. The pre-war model was imported into this country with 'Peugeot 402, Fab-en-France' cast inside body. 'z' means of French origin. Price 9d. Issued July 1939. Deleted 1940. 95mm. DC/TP/RT.   —   £650   £300

No. 25J Jeep
Red, green or pale blue with yellow hells. Tinplate windscreen. Spare wheel at the rear. Price 2/6. Issued 1947. Deleted 1948. 68mm. LHD/SW/DC/TP/RT.   —   £75   £35

No. 25Y Jeep
Red or dark green with maroon wheels. Tinplate windscreen and spare wheel on right of body. Price 4/4. Issued September 1952. Renumbered 405 in 1954. Deleted 1962. 90mm. LHD/SW/DC/RT/TP.   —   £100   £50

No. 27D Land Rover
Green with cream seats or orange with dark green seats. Screen and spare wheel behind orange driver. Not individually boxed until renumbered 340 in 1954. Price 3/9. Issued April 1950. Deleted 1962. 90mm. TP/RT/DC.   £60   £30   £20

No. 27D Land Rover
Orange and blue. Red wheels, black windscreen and beige driver. Otherwise details as above.   £75   £35   £20

No. 27F Estate Car
Brown and fawn or brown and grey (worth double). Price 2/10. Issued February 1950. Renumbered 344 in 1954. 105mm. DC/TP/RT.   £75   £35   £25

No. 30a Chrysler Airflow Saloon
Green, cream or dark blue (rare and worth double). Green and cream models were deleted in 1940. This model has no chassis and is almost identical to the earlier No. 32. Price 9d. Issued June 1935. Deleted 1936. 103mm. DC/RT.   —   £200   £75

No. 30A Chrysler Airflow Saloon
Green, cream or plate blue. No chassis. Price 1/11. Issued 1946. Deleted 1948. 103mm. DC/RT.   —   £200   £75

No. 30b Rolls Royce
Colours recorded: royal blue with black chassis, pale grey
with dark grey chassis, pale green with black chassis, and
dark grey with black chassis (rare and worth double).
Open chassis. Price 9d. Issued August 1935. Deleted 1950.
101mm. DC/RT.   —   £200   £75

No. 30B Rolls Royce
Dark blue or fawn with black chassis which is plain or
open. Price 1/11. Issued 1946. Deleted 1950. 101mm.
DC/RT.   —   £200   £75

No. 30c Daimler
Green or cream with open black chassis. Price 9d. Issued
August 1935. Deleted 1940. 98mm. DC/RT.   —   £450   £100

No. 30C Daimler
Fawn, green or cream. The last two colours are worth at
least double. Open or plain black chassis. Price 1/11.
Issued 1946. Deleted 1950. 98mm. DC/RT.   —   £250   £75

No. 30d Vauxhall
Yellow body and brown chassis, yellow body with black
chassis, or maroon body with black chassis. There are two
varieties of this model: with or without spare wheel.
There are also two varieties without spare wheels, and
the model with spare wheel is worth at least double.
Squared or shield radiator. Price 9d. Issued August 1935.
Deleted 1940. 102mm. DC/RT.   —   £750   £250

No. 30d Vauxhall
Yellow body with open brown chassis. Squared or shield
radiator. With or without spare wheel, although the latter
is worth double. Price 9d. Issued April 1939. Deleted 1940.
100mm. DC/RT.   —   £600   £200

No. 30D Vauxhall
Brown or green body with black chassis which is open or
plain. Shield radiator and no spare wheel. Price 1/11.
Issued 1946. Deleted 1948. 98mm. DC/RT.   —   £250   £100

No. 32 Chrysler Airflow Saloon
Maroon or blue (rare and worth double). Plated wheels.
Otherwise details as No. 30A. Price 9d. Issued January
1935. Renumbered 30a in June 1935. 103mm. DC/RT.
Single   —   £350   £150
Box of six   £4000   —   —

No. 35a Austin 7 Saloon
Colours recorded: grey, red, turquoise, dark blue, mid-blue, pale pink and dark brown. The last two colours are quite rare and worth double. On some models the spare wheel cover was picked out in a contrasting livery, e.g. a pale blue on a dark blue car. The change from white to black tyres occurred in 1939. Price 3d. Issued 1936. Deleted 1940. 51mm. DC/RW.

| | — | £200 | £75 |

No. 35A Austin 7 Saloon
Red, blue or grey with solid black rubber wheels. Issued 1946. Deleted 1948. 51mm. DC. Went to retailers in boxes of six.

| | — | £100 | £50 |

No. 35az Fiat Two Seater Saloon
Red, green blue or pale grey. The metal wheeled version was for the French market only. For the export market the model had white rubber tyres similar to the English '35' series. Marked on model 'Fab-en-France'. Price 4d. Issued July 1939. Deleted 1940. 59mm.

| | — | £175 | £75 |

No. 35b Racer
Silver or dark blue with white rubber wheels only. No driver. Price 3d. Issued 1935. Deleted 1939. 57mm. DC.

| | — | £250 | £50 |

No. 35b Racer
Blue, yellow or red with driver and white rubber wheels, although late pre-war models had black wheels. Price 3d. Issued 1939. Deleted 1940. 57mm. DC/RW.

| | — | £250 | £50 |

No. 35B Racer
Silver or red (worth almost double). Price 1/9. Issued 1946. Renumbered 200 in 1954. Deleted 1957. 57mm. DC.

| | — | £100 | £50 |

No. 35c MG Sports Car
Red, green, dark blue or maroon. Solid white rubber tyres, except for the later models which all had solid black rubber wheels. All pre-war models had windscreen, steering wheel and spare wheel picked out in silver. Price 3d. Issued 1936. Deleted 1940. 52mm. DC/RW.

| | — | £250 | £50 |

No. 35C MG Sports Car
Red or green (worth almost double). Solid black rubber wheels. Price 1/11. Issued 1946. Deleted 1948. 52mm. DC/RW.

| | — | £250 | £100 |

No. 35d Austin 7 Tourer
Blue, yellow or green. Solid white rubber wheels and wire windscreen. Late pre-war model had casting with hole in seat for driver, even though it was never issued

with a driver. As with No. 35A, some models had the
spare wheel cover picked out, e.g. orange cover on yellow
car with the steering wheel painted silver. Price 4d.
Issued 1938. Deleted 1940. 50mm. DC/RW.

| | — | £250 | £100 |

No. 35D Austin 7 Tourer
Fawn, pale blue, red or grey (very rare and worth
double). Solid black rubber wheels and no windscreen.
Price 2/6. Issued 1946. Deleted 1948. 50mm. DC/RW.

| | — | £150 | £45 |

No. 36a Armstrong Siddeley Limousine
Grey or dark blue with black moulded chassis and no
driver. The '36' series was issued late pre-war with no
figures but still had the slot in the baseplate. Many early
post-war models have the slots. Early pre-war model had
figures. Price 11d. Issued July 1938. Deleted 1940. 97mm.
DC/RT.

| With figures | £250 | £200 | £100 |
| Without figures | £150 | £65 | £50 |

No. 36A Armstrong Siddeley
Colours recorded: grey, maroon, pale blue, dark blue,
shire green and off-white with black chassis. No drivers
and Armstrong Siddeley radiator. Vertical bonnet
louvres. Price 2/11. Issued 1946. Deleted 1948. 97mm.
DC/RT.

| | £90 | £30 | £20 |

No. 36b Bentley Two Seater Sports Coupé
Colours recorded: yellow with black chassis, cream with
black chassis, two-tone grey, and yellow with maroon
chassis. Moulded chassis with seats for passengers.
Bentley radiator and no spare wheel. With or without
tinplate figures. Price 11d. Issued July 1938. Deleted 1940.
100mm. DC/RT.

| With figures | — | £250 | £150 |
| Without figures | — | £150 | £50 |

No. 36B Bentley Two Seater Sports Coupé
Colours recorded: green, cream, brown and grey. Bentley
radiator and no driver. Price 2/-. Issued 1946. Deleted
1958. 100mm. DC/RT.

| | — | £35 | £20 |

No. 36c Humber Vogue Saloon
Light blue, two-tone green, silver-grey with black
moulded chassis. With or without figures. Price 11d.
Issued July 1938. Deleted 1940. 100mm. DC/RT.

| With figures | — | £275 | £150 |
| Without figures | — | £150 | £40 |

No. 36C Humber Vogue
Brown or light blue with black moulded chassis. Humber
radiator and no driver. Price 2/-. Issued 1946. Deleted
1948. 97mm. DC/RT.   —   £150   £30

No. 36d Streamlined Rover Saloon
Colours recorded: light blue, two-tone green, two-tone
red and brown (very rare and worth double). Black
moulded chassis with slot for driver and double sided
window. No spare wheel. With or without tinplate
figures. Price 11d. Issued July 1938. Deleted 1940. 100mm.
DC/RT.
With figures   —   £275   £125
Without figures   —   £150   £50

No. 36D Rover Saloon
Colours recorded: pale green, dark green, pale blue, dark
blue and medium green with black moulded chassis.
Rover radiator and no driver. Price 1/11. Issued 1946.
Deleted 1948. 94mm. DC/RT.   —   £150   £70

No. 36e Two Seater Sports British Salmson
Colours recorded: grey body with red chassis, royal blue
with black chassis, black body with red chassis, two-tone
grey and two-tone red. Hole in seat for driver. With or
without spare rubber wheel. Salmson radiator. Price 11d.
Issued July 1938. Deleted 1940. 99mm. DC/RT.
With figures   —   £275   £150
Without figures   —   £150   £50

No. 36E Two Seater British Salmson
Red, light brown or mid-blue with black moulded chassis
and no driver. Solid screen, Salmson radiator and
steering wheel cast in. Price 1/11. Issued 1946. Deleted
1948. 93mm. DC/RT.   —   £250   £75

No. 36f Four Seater Sports British Salmson
Dark red or salmon-pink moulded chassis and red body.
Also dark green chassis and green body (very rare and
worth double). Hole in seat for driver. Spare wheel
optional and Salmson radiator. Price 11d. Issued July
1938. Deleted 1940. 98mm. DC/RT.
With figures   —   £350   £250
Without figures   —   £75   £50

No. 36F Four Seater British Salmson
Colours recorded: light green, dark green, light grey,
dark grey, beige and maroon (very rare and worth
double). Black chassis. Salmson radiator and no driver.
Steering wheel cast in solid green. Price 1/11. Issued 1946.
Deleted 1948. 96mm. DC/RT.   —   £250   £100

SPORTS CARS AND SALOONS	MB	MU	GC

No. 38a Frazer Nash (BMW) Sports Car
Light blue, light grey or dark grey (rare). Bare metal
baseplate. Black or khaki seats. Price 10d. Issued June
1939. Deleted 1940. 82mm. DC/TP. All prices for the '38'
series are for models with perfect screens.

	—	£250	£75

No. 38A Frazer Nash (BMW) Sports Car
Blue or light grey with black painted baseplate. Khaki
seats, but all the late export models had red seats and red
wheels. Price 1/11. Issued 1946. Deleted 1949. 82mm.
DC/TP.

	—	£200	£75

No. 38b Sunbeam Talbot Sports Car
Pale blue or dark blue with dark blue seats, or red with
maroon seats. Bare metal baseplate. Price 10d. Issued
1939. Deleted 1940. 92mm. S/SW/WS/DC/TP.

	—	£225	£75

No. 38B Sunbeam Talbot Sports Car
Colours recorded: red with maroon seats, blue with fawn
seats, pale green with dark green seats, yellow with fawn
seats, pale brown with khaki seats, and chocolate with
fawn seats (rare and worth double). Black painted
baseplate and black chassis. Price 2/6. Issued 1946.
Deleted 1949. 92mm. DC/TP.

	—	£150	£50

No. 38C Lagonda Sports Coupé
Red with dark red seats, dark green with black seats, grey
with fawn seats, and brown with fawn seats. Black
painted baseplate. Price 2/6. Issued February 1946.
Deleted 1951. 102mm. DC/TP.

	—	£175	£40

No. 38d Alvis Sports Tourer
Green body with brown seats. Bare metal baseplate. Price
10d. Issued 1939. Deleted 1940. 95mm.
SW/S/WS/DC/TP.

	—	£195	£60

No. 38D Alvis Sports Tourer
Green with brown or black seats, maroon with red or
black seats, and grey with black seats. Price 2/6. Issued
1946. Deleted 1949. 95mm. DC/TP.

	—	£155	£40

No. 38E Armstrong Siddeley Coupé
Pale grey with blue seats, light grey with pale blue seats,
pale green with grey seats, or cream with black seats (rare
and worth double). Black chassis and black painted
baseplate. Price 2/6. Issued December 1946. Deleted 1950.
96mm. DC/TP.

	—	£100	£50

No. 38F Jaguar Sports Car
Red with maroon seats, pale grey with black seats, pale
or dark blue with fawn seats, or red with black seats.
Black chassis and black painted baseplate. Price 2/9.
Issued November 1946. Deleted 1949. 80mm. DC/TP. — £100 £50

No. 39B Oldsmobile Six
Colours recorded: light grey, cream, dark grey, dark
brown, dark blue and green (rare and worth double).
Black chassis and black painted baseplate. Price 2/9.
Issued 1946. Deleted 1950. 100mm. DC/RT/TP. — £100 £50

No. 39c Lincoln Zephyr
Colours recorded: grey, light grey, yellow and cream.
Bare metal baseplate. Price 10d. Issued 1939. Deleted
1940. 106mm. DC/RT/TP. — £175 £40

No. 39C Lincoln Zephyr
Grey or brown with black chassis and black painted
baseplate. Price 2/9. Issued 1946. Deleted 1950. 106mm.
DC/RT/TP. — £100 £50

No. 39d Buick Viceroy
Colours recorded: maroon, bright green, deep blue and
chocolate (rare and worth double). Bare metal baseplate.
Price 10d. Issued 1939. Deleted 1940. 103mm.
DC/TP/RT. — £175 £50

No. 39D Buick Viceroy
Colours recorded: maroon, dark grey, pale grey, dull
yellow, putty, dark brown and dark red. Black chassis
and black painted baseplate. Price 2/9. Issued 1946.
Deleted 1950. 103mm. DC/TP/RT. — £100 £50

No. 39e Chrysler Royal
Blue, grey, green or cream (very rare). Bare metal
baseplate. Price 10d. Issued 1939. Deleted 1940. 106mm.
DC/RT/TP. — £175 £60

No. 39E Chrysler Royal
Many shade of green. Also blue, cream or grey. Black
chassis and painted black baseplate. Price 2/9. Issued
1946. Deleted 1950. 106mm. DC/TP/RT. — £100 £50

No. 39f Studebaker State Commander
Green or yellow with bare metal baseplate. Price 10d.
Issued 1939. Deleted 1940. 103mm. DC/TP/RT. — £175 £60

No. 39F Studebaker State Commander
Colours recorded: light blue, dark blue, olive green, light
green, light grey, dark grey, dark brown and chocolate
(the latter two-tone model very rare and worth five times
the normal colour). Price 2/9. Issued 1946. Deleted 1950.
103mm. DC/TP/RT.   —   £100   £50

No. 40A Riley Saloon
Medium, dull or light green, light or dark grey, dark blue
and cream with black baseplate. Price 2/6. Issued July
1947. Renumbered 158 in 1954. Deleted 1960.
DC/TTP/RT.   £175   £60   £25

No. 40B Triumph 1800 Saloon
Mid-blue, fawn, black and light grey, which was the first
type with rear axle pillars. Price 2/6. Issued July 1948.
Deleted 1949. 91mm. DC/TP/RT.   —   £150   £45

No. 40B Triumph 1800 Saloon
Mid-blue, dark blue, dark grey or bright beige. This
model was a second type with the rear axle held by a tin
baseplate. Price 2/2. Issued February 1949. Renumbered
151 in 1955. 91mm. DC/TP/RT.   £60   £30   £15

No. 40D Austin Devon
Maroon, dark blue, grey, suede green and black (rare and
worth considerably more). Price 1/9. Issued January
1949. Renumbered 152 in 1954. Deleted 1956. 86mm.
DC/TP/RT.   £60   £30   £15

No. 40E Standard Vanguard
Fawn, maroon or grey (rare). Open rear wheels, plain
boot with small print baseplate lettering and black
chassis. Price 1/9. Issued November 1948. Deleted 1950.
91mm. DC/TP/RT.   —   £155   £45

No. 40E Standard Vanguard
Fawn or blue. Covered rear wheels, plain boot, small
baseplate lettering. Price 2/6. Issued April 1950.
Renumbered 153 in 1954. Deleted 1960. 91mm.
DC/TP/RT.   £250   £75   £35

No. 40F Hillman Minx
Light green, dark green, light brown or dark brown. Price
2/6. Issued February 1951. Renumbered 154 in 1954.
Deleted 1956. 88mm. DC/TP/RT.   £250   £75   £50

No. 40G Morris Oxford
Dark green, very dark green, grey and fawn. Price 1/11.
Issued June 1950. Renumbered 159 in 1954. Deleted 1956.
93mm. DC/TP/RT.

	MB	MU	GC
No. 40G Morris Oxford	£250	£75	£50

No. 40J Austin Somerset
Red and pale blue or dark blue and maroon. Price 2/4.
Issued March 1953. Renumbered 161 in 1956. Deleted
1960. 89mm. DC/TP/RT.

£250   £100   £50

No. 100 Lady Penelope's Fab 1
Pink with firing rocket, silver trim and six wheels. Driver
and Lady Penelope figure inside plastic opening hood.
Price 15/11. Issued 1966. Deleted 1977. 147mm. Prices for
this model vary according to availability, and the model
in the cardboard box is worth double that in the plastic
bubble pack.

£500   £150   £50

No. 100A Lady Penelope's Fab 1
White. Lady Penelope figure with driver, pink interior,
silver trim, wheels etc. Price 15/11. Issued 1972. 147mm.
DC/TP/RT. Rare.

£1000   £300   £150

No. 100B Lady Penelope's Fab 1
Red. Figures and firing rocket. Price 15/11. Issued 1966.
Deleted 1977. 147mm. DC/TP/RT. Rare.

£1000   £350   £100

No. 101 Thunderbird 4
Dark green with gold. Space car with '4' in black on sides.
Stars, numbers and 'Thunderbird 4' in white on the large
model itself. All working parts. Price 12/11. Issued 1967.
Replaced in 1974 by No. 106. 143mm. DC/P.

£300   £100   £50

No. 101 Sunbeam Alpine Tourer
Blue or pink (rarer and worth double). Civilian driver
and no numbers. Price 3/-. Issued August 1957. Deleted
1960. 94mm. SW/S/D/WS/DC/TP/P/RT.

£250   £100   £50

No. 102 Joe's Car
Green and grey with red cab interior. Working parts and
rocker. Automatic opening wings and extending tail fins.
Flashing engine, exhaust and independent super
suspension. From the TV series Joe 90. Price £1/5/11.
Issued 1969. Deleted 1976. 139mm. DC/TP.

£100   £50   £25

No. 102 Joe's Car
Blue, silver or grey. Otherwise as above. Rare colours.

£300   £250   £100

No. 102 MG Midget
Yellow or green. Civilian driver and no numbers. Price
3/-. Issued September 1957. Deleted 1960. 83mm.
SW/S/D/WS/DC/TP/P/RT.   £250   £100   £50

No. 103 Spectrum Patrol Car
Metallic red with white interior, silver hubs and trim.
From the TV series Captain Scarlet. Price 9/11. Issued
1968. Deleted 1976. 121mm. DC/P.   £250   £100   £50

No. 103 Spectrum Patrol Car
Metallic blue. Otherwise as above. Rare.   £750   £250   £100

No. 103 Austin Healey 100
Red or cream. Civilian driver and no numbers. Price 3/-.
Issued November 1957. Deleted 1960. 85mm.
SW/S/D/WS/DC/TP/P/RT   £200   £100   £50

No. 104 Aston Martin DB3S
Blue or salmon. Civilian driver and no numbers. Price
3/-. Issued September 1957. Deleted 1960. 87mm.
SW/S/D/DC/TP/RT.   £250   £75   £50

No. 104 Spectrum Pursuit Vessel
Blue and white with red interior. All rocket action. From
the TV series Captain Scarlet. Price £1/2/11. Issued 1968.
Deleted 1977. 160mm. DC/P.   £250   £100   £50

No. 105 Maximum Security Vehicle
White with red stripes and red interior. Opening doors
and aerial. From the TV series Captain Scarlet. Price 13/9.
Issued 1968. Deleted 1975. 137mm. DC/P.   £250   £100   £50

No. 105 Maximum Security Vehicle
Grey with black flashes on sides. Otherwise as above.
Rare.   £500   £200   £100

No. 105 Triumph TR2 Sports Tourer
Yellow or grey. Civilian driver and no numbers. Price 3/-.
Issued August 1957. Deleted 1960. 84mm.
SW/S/D/WS/DC/TP/P/RT.   £250   £100   £50

No. 106 The Prisoner Mini-Moke
White with red and white canopy. Opening bonnet and
spare wheel. From the TV series The Prisoner. Price 6/9.
Issued 1968. Deleted 1971. 73mm. DC/P.   £100   £50   £25

No. 106 The Prisoner Mini-Moke
Cream with blue canopy. Otherwise as above. Rare.   £350   £150   £50

No. 106 Thunderbird 2
Blue and white with black marking, or very dark blue
with brown and dark yellow (rare and worth double).
Price 15/11. Redesigned 1974. Deleted 1978. 153mm.
DC/P.

| | £350 | £150 | £50 |

No. 106 Austin A90 Atlantic
Blue, pink or black. Originally numbered 140A. Price 3/-.
Renumbered in 1954. Deleted 1958. 95mm.
SW/S/DC/TPO/RT.

Blue	£250	£100	£50
Pink	£300	£100	£50
Black	£350	£100	£75

No. 107 Sunbeam Alpine Competition Finish
Blue or pink. White circles with racing number. Special
competition model. Price 3/11. Issued November 1955.
Deleted 1959. SW/S/D/WS/DC/TP/P/RT.

| | £100 | £50 | £25 |

No. 107 Stripey the Magic Mini
White, yellow, red and blue with the figures Candy Andy
and the Bearandas. Price 10/9. Issued 1967. Deleted 1970.
75mm. DC/P.

| | £250 | £100 | £50 |

No. 108 Sam's Car
Beautiful model made in gold with a keyless clockwork
motor and automatic drive. Red interior and a first of its
kind in the world of diecasts. World intelligence network
lapel badge given with the model. Price 13/9. Issued
1969. Deleted 1975. 111mm. DC/P.

| | £250 | £100 | £50 |

No. 108 Sam's Car
Red. Also metallic green or metallic blue (rarer and worth
treble). Otherwise details as above.

| | £500 | £300 | £150 |

No. 108 MG Midget Competition Model
Red or white with racing driver and competition
numbers which vary. Price 3/9. Issued April 1955.
Deleted 1959. 83mm. DC/TP/P/RT.

| | £150 | £100 | £50 |

No. 109 Austin Healey 100
Cream or yellow. Competition numbers, racing driver
and white circles. Price 3/9. Issued June 1955. Deleted
1959. 85mm. SW/S/D/SW/DC/TP/P/RT.

| | £250 | £100 | £50 |

No. 109 Gabriel's Model T Ford
Black and yellow with driver. From TV series. Price 7/11.
Issued 1969. Deleted 1970. 79mm. DC/P.

| | £250 | £100 | £50 |

No. 109 Gabriel's Model T Ford
Black, red and white with black driver. Otherwise as above. Rare.

	MB	MU	GC
No. 109	£500	£250	£100

No. 110 Aston Martin DBS
Green or grey. Racing driver and competition numbers with white circles. Prices 3/6. Issued March 1956. Deleted 1959. 87mm. DC/RT/TP.

£250   £100   £50

No. 110 Aston Martin DBS
Metallic red or metallic blue (very rare and worth treble). Black interior, opening bonnet, silver bumpers, radiator and headlights. Price 9/11. Issued 1965. Deleted 1971. 111mm. DC/P/RT.

£150   £100   £50

No. 111 Triumph TR2
Pink or turquoise with white circles, racing driver and competition numbers. Prices 3/6. Issued February 1956. Deleted 1959. 84mm. DC/TP/P/RT.

£150   £100   £50

No. 112 Purdey's TR7
Bright yellow or green (rarer and worth double). Silver flashes on doors and sides, black and silver trim with white interior. Black 'P' is on bonnet and the model is designed with a double 'V' in silver at the front. Some models have the full word 'Purdey' and are worth slightly more than the ones with the individual letter. Issued 1978. Deleted 1980. 98mm. DC/P.

£750   £200   £100

No. 112 Austin Healey Sprite Mk II
Red. Price 4/-. Issued November 1961. Deleted 1966. 78mm. SW/SS/FTS/S/WS/DC/TP/RT.

£200   £100   £50

No. 113 Steed's Special Leyland Jaguar
This model was advertised but never issued for sale to the public. There were several prototype models handled by salesmen and others which came out of the factory illegally; therefore this model is very rare and worth a great deal of money. Greenish blue, medium green or medium blue with gold stripes along each side. Also known to exist with long orange flash, with silver wheels, bumpers etc. White or fawn interior with the figure of Steed in the driving seat. From the TV series The New Avengers. Price 75p. Advertised 1977. 137mm. DC/P.

£100   —   —

No. 113 MGB
Off-white with several shades, or cream. Price 5/9. Issued October 1962. Deleted 1969. 85mm. SW/SS/FTS/SD/WS/OD/DC/TP/P/RT.

£100   £50   £25

No. 114 Triumph Spitfire
Red, silver-grey. Gold from 1968, then purple from 1970.
Lady driver wearing safety belt. Price 6/6. Issued
September 1963. Deleted 1971. 88mm. SW/SS/S/D/
WS/OB/DC/TP/P/RT.

| | £150 | £75 | £35 |

No. 115 Plymouth Fury Sports
White or silver-grey (rarer and worth double). Driver,
passenger and pull-out twin aerials. Silver trim and red
interior with opening bonnet. Price 7/11. Issued 1965.
Deleted 1969. 122mm. DC/P/RT.

| | £75 | £50 | £25 |

No. 116 Volvo 1800S
Red with white or pink interior, opening bonnet, boot
and doors. Spoked wheels, silver bumper, grille and
headlights. Price 9/11. Issued 1966. Deleted 1976. 105mm.
DC/RT/P.

| | £75 | £50 | £20 |

No. 116 Volvo 1800S
Red or black (rarer and worth double). Blue or white
interior with opening doors, boot and bonnet and
all-silver trim. Price 9/11. Issued 1966. Deleted 1976.
105mm. DC/P.

| | £100 | £50 | £25 |

No. 120 Jaguar E Type
Red or blue (worth double). Black roof with removable
hard top. Price 6/-. Issued March 1962. Deleted 1970.
91mm. DC/TP/P/RT.

| | £150 | £50 | £25 |

No. 122 Volvo 265DL Estate Car
Blue with white interior, silver wheels etc. Price 76p.
Issued 1977. Deleted 1979. 141mm

| | £75 | £35 | £25 |

No. 122A Volvo 265DL Estate Car
Dark blue or medium blue with opening rear doors,
white interior and silver trim. All-plastic Speediwheels.
Issued 1978. Deleted 1985. 128mm.

| | £75 | £40 | £25 |

No. 123 Princess 2200HL Saloon
Metallic gold with white interior. All-silver trim and
plastic Speediwheels. Price 76p. Issued 1977. Deleted
1979. 128mm. DC/P.

| | £75 | £50 | £25 |

No. 123 Princess 2200HL Saloon
Rich tan with white interior, silver wheels, plastic
bumper etc. Price 76p. Issued 1977. Deleted 1985. 128mm.
DC/P.

| | £150 | £50 | £30 |

No. 123 Princess 2200HL Saloon
Bronze metallic with black roof and black bonnet and
boot. There are several plain all-metallic gold models
which have white interiors and silver trims. Keen
collectors will have to pay collector's prices. Black plastic
tyres on metal hubs in place of all-plastic wheels and
tyres. Price 89p. Issued 1978. Deleted 1980. 128mm.

£100   £50   £25

No. 124 Rolls Royce Phantom V
Metallic sky-blue with silver tint. Cream or white
interior, silver bumpers, grille, headlights etc. with the
number plate 'RP1'. Opening boot, although the bonnet
does not open on this model. This is a retooled reissue of
No. 152, on which the bonnet opened. The second change
is the absence of passengers, but there is a driver. Price
£1.25. Issued 1977. Deleted 1979. 141mm. DC/P.

£100   £50   £25

No. 124 Rolls Royce Phantom V
Medium blue, matt or metallic finish. Opening boot and
doors. Driver and no passengers. Issued 1977. Deleted
1979.

£75   £50   £25

No. 127 Rolls Royce Silver Cloud III
Metallic green, metallic gold and dark blue. Price 9/11.
Issued November 1964. Deleted 1972. 124mm.
SW/SS/S/W/OD/OB/TS/DC/P/RT.

£150   £50   £25

No. 128 Mercedes Benz 600
Metallic red with luggage, driver and two passengers.
All-opening doors, bonnet and boot. Price 14/11. Issued
October 1964. Deleted 1978. 147mm. DC/P/RT. One of
the longest running models made by Dinky, but still a
good investment.

£100   £50   £25

No. 128 Mercedes Benz 600
Metallic blue with white interior, silver trim, bumpers
etc. This last version has no passengers. Price £1/1/-.
Issued 1968. Deleted 1979. 147mm. DC/P.

£20   £10   £50

No. 129 MG Special American Issue
Pink and maroon or red and white (rarer and worth
double). Equivalent price 5/9. Issued 1960 with the same
casting as Nos. 102 and 108 but without any driver.
Deleted 1966, although the model had disappeared from
the shops by this time. The model had a special
presentation box with most of the early models and is a
collector's dream. 83mm. DC/RT.

£300   £150   £50

No. 129 Volkswagen De Luxe 1300 Sedan
Metallic blue with cream interior, opening doors, boot
and bonnet. Speediwheels and silver trim after 1971.
Price 8/11. Issued 1965. Deleted 1976. 100mm.
DC/RT/P.

	MB	MU	GC
With metal wheels	£100	£50	£25
With Speediwheels	£75	£40	£20

No. 129 Volkswagen 1300 Sedan
Metallic green or metallic grey. Otherwise as above. Rare. £750 £100 £50

No. 130 Ford Consul Corsair
Metallic red, light blue or medium blue with grey, white
or fawn interior. Sliding windows and opening bonnet.
Price 5/11. Issued June 1965. Deleted 1969. 106mm.
DC/P/RT.   £75   £50   £25

No. 130 Ford Consul Corsair
Metallic emerald green. Otherwise as above. Rare.   £250 £100 £50

No. 131 Jaguar E Type 2 + 2
Gold, yellow, metallic tan, mauve, metallic blue or
metallic red. Opening doors, boot and bonnet, spoked
wheels and silver bumpers, headlights etc. Speediwheels
were introduced in 1971 and deleted in 1978. Price 13/11.
Issued 1968. Deleted 1975. 112mm. DC/RT/P.

	MB	MU	GC
Spoked wheels	£100	£50	£25
Speediwheels	£75	£40	£20
Rare colour of mauve and white, or purple and white two-tone with spoked wheels and white interior	£750	—	—

No. 131 Cadillac Eldorado
Pink and yellow. Also fawn (rare and worth double).
Apart from one-colour versions there do exist two-tone
colours. Price 4/6. Issued June 1956. Deleted 1963.

	MB	MU	GC
118mm. DC/TP/RT/P.	£200	£100	£50
Red and yellow. New colour for 1970	£150	£75	£35

No. 132 Ford 40-RV
Silver-grey. Also metallic green at a later date. Opening
bonnet, spoked wheels and suspension details. Red
interior. Price 9/6. Issued 1967. Deleted 1970. 100mm.

	MB	MU	GC
DC/P.	£100	£75	£35
Red and yellow (rare)	£300	£100	£50

No. 132 Packard Convertible
Fawn or green. Price 4/6. Issued November 1955. Deleted
1961. 112mm. SW/LHD/WS/S/D/DC/TP/RT/P.   £200   £75   £50

No. 133 Cunningham C5R
White with blue stripes. Racing number '31' in blue. Price
4/3. Issued March 1955. Deleted 1960. 99mm.
SW/LHD/S/WS/D/DC/TP/RT/P.   £100   £50   £25

No. 133 Ford Cortina (1965)
Gold with white roof, then replaced by all-yellow in 1966.
Tipping seats, jewelled headlights and rear lights, and
number plates. Price 6/11. Issued November 1964.
Deleted 1971. 101mm. DC/TP/RT/P/SW/SS/S/
W/OD.   £100   £50   £25

No. 134 Triumph Vitesse
Metallic green with flashes on body sides in white or dark
red (the latter flash worth double). Price 3/11. Issued
February 1964. Deleted 1969. 85mm. SW/SS/W/
DC/TP/RT/P.   £100   £50   £25

No. 134 Triumph Vitesse
Metallic blue. Otherwise as above. Rare.   £650   —   —

No. 135 Triumph 2000
Metallic green with white roof; pale or medium blue with
white roof; black with white roof and red interior (rare
and worth double). Luggage. Price 5/11. Issued October
1963. Deleted 1969. 105mm. S/W/SS/S/W/OB/
OR/DC/RT/P.   £75   £30   £15

No. 136 Vauxhall Viva
Off-white, dark blue, medium blue and metallic blue.
Also mauve with off-white interior (rare and worth
double). Price 4/11. Issued 1964. Deleted 1973. 93mm.
SW/SS/S/W/OB/OR/DC/RT/P.   £40   £20   £10

No. 137 Plymouth Fury Convertible
Metallic grey, green or blue (rare and worth double).
Removable hard top. Price 5/11. Issued October 1963.
Deleted 1966. 22mm. SW/LHD/SS/FTS/S/WS/OB/
DC/TP/RT/P.   £110   £40   £15

No. 138 Hillman Imp
Metallic green or red. Luggage. Price 4/11. Issued
November 1963. Deleted 1973. 85mm. SW/SS/S/W/
OB/OR/DC/RT/P.   £40   £20   £10

No. 139 Ford Cortina
First appeared in pale blue, then in metallic and in red
metallic (rare and worth treble). Price 5/3. Issued June
1963. Deleted 1964. 102mm. SW/SS/S/W/OD/
FS/DC/TP/RT/P.   £70   £40   £20

No. 139A Ford Fordor Sedan
Red, brown, pale green or yellow. Brown model has matching wheels. Price 2/6. First issued without an individual box in August 1949. Renumbered 170 in 1954. Deleted 1965. 102mm. DC/TP/RT.

£90 £20 £10

No. 139B Hudson Commodore Sedan
Maroon, maroon and fawn or fawn and blue. The first models were not individually boxed. Price 2/9. Issued July 1950. Renumbered 171 in 1954. Deleted 1965. 111mm. DC/RT/TP.

£95 £40 £15

No. 140 Morris 1100
Various shades of blue with red interior. Opening bonnet to reveal silver engine. Silver bumpers, grille etc. Price 4/6. Issued February 1963. Deleted 1969. 87mm. SW/SS/S/W/OB/DC/TP/RT/P.

£80 £30 £15

No. 140B Rover 75 Saloon
Maroon or cream. The first models were not individually boxed. Price 3/2. Issued April 1951. Renumbered 156 in 1954. Deleted 1969. 101mm. DC/TP/RT.

£75 £30 £15

No. 141 Vauxhall Victor Estate Car
Yellow or white (rare and worth double). Opening rear door. Price 4/11. Issued April 1963. Deleted 1967. 92mm. SW/SS/S/W/DC/RT/TP/P. Model was also issued as ambulance No. 278 in 1964 and deleted in 1970.

£60 £30 £15

No. 142 Jaguar Mk X
Metallic blue from electric to mid-blue. Also metallic green or metallic dark red (rare and worth double). Luggage. Price 5/6. Issued November 1962. Deleted 1969. 106mm. SW/SS/FTS/S/W/OR/RT/P/DC.

£100 £30 £15

No. 143 Ford Capri
Green and white. Luggage. Price 3/11. Issued August 1962. Deleted 1967. 106mm. SW/SS/FTS/S/W/OR/DC/P/RT.

£70 £30 £15

No. 144 Volkswagen 1500
White and later in gold from 1965. Opening bonnet and luggage. Price 4/6. Issued March 1963. Deleted 1967. 93mm. SW/LHD/SS/FTS/S/W/DC/TP/RT/P.

£40 £20 £10

No. 145 Singer Vogue
Metallic green or orange (rare and worth double). Price 3/11. Issued December 1962. Deleted 1967. 93mm. SW/SS/FTS/S/W/DC/TP/P/RT.

£50 £20 £10

No. 146 Daimler V8 2½ Litre
Metallic green or metallic blue (rare and worth double).
Price 3/9. Issued January 1963. Deleted 1967. 95mm.
SW/SS/FTS/S/W/DC/TP/RT/P.

| | £75 | £30 | £15 |

No. 147 Cadillac 62
Metallic green or metallic red (rare and worth double).
Price 4/11. Issued October 1962. Deleted 1968. 113mm.
SW/SS/FTS/LHD/S/W/DC/TP/RT/P.

| | £100 | £50 | £20 |

No. 148 Ford Fairlaine
Green or metallic green (rare and worth double). Price
4/11. Issued February 1962. Deleted 1966. 111mm.
SW/SS/FTS/S/W/LHD/DC/TP/RT/P.

| | £60 | £20 | £10 |

No. 149 Citroën Dyane
Gold with black roof. Also red or purple with red interior
(rare and worth treble). Plastic Speediwheels. Opening
rear door and bonnet. Price 75p. Issued 1971. Deleted
1975. 91mm. DC/P.

| | £75 | £30 | £15 |

No. 150 Rolls Royce Silver Wraith
Grey and dark grey with windows and four wheel
suspension. All-chromed parts. Price 5/6. Issued
February 1959. Deleted 1964. 117mm. DC/TP/RT.

| | £115 | £50 | £20 |

No. 151 Triumph 1800
Blue or brown. Renumbering of 40B. Price 2/2. Issued
1958. Deleted 1960. 91mm. DC/TP/RT.

| | £65 | £25 | £10 |

No. 151 Vauxhall Victor 101
Lemon, lime green or metallic red. Also cream with white
interior (rare and worth double). Opening boot and
bonnet, and full silver trim. Price 7/-. Issued 1965.
Deleted 1969. 105mm. DC/TP/RT/P.

| | £55 | £20 | £10 |

No. 152 Rolls Royce Phantom V Limousine
Black, very deep blue, or metallic dark green (rare and
worth double). All opening doors, bonnet and boot. Fawn
interior with driver. Price 14/11. Issued 1965. Replaced
by No. 124 in 1977. Finally deleted 1978. This model was
also issued as Action Kit No. 1001 in 1971 and deleted in
1978. 141mm. DC/P/RT/TP.

| | £80 | £40 | £20 |

No. 152 Austin Devon
Maroon, blue or suede green. Renumbering of 40D. Price
2/2. Reissued 1954. Deleted 1956. 86mm. DC/TP/RT.

| | £95 | £40 | £20 |

No. 152 Austin Devon
Two-tone colours of various shades: blue, green, purple and black (rare and worth double). Also blue and yellow or grey and cerise. Price 2/6. Issued August 1956. Deleted 1960. 86mm. DC/TP/RT.

	MB	MU	GC
	£95	£40	£20

No. 152c Austin 7 Car
This is the military version of No. 35d and should for consistency appear in the military section as well. Never issued in an individual box, although it appeared in two boxed sets. Matt green. Wire screen and hole in seat for driver. Price 4d. Issued February 1938. Deleted 1940. This model was approx. 51mm originally, but metal does expand with age and several models are now between 51 and 55mm. DC/RW.

	—	£75	£25
Boxed set	£60	—	—

No. 153 Standard Vanguard
Blue, fawn or cream. Covered rear wheels similar to those of No. 40E with ridged boot. Large print baseplate lettering. Price 2/2. Issued August 1954. Deleted 1960. 91mm. DC/TP/RT.

	£90	£30	£10

No. 153 Aston Martin DB6
Silver blue or metallic green. Also two-tone green and blue (rare and worth treble). Red interior, opening boot, bonnet and doors, with spoked silver wheels, hubs, bumpers etc. Price 14/11. Issued 1967. Deleted 1971. 111mm. DC.

	£55	£25	£10

No. 154 Hillman Minx
Green or brown. Renumbering of 40F. Price 2/2. Issued May 1954. Deleted 1956. 87mm. DC/TP/RT.

	£60	£25	£10

No. 154 Hillman Minx Two-Tone
Green and cream or cerise and blue (rare and worth double). Price 2/6. Issued September 1956. Deleted 1958. 87mm. DC/TP/RT.

	£120	£30	£15

No. 154 Ford Taunus 17M
Yellow, various shades with white roof and red interior. Opening boot and bonnet with silver grille etc. Price 9/11. Issued 1966. Deleted 1976. 110mm. DC/RT/P.

	£75	£35	£15

No. 155 Ford Anglia
Green. Price 3/9. Issued July 1961. Deleted 1966. 81mm. SW/SS/S/W/DC/TP.

	£50	£20	£10

No. 156 Rover 75
Cream. Renumbering of 140B. Price 2/5. Issued May 1954. Deleted 1956. 101mm. DC/RT/TP.

	£65	£25	£10

No. 156 Rover 75 Two-Tone
Blue and cream, two shades of green, or red and black
(rare and worth treble). Price 3/-. Issued January 1956.
Deleted 1960. 101mm. DC/TP/RT.   £100   £40   £20

No. 156 Saab 96
Red with light fawn or white interior. Also rare metallic
blue worth at least treble. Price 7/-. Issued 1966. Deleted
1971. 98mm. DC/P/RT.   £65   £30   £15

No. 157 Jaguar XK120
Red or green with shiny aluminium hubs. It also appears
in a 1959/60 and 1961 catalogue in red with shiny wheels.
The single and two-colour versions were available at
various times from 1956 to 1958 when the two-colour
versions were dropped as they were not very good. There
is also a white or yellow version which is rare and worth
more. A further range of two-tone colours are worth
double; these are cerise and turquoise, grey and yellow,
and two-tone green (extremely rare). Price 2/5. Issued
March 1956. Deleted 1962. 97mm. DC/TP/RT.   £150   £75   £50

No. 157 BMW 2000 Tilux
Blue and white with flashing indicators. White interior
and silver wheels, bumpers etc. Price 13/11. Issued 1968.
Deleted 1973. 121mm. DC/P.   £100   £50   £25

No. 158 Rolls Royce Silver Shadow
Metallic red and later in metallic blue. Four opening
doors, opening bonnet and boot, fawn or white interior
with silver hubs, bumpers etc. Price 14/11. Issued 1962.
Deleted 1973. 125mm. DC/P.   £100   £50   £25

No. 158 Riley
Blue, cream or pale green. Price 2/2. Issued March 1954.
Deleted 1960. 93mm. DC/TP/RT.   £150   £50   £25

No. 159 Ford Cortina
White with opening doors, bonnet and boot, and red flash
on sides. Silver engine, wheels, bumpers etc. Price 9/3.
Issued 1967. Deleted 1970. 105mm. DC/P.   £100   £50   £25

No. 159 Morris Oxford
Fawn or green. Renumbering of 40G. Price 2/2. Issued
March 1954. Deleted January 1956. 97mm. DC/TP/RT.   £100   £50   £25

No. 159 Morris Oxford Two-Tone
Green and cream or white and red. Price 2/9. Issued
January 1956. Deleted 1960. 97mm. DC/TP/RT.   £250   £100   £50

No. 160 Austin A30
Fawn or blue. Smooth or ridged plastic wheels. Price 2/4.
Issued June 1958. Deleted 1962. 77mm. DC/TP/P.

| | £100 | £50 | £25 |

No. 160 Mercedes Benz 250SE
Metallic blue with stop lights which work by pressing the
car. White interior with silver bumpers and wheels etc.
Price 9/3. Issued 1967. Deleted 1974. 117mm. DC/P.

| | £100 | £50 | £25 |

No. 161 Ford Mustang Fastback 2 + 2
White, yellow or orange (the last colour being made from
1970). Red interior, opening doors, boot and bonnet with
silver trim etc. Price 10/9. Issued 1965. Deleted 1973.
111mm. DC/P.

| | £100 | £50 | £25 |

No. 161C Austin Somerset
Blue or red. Price 2/2. Issued March 1964. Deleted 1970.
89mm. DC/TP/RT.

| | £200 | £100 | £50 |

No. 161D Austin Somerset Two-Tone
Black and white or yellow and red. Renumbering of 40J.
Price 2/6. Issued August 1956. Deleted 1960. 89mm.
DC/TP/RT.

| Black and white | £175 | £100 | £50 |
| Yellow and red | £300 | £75 | £50 |

No. 162 Ford Zephyr Saloon
Two-tone blue, very pale on the upper part, medium or
dark on the lower. Silver radiator grille, bumpers and
wheels with black tyres. Issued 1957. Deleted 1960. Price
3/-. 96mm. DC/TP/RT.

| | £75 | £50 | £25 |

No. 162G Ford Zephyr Saloon
Two-tone green or light green and cream (rare and worth
double). Price 3/-. Issued April 1956. Deleted 1960.
96mm. DC/TP/RT.

| | £250 | £100 | £50 |

No. 162H Triumph 1300
Light blue with red interior or with red and white interior
(rare and worth double). Opening boot and bonnet,
all-silver bumpers, headlights, grille, hubs etc. Price 6/-.
Issued 1966. Deleted 1970. 92mm.

| | £100 | £50 | £25 |

No. 163 VW 1600TL Fastback
Red with fawn interior, opening doors, bonnet and boot.
Silver grille, bumpers, headlights and wheels with spare
wheel inside bonnet. Price 9/6. Issued 1966. Deleted 1971.
102mm. DC/P/RT.

| | £100 | £50 | £25 |

No. 163A Bristol 450
Green. White circles with racing number. Price 2/9.
Issued July 1956. Deleted 1960. 98mm. DC/TP/RT.

| | £100 | £50 | £25 |

No. 164 Ford Zodiac
Silver with red interior. Also bronze, which is scarce as it
was made for export only (worth treble). Opening doors,
bonnet and boot, silver hubs, bumpers, grille and
headlights. Price 13/11. Issued March 1966. Deleted 1971.
114mm. DC/P.

| | £100 | £50 | £25 |

No. 164A Vauxhall Cresta
Green and grey. Rare grey and black or maroon and
cream worth double. Price 3/-. Issued March 1957.
Deleted 1960. 96mm. DC/TP/RT.

| | £100 | £50 | £25 |

No. 165 Humber Hawk
Green and black or maroon and cream (rare and worth
double). Windows and four wheel suspension. Price 3/9.
Issued July 1959. Deleted 1963. 102mm. DC/TP/P/RT.

| | £100 | £50 | £25 |

No. 165A Ford Capri
Green or purple and yellow with a metallic finish (rare
and worth double). Also two-tone green (scarce and
therefore valuable). Red interior, silver wheels, bumpers
etc. Price 6/11. Issued 1969. Deleted 1976. 102mm. DC/P.

| | £100 | £50 | £25 |

No. 166 Renault R16
Blue. Borrowed French Dinky body casting but chassis
made in England. '1/43' and '65' still cast into baseplate
French Dinky style. Numbers indicate scale and year of
introduction. Price 6/11. Issued 1965. Deleted 1970.
86mm. DC/RT.

| | £100 | £50 | £25 |

No. 166A Sunbeam Rapier
Two-tone blue or cream and orange (rare and worth
double). Windows. Price 2/11. Issued June 1958. Deleted
1963. 89mm. DC/TP/RT/P.

| | £100 | £50 | £25 |

No. 167 AC Aceca Coupé
Red and grey, cream and brown, and cream with maroon
roof, a late colour only seen with shiny aluminium
wheels. Price 2/11. Issued November 1958. Deleted 1963.
89mm. DC/TP/RT.

| | £250 | £150 | £75 |

No. 168 Ford Escort
Light blue or metallic red with cream or yellow interior.
Also black (rare). Opening doors, bonnet and boot. Price
8/6. Issued 1968. Also available as Dinky Action Kit No.
1006 with rally stripes as per Ford Escort Mexico:
1973/78. Deleted 1977. 97mm. DC/P.

	MB	MU	GC
Light blue	£100	£50	£25
Metallic red	£250	£100	£50
Black	£750	—	—

No. 168A Singer Gazelle
Grey and green or cream and brown (worth double).
All-silver reported but not verified. Windows. Price 2/11.
Issued January 1959. Deleted 1963. 92mm. DC/TP/RT/P. £100 £50 £25

No. 169 Ford Corsair 2000E
Silver with black roof. Price 5/11. Issued 1967. Deleted
1969. 108mm. DC/P. £85 £50 £25

No. 169A Studebaker Golden Hawk
Green and cream, fawn and red or green and fawn. Red
and later cream flashes. Windows. Price 3/5. Issued
November 1958. Deleted 1963. 106mm. DC/TP/P/RT. £100 £50 £25

No. 170 Ford Fordor
Sedan model in yellow, red or fawn with red wheels.
Renumbering of 139A. Price 2/3. Issued 1954. Deleted
1956. 102mm. DC/TP/RT. £150 £100 £50

No. 170 Ford Fordor Two-Tone
Cream and red or pink and blue. Price 2/11. Issued March
1956. Deleted 1959. 102mm. DC/TP/RT. £400 — —

No. 170A Lincoln Continental
Metallic orange or medium blue with white roof. There
was a series of 1/42nd scale Dinky Toy American cars
which were made in Hong Kong in 1965, but this model
is not one of them. 'Made in England' on the baseplate,
although on the boxes it said 'Made in Hong Kong for
Dinky'. All-chrome parts. Price 14/11. Issued October
1964. Deleted 1970. 127mm. LHD/SW/FTS/S/
W/OB/DC/RT/P. £250 £100 £50

No. 170 Granada Ghia
This was a new model for 1978, made in a very limited
number. There was a wooden mock-up for the Dinky
stand in the 1979 Exhibition at Earls Court, London where
I was invited as a guest by Mr Hudson, the head of Dinky
at Binns Road, Liverpool. However, the sit-in by the

workers kept the factory and offices closed, which made
it very difficult for the company. Metallic silver with
all-silver finish. Price £1.50. Deleted soon after it was
issued. 127.5mm. DC/P. Extremely rare.

	MB	MU	GC
	£500	£250	£50

No. 171 Hudson Commodore
Maroon and fawn or fawn and blue. Price 2/8. Issued
1954. Deleted 1956. 111mm. DC/TP/RT.

	£150	£50	£25

No. 171A Hudson Commodore Two-Tone
Red and blue or blue and grey. Price 2/9. Issued January
1956. Deleted 1958. 111mm. DC/TP/RT.

	£160	£70	£30

No. 171B Austin 1800
Blue with red interior or red with white interior (rare and
worth double). Silver trim and opening boot and bonnet.
Price 7/-. Issued 1965. Deleted 1968. DC/P/RT.

	£80	£40	£10

No. 172 Studebaker Land Cruiser
Green or blue. Price 2/8. Issued April 1954. Deleted July
1956. 107mm. DC/RT/PT.

	£125	£50	£25

No. 172 Studebaker Land Cruiser Two-Tone
Maroon and cream or fawn and brown. Price 2/9. Issued
July 1956. Deleted 1958. DC/TP/RT.

	£125	£50	£25

No. 172 Fiat 2300 Station Wagon
Off-white with dark blue roof; green with white roof (rare
and worth double); light blue with white or blue roof
(very rare and worth at least treble). Opening bonnet and
opening rear doors with full silver trim. Price 7/11.
Issued 1965. Deleted 1969. 108mm. DC/P.

	£55	£30	£20

No. 173 Nash Rambler
Pale green with pink and maroon side flashes; pale pink
with blue side flashes; green with purple flashes; or blue
with red flashes (rare and worth treble). Price 3/5. Issued
May 1958. Deleted 1962. 101mm. DC/TP/RT.

	£75	£30	£15

No. 173 Pontiac Parisienne
Maroon or metallic blue; pink or purple, and red. All
models had pink or white interior with retractable aerials
and full silver trim. This model always had
Speediwheels. The first variety made in 1968 had rubber
tyres on metal hubs, the second variety made in 1970 had
wheels entirely of plastic. Price 8/11. Issued 1968. Deleted
1975. 132mm. DC/P.

	MB	MU	GC
Metal wheels and rubber tyres	£125	£50	£25
Plastic wheels	£65	£50	£15

No. 174 Hudson Hornet
Red and cream, red and yellow or yellow and grey.
Windows. Price 3/5. Issued August 1958. Deleted 1963.
111mm. DC/TP/RT/P.

	MB	MU	GC
	£95	£40	£25

No. 174A Ford Mercury Cougar
Metallic blue, metallic sand, metallic purple or metallic
red. Retractable aerial, silver bumpers and white interior
with opening doors. Price 8/11. Issued 1960. Deleted
1969. 122mm. DC/P.

	MB	MU	GC
	£80	£30	£15

No. 175 Hillman Minx
Green and mustard, pink and green or grey and blue.
Windows. Price 2/11. Issued August 1958. Deleted 1961.
88mm. DC/TP/RT/P.

	MB	MU	GC
	£80	£30	£15

No. 175A Cadillac Eldorado
Mauve with black roof or blue with black roof. In 1969 a
new model in gold with black roof appeared. White
interior and full silver trim, bumpers etc. Price 9/6.
Issued 1969. Deleted 1973. 133mm. DC/P.

	MB	MU	GC
Mauve with black roof	£190	£100	£50
Blue with black roof	£190	£100	£50
Gold with black roof	£95	£50	£25

No. 176 Austin A105 Saloon
Grey with red flash, some with red roof; cream with blue
flash, some with blue roof; grey with red flash, some with
red roof; or blue yellow flash, some with yellow roof (rare
and worth double). Windows. Price 3/5. Issued April
1958. Deleted 1963. 102mm. DC/TP/RT/P.

	MB	MU	GC
	£95	£30	£15

No. 176A NSU RO80
Metallic maroon with or without black roof, or metallic
blue with white or fawn interior. Silver trim, bumpers,
headlights etc. Luminous seats and battery operated
head and tail lights. Price 10/6. Issued 1969. Deleted 1974.
114mm. DC/P.

	MB	MU	GC
	£55	£20	£10

No. 177 Opel Kapitan
Mid- or pale blue. Price 4/6. Issued August 1961. Deleted
1966. 100mm. SW/LHD/SS/FTS/S/W/DC/TP/RT/P.

	MB	MU	GC
	£55	£25	£15

No. 178 Plymouth Plaza
Pink and light green. Also light blue with darker roof and
flash. Windows. Price 3/5. Issued January 1959. Deleted
1963. 100mm. DC/TP/P/RT.

	MB	MU	GC
	£125	£50	£25

No. 178 Mini-Clubman
Metallic bronze with various shades as years progressed.
White or black interior. Price 75p. Issued 1975. Deleted
1979.

No. 179 Studebaker President
Blue with blue flash or yellow with blue flash (rare and
worth more). Windows. Price 3/5. Issued October 1958.
Deleted 1963. 108mm. DC/TP/RT/P.

No. 179A Opel Commodore
This was a borrowed French Dinky Toy casting. Fitted
with plastic Speediwheels. Metallic blue with black roof
or metallic green (rare and worth double). Price 9/6.
Issued 1971. Deleted 1975. 107mm. DC/P.

No. 180 Packard Clipper
Fawn and pink or orange and grey. Windows. Price 3/5.
Issued September 1958. Deleted 1963. 112mm.
DC/TP/RT/P.

No. 180 Rover 3500
White with black plastic chassis and black plastic
Speediwheels. On the chassis 'Made in Hong Kong', the
first Dinky Toy to be marked this way since 1965. Price
£1.35. Issued 1978. Deleted 1979/80. 131mm. DC/P.

No. 181 Volkswagen
Grey and pale blue or grey and sky blue. Green or
mid-blue are worth double. Price 2/5. Issued February
1956. Deleted 1971. 90mm. DC/TP/RT.

No. 182 Porsche 356A Coupé
Blue, cream or red. Windows. Price 2/10. Issued
September 1958. Deleted 1964. 87mm. DC/TP/RT/P.

No. 183 Fiat 600 Saloon
Red or green with solid plastic wheels. There is a version
in red with rubber tyres which is very rare and worth at
least quadruple. Price 2/3. Issued May 1958. Deleted
1960. 71mm. DC.

No. 183A Morris Mini-Minor Automatic
White body with black roof, red body with black roof, or
blue with darker blue roof (very rare and worth double).
Plastic Speediwheels from 1972. Price 7/-. Issued 1966.
Deleted 1975. 75mm. DC/P.

	MB	MU	GC
No. 178 Mini-Clubman	£45	£25	£10
No. 179 Studebaker President	£115	£50	£25
No. 179A Opel Commodore	£125	£50	£25
No. 180 Packard Clipper	£115	£50	£25
No. 180 Rover 3500	£75	£40	£20
No. 181 Volkswagen	£60	£30	£15
No. 182 Porsche 356A Coupé	£90	£40	£20
No. 183 Fiat 600 Saloon	£60	£20	£10
Metal wheels and rubber tyres	£65	£20	£10
Speediwheels	£50	£20	£10

No. 184   Volvo 122S
Red. Price 4/5. Issued December 1961. Deleted 1964.
98mm. SW/SS/S/W/DC/TP/RT/P.

No. 186   Mercedes Benz 220SE
Pale or mid-blue with all-chromed parts. Price 5/9.
Issued February 1961. Deleted 1967. 102mm.
LHD/SW/SS/FTS/S/W/DC/TP/RT/P.

No. 187   Volkswagen Karmann Ghia Coupé
Red with black roof and green with off-white or cream
roof. Windows and four-wheel suspension. Price 3/6.
Issued November 1959. Deleted 1964. 96mm.
DC/TP/RT/P.

No. 187A   De Tomaso Mangusta 5000
Metallic red and white, although shades vary. Opening
bonnet and boot. White interior. Price 10/9. Issued 1968.
Deleted 1977. 109mm. DC/P.

No. 188   Jensen FF
This model was mostly in yellow, although there are the
rare colours of yellow with black roof and cream and blue
(worth double). Metal hubs, rubber tyres and
Speediwheels. Opening doors and bonnet. Price 10/9.
Issued 1968. Deleted 1975. 121mm. DC/P.

No. 189   Triumph Herald
Green and white or blue and white (rare). Windows. Price
3/3. Issued May 1959. Deleted 1964. 86mm.
SS/W/DC/TP/RT/P.

No. 189A   Lamborghini Marzal
Green and white with red interior; metallic dark green
and yellow; red; metallic blue and white; and metallic
blue with plastic Speediwheels and red interior. Price
9/6. Issued 1969. Deleted 1978. 108mm. DC/P.

No. 190   Monteverdi 375L
Metallic red or metallic maroon with Speediwheels and
rubber tyres, and a metal hub variety. Pink or white
interior. Price 9/6. Issued 1971. Deleted 1974. 116mm.
DC/P.

	MB	MU	GC
No. 184 Volvo 122S	£120	£50	£25
No. 186 Mercedes Benz 220SE	£100	£50	£25
No. 187 Volkswagen Karmann Ghia Coupé	£100	£50	£25
No. 187A De Tomaso Mangusta 5000	£100	£50	£25
No. 188 Jensen FF	100	£50	£25
No. 189 Triumph Herald	£100	£50	£25
No. 189A Lamborghini Marzal			
Green and white	£50	£25	£15
Metallic dark green and yellow	£65	£20	£10
Red	£65	£20	£10
Metallic blue and white	£80	£40	£20
Metallic blue	£80	£40	£20
No. 190 Monteverdi 375L	£55	£20	£10

No. 191 Dodge Royal Sedan
Cream with blue or brown flashes and green with black
flashes. Windows. Price 3/5. Issued March 1959. Deleted
1964. 111mm. DC/TP/RT/P.

No. 192 De Soto Fireflite
Blue body with orange roof and orange flashes; grey with
red roof; green with fawn roof; and blue with orange roof
and flashes (rare and worth treble). Price 3/5. Issued
December 1958. Deleted 1964. 114mm. DC/TP/RT/P.

No. 192 Range Rover
Gold with pale blue interior; metallic bronze with white
interior; white or grey (last two versions rare and worth
double). Plastic Speediwheels from 1977. Price 10/6.
Issued 1971. Deleted 1980. 109mm. DC/P.

No. 193 Rambler Cross Country Station Wagon
Yellow and white or blue and yellow (worth double).
All-chrome parts. Price 6/3. Issued 1961. Deleted 1969.
102mm. DC/TP/RT/P.

No. 194 Bentley S Coupé
Grey with red seats, brown plastic dashboard and grey
suited driver. Later gold with cream seats. Grey type is
worth double as it is now quite scarce. All-chromed parts.
Price 6/3. Issued March 1964. Deleted 1967. 112mm.
SW/SS/FTS/S/WS/D/DC/RT/TP/P.

No. 195 Alfa Romeo 1900 Sprint
Red or yellow. Price 4/3. Issued January 1961. Deleted
1963. 102mm. SW/LHD/SS/FTS/W/S/DC/TP/RT/P.

No. 195 Jaguar 3.4 Litre Saloon
Cream and yellow, grey, maroon or dark green (worth
double). Window seats, four-wheel suspension and
steering wheel. Price 3/11. Issued August 1960. Deleted
1966. 95mm. DC/TP/RT/P.

No. 195A Range Rover Fire Chief
Metallic red and later plain red. Price 9/6. Issued 1971.
Deleted 1978. 109mm. DC/P.

No. 196 Holden Special Sedan
Metallic bronze with white roof, light blue with white
roof, and black with white roof (worth double). Opening
boot and bonnet. This model was not a success in England
but proved to be a good seller in Australia, Canada and
the USA. Price 7/-. Issued 1967. Deleted 1970. 108mm.
DC.

	MB	MU	GC
No. 191 Dodge Royal Sedan	£80	£40	£20
No. 192 De Soto Fireflite	£70	£30	£15
No. 192 Range Rover	£65	£30	£15
No. 193 Rambler Cross Country Station Wagon	£50	£25	£10
No. 194 Bentley S Coupé	£95	£40	£15
No. 195 Alfa Romeo 1900 Sprint	£70	£30	£15
No. 195 Jaguar 3.4 Litre Saloon	£80	£30	£15
No. 195A Range Rover Fire Chief	£45	£20	£10
No. 196 Holden Special Sedan	£60	£20	£10

No. 197 Morris Mini-Traveller
Cream or green with imitation wood panels in brown.
Also red (worth double). Good seller, especially the first
model. Price 3/5. Issued 1961. Deleted 1970. 72mm.
SW/SS/FTS/S/W/DC/RT/P.   £50   £20   £10

No. 198 Rolls Royce Phantom V
Metallic pale green, cream and grey, off-white or black
and silver (worth treble). All-chromed parts. Price 6/11.
Issued November 1962. Deleted 1965/66. 125mm.
SW/SS/FTS/S/W/D/DC/TP/RT/P.   £95   £50   £25

No. 199 Austin 7 Countryman
Originally pale blue with imitation wood panel in brown
at rear. Later orange. Price 3/5. Issued May 1961. Deleted
1970. 72mm. SW/SS/FTS/S/W/DC/TP/RT/P.   £50   £20   £10

No. 200 Midget Racer
Red or silver. Renumbering of 35B. Price 11d. Issued 1954.
Deleted 1957. 57mm. DC/RT. This model never had an
individual box but came in boxes of six.   —   £45   £10

No. 200A Matra 630
Blue. A borrowed French Dinky casting, it was rather
spoilt by the small plastic Speediwheels. Price 3/5. Issued
1971. Deleted 1975. 105mm. DC/P.   £35   £20   £10

No. 201 Stock Car
Dark blue with yellow stickers. This stock car was based
on the 278/244 Plymouth casting but had large racing
tyres and wheels. Price £2.25. Issued 1979. Deleted 1980.
134.5mm. DC/P. This model appeared in the catalogue
under 'Meccano & Kits' section.   £35   £20   £10

No. 202 Fiat Abarth 2000
Red or orange and white. Another borrowed French
Dinky with the same plastic wheels as No. 200A. Price
3/5. Issued 1970 but not released until 1971. Deleted 1975.
91mm. DC/P.   £35   £20   £10

No. 202 Custom Land Rover
Black with yellow stickers. Casting was No. 344 with
racing wheels, large tyres and plastic bumpers. Price
£2.25. Issued 1979. Deleted 1980. 115mm. DC/P.   £45   £20   £10

No. 203 Custom Range Rover
Black body with white plastic chassis. Casting is No. 192
with racing wheels and large black tyres. Plastic frame
with large bumpers front and rear. Price £2.50. Issued
1979. Deleted 1980. 115mm. DC/P.   £45   £20   £10

No. 204 Ferrari 312P
Metallic red with white doors but deep metallic maroon
from 1972. Also green metallic with white doors (worth
double). Another borrowed French Dinky. Price 4/11.
Issued 1971. Deleted 1975. 99mm. DC/P.

	£55	£20	£10

No. 205 Talbot Lago
Blue. In bubble pack, which was for the export market
only, although some remained in England. Price 3/3.
Issued May 1962. Deleted 1964. 103mm. DC/TP/RT/P.

	£65	£30	£15

No. 205A Lotus Cortina Rally Car
Cream and red with red flash on sides and stripes on roof
at one side. Opening boot, bonnet and doors with yellow
squares with '7' in black. White interior. Chrome
bumpers etc. Speediwheels from approx. 1970. Price
10/9. Issued 1968. Deleted 1973. 105mm. DC/P.

	£55	£20	£10

No. 206 Maserati
Red. Another borrowed French dinky. Price 3/3. Issued
May 1962. Deleted 1964. 94mm. DC/RT/TP/P.

	£50	£25	£10

No. 206 Customised Corvette Stingray
Bright red with flame flashes in red, white and yellow,
with black chassis and silver trim. This was the same as
No. 221 without opening features, a last minute effort by
Dinky to revive old moulds. Price £2.25. Issued 1979.
Deleted 1980. 113mm. DC/P.

	£55	£20	£10

No. 207 Alfa Romeo
Red. In bubble pack. Price 3/3. Issued May 1962. Deleted
1964. 100mm. DC/RT/TP/P. See also comments for No.
205.

	£55	£20	£10

No. 207A Triumph TR7 Rally Car
White with red and purple design on bonnet. Black
interior and '8' on doors. Price £1.25. Issued 1978. Deleted
1980. 98mm. DC/P.

	£50	£20	£10

No. 208 Cooper Bristol
Green. In bubble pack. Price 3/3. Issued May 1962.
Deleted 1964. 89mm. DC/TP/RT/P. See also comments
for No. 205.

	£50	£20	£10

No. 208A   Porsche 914
Yellow with black interior. Metallic mid-blue with black bonnet and red interior from 1976. Metallic blue with white bonnet also from 1976. Colours may vary. Rubber tyres, metal hubs and Speediwheels. Price 75p. Issued 1971. Deleted by 1979. 89mm. DC/RT/P.

	MB	MU	GC
Yellow	£50	£20	£10
Metallic mid-blue	£50	£20	£10
Metallic blue	£75	£40	£20

No. 209   Ferrari
Blue and yellow. In bubble pack. Price 3/3. Issued May 1962. Deleted 1964. 101mm. DC/RT/TP/P. See also comments for No. 205.

	£65	£30	£15

No. 210   Vanwall
Green. In bubble pack. Price 3/3. Issued May 1962. Deleted 1964. 95mm. DC/TP/RT/P. See also comments for No. 205.

	£50	£20	£10

No. 210A   Alfa Romeo 33 Tipo-Le-Mans
Orange with red or white interior and with '36' in white circle on sides and front. Price 8/6. Issued 1970. Deleted 1978. 107mm. DC/P.

	£50	£20	£10

No. 211   Triumph TR7 Sports Car
Red with black or white interior and black plastic chassis with black or grey plastic bumper. Price £1.20. Issued 1976. Deleted 1980. 98mm. DC/P.

	£50	£20	£10

No. 212   Ford Cortina Rally Car
Cream and black with black bonnet and black circle with white '8'. Opening doors, light on roof and silver trim. Price 7/-. Issued 1965. Deleted 1970. 102mm. DC/P.

	£75	£30	£15

No. 213   Ford Rally Car
Red with black bonnet with white flash and '20' on opening doors. Originally issued with metal hubs and rubber tyres. It had all-plastic Speediwheels from 1973. Price 70p. Issued 1970. Deleted 1975. 102mm. DC/RT/P.

	MB	MU	GC
Metal hubs and rubber wheels	£75	£40	£20
All-plastic Speediwheels	£50	£20	£10

No. 214   Hillman Imp Rally Car
Blue with white flash, red interior and silver trim. Opening boot and bonnet showing '35' on side. Rally signs on model. Price 6/-. Issued 1966. Deleted 1969. 86mm. DC/P.

	£50	£20	£10

No. 215 Ford GT Racing Car
Cream with red interior and black '7' on sides. Also green with red flash. Opening bonnet at each end to reveal engine workings. The model was originally issued with plain silver disc wheels, but later it had spoked wheels in white and later still in metallic green. The plain or spoked wheel model is worth double the Speediwheel type. Price 8/11. Issued 1965. Deleted 1974. 96mm. DC/RT/P.

£75   £40   £20

No. 216 Dino Ferrari
Red with opening doors and large opening rear engine hatch showing a silver-blue racing engine. Blue from 1970. Both colours have stick-on paper racing numbers, normally '20'. Some red models have gold spoked wheels, and the blue version at first had a black engine cover which changed to white from 1973. Price 8/11. Issued 1969. Deleted 1975. 98mm. DC/P.

£50   £20   £10

No. 217 Alfa Romeo Scarabeo Osi
Orange with yellow interior, with rubber tyres and metal spoked hubs on Speediwheels on all models. No bumpers. Price 7/11. Issued 1969. Deleted 1974. 90mm. DC/P.

£50   £20   £10

No. 218 Lotus Europa
Dark blue and deep lemon with orange and black flashes on bonnet and silver wheels. Metal hubs and rubber tyre Speediwheels from 1969, and all-plastic Speediwheels from 1973. The price of the earlier model is almost double that of the later. Price 7/11. Issued 1969. Deleted 1975. 96mm. DC/P.

£80   £30   £10

No. 219 Leyland Jaguar XJ 5.3 Coupé
Purple and white with red stripes design. The number '2' on bonnet and doors. This model was first illustrated in the 1978 catalogue, but only a few models were released owing to the sit-in at the factory. Price £1.58. 137mm. DC/P. Good investment.

£250   £50   £25

No. 219 The Big Cat Jaguar
Deep purple or white (rarer). Face of a Jaguar animal on bonnet and figure of the same animal in full flight on each side of item. Twin headlights and silver trim. Another variation of the customised Leyland Jaguar coupé. Price £1.58. Issued 1978 is a very limited quantity, mostly brought out by reps during factory sit-in. 137mm. DC/P.

£350   £150   £50

No. 220 Small Open Racing Car
Silver with red flashes and red circles with silver '4' on sides. Renumbering of 23A. Price 1/6. Issued 1954. Deleted 1955. 94mm. DC/RT. Never issued in an individual box but came in cartons of six.

	—	£45	£20

No. 220A Ferrari P5
Red body and white or cream interior and opening doors. Metal hubs and rubber tyre Speediwheels, then all-plastic Speediwheels from 1973. Price 7/11. Issued 1970. Deleted 1975. 96mm. DC/P.

	MB	MU	GC
Metal hubs and rubber tyres	£50	£20	£10
All-plastic Speediwheels	£40	£15	£10

No. 221 Speed of the Wind Racing Car
Silver with red trim. Renumbering of 23E. Price 2/-. Issued 1954. Deleted 1957. 104mm. DC/RT/TP. Never issued in an individual box but came in cartons of six.

	—	£55	£20

No. 221A Corvette Stingray
Metallic bronze with swivelling headlights and speed wheels. Opening bonnet and doors with off-white or cream interior, silver bumpers etc. Rubber tyres and spoked metal hubs when issued in metallic bronze, it was later released in metallic orange with all-plastic Speediwheels, plus a white version with black bonnet which was issued from 1976. Metallic bronze or metallic orange model is worth double the white and black. Price £1.35. Issued 1970. Deleted 1978. 113mm. DC/P.

	£75	£40	£20

No. 222 Streamlined Racing Car
Silver or green with red or blue trim. Renumbering of 235. Price 2/4. Issued 1955. Deleted 1957. 126mm. DC/RT/TP. Never issued in an individual box but came delivered in cartons of six.

	—	£50	£20

No. 222 Hesketh 308E
Medium blue body with 'Olympus' on rear, front and sides in yellow. Driver in white and '24' in orange or yellow on sides and bonnet. Large tyres and silver hubs. Price £1.76. Issued 1978. Deleted 1985. 132mm. DC/P.

	£40	£20	£10

No. 223 MacLaren Can Am
Originally blue and white with metal hubs and rubber tyre Speediwheels. Then red and white from 1972. Then metallic green (always mottled) or lime from 1976 with all-plastic Speediwheels. Price 7/11. Issued 1970. Deleted 1978. 94mm. DC/P.

	MB	MU	GC
Blue and white or red and white	£50	£20	£10
Metallic green or lime	£40	£10	£5

No. 224 Mercedes Benz CIII
Metallic maroon and bright red with metal hubs and
rubber tyre Speediwheels. White interior, opening boot
and driver's door. Price 14/11. Issued 1970. Deleted 1977.
192mm. DC/P.

	MB	MU	GC
No. 224	£50	£20	£10

No. 225 Lotus F1 (No. 7)
Red body with gold nose and John Player racing team
transfers on sides. Metallic blue body from 1976. Price
7/6. Issued 1970. Deleted 1978. 127mm. DC/P.

Red	£50	£20	£10
Blue	£40	£15	£10

No. 226 Ferrari 312/B2
Red with '2'. Gold from 1976. Price 75p. Issued 1972.
Deleted 1978. 121mm.

Red	£60	£30	£10
Gold	£30	£15	£5

No. 227 Beach Buggy
Yellow, then later green with white interior. White or
green detachable hood. Price 47p. Issued 1975. Deleted
1977. 105mm. DC/P.

	£30	£15	£5

No. 228 Super Sprinter
Blue with metal hubs and rubber tyre Speediwheels.
Price 5/9. Issued 1970. Deleted 1972. 113mm.

	£30	£15	£5

No. 230 Talbot Lago
Light blue. Renumbering of 23K. Yellow '4'. Price 2/5.
Issued 1954. Deleted 1964. 103mm. DC/TP/RT.

	£100	£40	£20

No. 231 Maserati Racer
Red with white flash and white '9'. Renumbering of 23N.
Price 2/5. Issued 1954. Deleted 1964. 94mm. DC/RT/TP.

	£100	£40	£20

No. 232 Alfa Romeo Racer
Red with white '8' and driver cast in. Renumbering of
23F. Price 2/5. Issued 1954. Deleted 1964. 100mm.
DC/RT/TP.

	£140	£50	£25

No. 233 Cooper Bristol Racer
Green with driver cast in and white '6'. Renumbering of
23G. Price 2/5. Issued 1954. Deleted 1964. 89mm.
DC/TP/RT.

	£85	£40	£20

No. 234 Ferrari Racer
Blue with yellow '5' and driver cast in. Renumbering of
23H. Two varieties: the earlier has the nose all in yellow
and the later has a yellow triangle only. Issued 1954.
Deleted 1964. 101mm. DC/RT/TP.

Yellow nose	£100	£40	£20
Yellow triangle	£150	£60	£30

No. 235 HWM Racer
Green with yellow '7' and driver cast in. Renumbering of
23J. Price 2/5. Issued 1954. Deleted 1960. 99mm.
DC/RT/TP.

	£90	£40	£20

No. 236 Connaught Racer
Green with white number in circle. Price 3/6. Issued
December 1956. Deleted 1959. 96mm.
SW/D/DC/RT/TP.

	£80	£40	£20

No. 237 Mercedes Benz Racer
White or cream (worth double). Red '30'. Price 3/8.
Issued October 1956. Deleted 1969. 98mm.
SW/D/DC/RT/TP.

	£65	£30	£15

No. 238 Jaguar Type D Racing Car
Turquoise. When this model was released, Jaguar had
just won the Le Mans race for the third year running and
it was a great seller. Price 2/11. Issued September 1957.
Deleted 1965. 86mm. SW/D/DC/TP/RT.

	£100	£40	£20

No. 239 Vanwall Racer
Green with 'Vanwall' in white on sides and white '35'.
Price 2/11. Issued April 1958. Deleted 1964. 95mm.
DC/RT/TPS/WD.

	£110	£40	£20

No. 240 Cooper Racing Car
Blue with white stripes and white circles with racing
number. Cowling removable to show engine. Price 3/11.
Issued April 1963. Deleted 1970. 83mm.
SW/SS/WS/D/DC/RT/P.

	£40	£10	£5

No. 241 Lotus Racing Car
Green with white circles and racing number. Cowling
removable to show engine. Price 3/11. Issued 1963.
Deleted 1970. 83mm. SW/SS/WS/D/DC/RT/P.

	£40	£10	£5

No. 242 Ferrari Racing Car
Red with white circles and racing number. Cowling
removable to show engine. Wrap-round windscreen.
Larger than usual rear tyres (like those of the big car
itself). Price 3/11. Issued March 1963. Deleted 1971.
89mm. DC/RT/P/SW/SS/WS/D.

	£40	£10	£5

No. 243 BRM Racing Car
Metallic green with yellow engine cover of various
shades. Many shades tend to look like orange. Also blue
with dark blue engine cover (worth double). Removable
cowling to show engine and white circle with racing
number. Price 3/11. Issued April 1964. Deleted 1971.
83mm. SW/SS/WS/D/DC/RT/P.

No. 281 Pathé News Car
Black with opening rear doors and bonnet. Camera man
and camera with stand on roof. Price 9/11. Issued 1968.
Deleted 1970. 108mm. DC/P.

No. 340 Land Rover
Orange and green with green and cream interior. Also
red with green wheels and green interior plus driver
(worth more). Red or yellow plastic wheels, black plastic
steering wheel, blue plastic driver, seats and matching
wheels most of the time. Price 5/-. Issued 1967. Deleted
1971. 92mm. DC/P.

No. 340 Land Rover
Red body with any colour wheels.

No. 341 Land Rover Trailer
Orange, green or red. Price 2/11. Issued 1967. Deleted
1974. 79mm. DC/RT/P.
Orange or green
Red

No. 342 Austin Mini-Moke
Green with canopy. Speediwheels from 1972. Price 5/-.
Issued 1966. Deleted 1975. 73mm. DC/P.

No. 344 Estate Car
Fawn and brown. Renumbering of 27F. Price 2/11. Issued
1955. Deleted 1961. 105mm. DC/RT/TP.

No. 344 Land Rover
Medium blue with all-matching colour in back interior.
Cream or white interior of cab. Opening doors. Bonnet
opens to reveal silver engine. Metallic red model started
in 1973. Also green and two-tone green (rare). Price 7/11.
Issued 1970. Deleted 1978. 108mm.

	MB	MU	GC
No. 243 BRM Racing Car	£40	£10	£5
No. 281 Pathé News Car	£120	£50	£30
No. 340 Land Rover (orange and green)	50	£20	£10
No. 340 Land Rover (red body)	£50	£20	£10
No. 341 Land Rover Trailer — Orange or green	£30	£15	£5
No. 341 Land Rover Trailer — Red	£40	£20	£10
No. 342 Austin Mini-Moke	£35	£20	£10
No. 344 Estate Car	£55	£20	£10
Medium blue	£50	£25	£15
Metallic red	£40	£20	£10
Green	£60	£30	£15
Two-tone green	£125	£50	£20

No. 350 Tiny's Mini-Moke
Red and yellow with hole in canopy for the giraffe driver to put his head through. From the TV series The Enchanted House. Price 4/6. Issued 1970. Deleted 1973. 73mm. DC/P.

	MB	MU	GC
No. 350	£100	£30	£20

No. 475 Model T Ford
Medium blue and sky blue with yellow wheels, black chassis and mudguard. Gold headlights with radiator, grille and starting handle. One plastic male and one plastic female figure. Red interior seats. There is also a rare model with red body (worth treble). Price 8/11. Issued 1965. Deleted 1968. 79mm. DC/P.

£500 £250 £100

No. 476 1913 Morris Oxford
Yellow with blue chassis and black body with dark blue chassis (rare and worth treble). Canopy and driver. Red or black wheels. Price 8/11. Issued 1965. Deleted 1970. 92mm. DC/P.

£500 £200 £100

No. 477 Parsley's Car
Green and black with the friendly lion driver in plastic. From the TV series The Herbs. Price 11/3. Issued 1970. Deleted 1973. 92mm. DC/P.

£250 £100 £50

No. 485 Model T Ford with Santa Claus
Red and white with green Xmas motifs on doors, Santa Claus figure, sack of presents and tree. Price 9/11. Issued October 1964. Deleted 1968. 83mm. DC/RT/P.

£250 £100 £25

No. 486 Dinky Beats Car
Blue chassis with white or cream body and red wheels, with three figures in black, one with harmonica and the other two with guitars. Words like 'Kinky Gear' on sides. Price 9/11. Issued 1965. Deleted 1970. 92mm. D/DC/P.

£250 £100 £50

No. 518 Renault
Brown French Dinky toy imported into England for a few years. First issued in France in 1961. Available from 1962 until 1965, though toy was made in France until 1972, when grille was changed for a later one. There is nothing to distinguish the one imported into England except the price, if it is written on the box, from those available in France. This applies to all French Dinkies imported into England. Price 5/11. Issued July 1962. Deleted 1965. 85mm. SW/LHD/SS/FTS/S/W/DC/RT/TP/P.

£100 £50 £25

No. 524 Panhard 24C
Another French Dinky imported into England between 1965 and 1968, although made in France and sold between 1964 and 1970. Only available in England in metallic grey with red interior and shiny metal wheels. Issued in France in pale blue or white. With headlights and winding windows. Price 7/-. 100mm. DC/P.

	MB	MU	GC
Metallic grey	£250	£100	£50
Pale blue or white	£350	£150	£75

No. 535 2cv Citroën
Blue, also maroon with grey imitation canvas roof or very dark grey roof. Made in France from 1955 to 1965; from July 1962 imported into England where it was on sale for almost four years. Price 3/11. Deleted 1968. 88mm. DC/TP/RT.

	£250	£100	£50

No. 550 Chrysler Saratoga
Pink and white. Another model made in France from 1962 to 1965, and imported into England. There were models on sale in France in 1961, but it was only in limited numbers until the following year when supplies were made for England. Price 7/8. Deleted 1968. 129mm. SW/LHD/SS/FTS/S/W/DC/RT/TP/P.

	£250	£100	£50

No. 553 Peugeot 404
Light green. Made in France from 1961 to 1969; imported into England from July 1962. Price 7/11. Deleted 1967. 102mm. SW/LHD/SS/FTS/S/W/DC/RT/TP/P.

	£100	£50	£25

No. 555 Ford Thunderbird Convertible
White or red. Made in France from 1961 to 1969; imported into England from 1962. Price 7/8. Deleted 1967. 121mm. SW/LHD/D/SS/FTS/S/WS/DC/TP/RT/P.

	£150	£75	£50

STREET SIGNS, LETTERBOXES AND FURNITURE

No. 47 Road Signs

MODEL	MB	MU	GC
No. 12a GPO Pillar Box Red with 'Post Office', 'GR' and crown. Price 3d. Issued June 1935. Deleted 1940. 50mm high. DC. Box of six.	£75	—	—
No. 12b Air Mail Pillar Box Blue with 'Air Mail', 'GR' and crown. Price 3d. Issued June 1935. Deleted 1940. 50mm high. DC. Box of six.	£75	—	—
No. 12c Telephone Box Cream and silver. Price 4d. Issued April 1936. Deleted 1940. 62mm high. DC. Box of six.	£120	—	—
No. 12C Telephone Box Red and silver. Price 1/-. Issued 1948. Renumbered 750 in 1954. Deleted 1968. 58mm high. DC. Box of six.	£100	—	—
No. 46 Pavement Set Grey cardboard. Price 6d. Issued 1937. Deleted 1940.	£55	—	—
No. 46 Pavement Set Grey cardboard. Price 1/9. Issued 1948. Deleted 1950.	£30	—	—

No. 47 Road Signs
Set of 12. Black, white and red. Contains Nos. 47e 30-Mile Limit; 47f Derestriction; 47g School; 47h Steep Hill; 47k Bend; 47m Left Hand Corner; 47n Right Hand Corner; 47p Road Junction; 47q Right Hand Corner; 47r Main Road Ahead; 47s Crossing, No Gates; and 47t Roundabout. Price 1/6 (could also be bought in packets of two for 3d). Issued December 1935. Deleted 1940. DC.

£75 — —

No. 47 Road Signs
Set of 12. Contains Nos. 47E, 47F, 47G, 47H, 47K, 47M, 47N, 47P, 47Q, 47R, 47S and 47T. Made from pre-war castings. Price 2/3 (could also be bought in packets of two for 5d). Issued 1947. Deleted 1954.

£50 — —

No. 47a Four-Face Traffic Lights
Black and white. Price 3d. Issued June 1935. Deleted 1940. DC. Box of six.

£50 — —

No. 47A Four-Face Traffic Lights
Black and white. Price 4d. Issued 1947. Deleted 1954. 62mm high. DC. Box of six.

£50 — —

No. 47b Three-Face Traffic Lights
Price 3d. Issued 1935. Deleted 1940. DC. Box of six.

£50 — —

No. 48B Three-Face Traffic Lights
Price 4d. Issued 1947. Deleted 1954. Box of six.

£35 — —

No. 47c Two-Face Traffic Lights (Right Angle)
Black and white. Price 3d. Issued October 1935. Deleted 1940. DC. Box of six.

£55 — —

No. 47c Two-Face Traffic Lights (Back to Back)
Black and white. Price 3d. Issued August 1935. Deleted 1940. DC. Box of six.

£50 — —

No. 47C Two-Face Traffic Lights
Black and white. Price 4d. Issued 1947. Deleted 1954. DC. Box of six.

£45 — —

No. 47C Two-Face Traffic Signs (Back to Back)
Black and white. Price 4d. Issued 1947. Deleted 1954. DC. Box of six.

£35 — —

No. 47d Belisha Beacon (Safety)
Black, white and orange. Price 3d. Issued June 1935. Deleted 1940. Box of six.

£50 — —

No. 47D Belisha Beacon
Black, white and orange. Price 4d. Issued 1946. Deleted
1954. 51mm high. DC. Box of six. £35 — —

No. 750 Telephone Call Box
Red. Price 1/-. Renumbering of 12C in 1954. Deleted 1960.
58mm high. DC. Box of six. £75 — —

No. 753 Police Controlled Crossing
Grey base and black and white. Revolving policeman.
Price 3/6. Issued November 1962. Deleted 1967. 151mm.
P. £25 £10 £5

No. 754 Pavement Set
Cardboard. Vastly different from the pre-war set. Price
2/5. Issued November 1948. Deleted 1962. £15 £8 £4

No. 755 Lamp Standard Single Arm
Grey and fawn with diecast base and plastic standard.
Orange lights. Price 1/11. Issued March 1960. Deleted
1964. 145mm high. DC/P. £25 £10 £4

No. 756 Lamp Standard Double Arm
Grey and fawn or yellow and fawn with orange lights.
Price 2/6. Issued March 1960. Deleted 1964. 145mm high.
DC/P. £30 £10 £5

No. 760 Pillar Box
Red and black. Different casting from No. 12b, being
stouter and with the 'Post Office' sign above 'EIIR'. Price
10d. Issued July 1954. Deleted 1960. 42mm high. DC. Box
of six. £65 — —

No. 763 Posters for Road Hoardings
Six paper posters in various colours. Price 2/6. Issued
September 1959. Deleted 1964. £15 £8 £4

No. 764 Posters for Road Hoardings
Six more paper posters with self-adhesive labels in
various colours and adverts. Price 9d. Issued September
1959. Deleted 1963. £15 £8 £4

No. 765 Road Hoardings
Green plastic with 'David Allen & Sons Ltd', with six
posters. Price 3/3. Issued September 1959. Deleted 1964.
205mm. £15 £8 £4

No. 766 British Road Signs Country Set A
Set of six. Price 2/8. Issued 1960. Deleted 1964. £50 — —

No. 767 British Road Signs Country Set B
Set of six. Price 2/8. Issued 1960. Deleted 1964.   £35   —   —

No. 768 British Road Signs Town Set A
Set of six. Black, white and red. Price 2/8. Issued 1960.
Deleted 1964. Average height 55mm. DC.   £35   —   —

No. 769 British Road Signs Town Set B
Set of six. Black, white and red. Price 2/8. Issued 1960.
Deleted 1964. Average height 55mm. DC.   £35   —   —

No. 771 International Road Signs
Set of 12 signs in various colours. Price 3/9. Issued
August 1953. Deleted 1965. Average height 35–45mm.
DC.   £95   —   —

No. 772 British Road Signs
Set of 24 signs in various colours. Price 10/6. Issued 1959.
Deleted 1964. Average height 55mm. DC.   £125   —   —

No. 773 Four-Face Traffic Lights
Black and white. Same casting as No. 47A but without
orange beacon on top. Price 1/-. Issued 1959. Deleted
1963. 62mm high. DC. Never individually boxed.   —   £5   £2

No. 777 Belisha Beacon
Black, white and orange. Same casting as No. 47D but
without orange beacon on top. Price 8d. Issued 1962.
Deleted 1963. DC. Box of six.   £45   —   —

No. 787 Building Light Kit
Made for Dinky Toy Buildings. Price 2/11. Issued 1960.
Deleted 1964.   £15   £5   £2

No. 788 Spare Bucket for No. 966
Grey. Price 1/9. Issued December 1960. Deleted 1969.
68mm. DC/TP.   £10   £4   £2

No. 790 Imitation Granite Chippings
Made for Dinky Wagons and Hornby Dublo Railways.
Came in clear packets. Price 9d. Issued 1961. Deleted
1964. Packet only.   £5   —   —

No. 791 Imitation Coal
Made for Dinky Wagons. Came in clear packets. Price 9d.
Issued 1961. Deleted 1964. Packet only.   £5   —   —

No. 792 Packing Cases
Three packing cases and lids in fawn with 'Hornby
Dublo' on sides. Price 1/6. Issued 1960/61. Deleted 1969.
30 x 28 x 19mm. P.   £5   £3   £1

No. 793 Pallets
Packet of three. Orange. To be used with No. 930 Bedford
Pallet Jekta Van. Also used with No. 404. Price 1/11.
Issued 1960. Deleted 1969.   £10   —   —

No. 794 Loading Ramp
For the Pullmore Car Transporter. Price 1/6. Issued
December 1954 or January 1955. Renumbered 794 in 1960.
Deleted 1964.   £12   —   —

No. 846 Six Oil Drums
French Dinky import from 1960/61. Made in France 1959.
Equivalent price 1/4. Deleted 1970. Box of six.   £15   —   —

No. 847 Six Barrels
French Dinky import from 1960/61. Made in France 1959.
Equivalent price 1/4. Deleted 1970. Box of six.   £15   —   —

No. 849 Six Packing Cases
French Dinky import from 1960/61. Made in France 1959.
Equivalent price 1/4. Deleted 1970. Box of six.   £15   —   —

No. 850 Six Crates of Bottles
French Dinky import from 1960/61. Made in France 1959.
Equivalent price 1/4. Deleted 1970. Box of six.   £15   —   —

No. 851 Pairs Sets (Nos. 846, 847, 849 and 850)
Set of eight. French Dinky import from 1960/61. Made in
France in 1959. Equivalent price 1/6. Issued September
1961. Deleted 1970.   £15   —   —

No. 0036 1½-Volt Battery
Novelty collector's item to go with Nos. 276 and 277. Price
5d. Issued August 1962. Deleted 1964. Never individually
boxed.   —   £5   —

No. 0037 Red Lamp
Price 5d. Issued December 1962. Deleted 1964. Never
individually boxed.   —   £10   —

No. 0038 Blue Lamp
Novelty collector's item to go with No. 276. Price 10d.
Issued August 1962. Deleted 1964. Never individually
boxed.   —   £10   —

TAXIS

No. 40H   Austin Taxi

MODEL	MB	MU	GC
No. 36g Taxi with Driver Green. Promotional model for the Old London Cab Company. Sold or given away at several taxi stands to tourists. 'Taxi' cast on roof. Price 11d. Limited issue in 1938. Deleted 1938. 72mm. DC/RT. Never individually boxed.	—	£750	£300
No. 36g Taxi with Driver Yellow and black, light green and black, or royal blue and black. Open rear window. 'Taxi' cast on roof. Price 11d. Issued 1938. Deleted 1940. 72mm. DC/RT. Never individually boxed.	—	£95	£40
No. 36G Taxi with Open Rear Window Maroon and black, light green and black or dark green and black. 'Taxi' cast on roof. Price 2/6. Issued 1946. Deleted 1947. 72mm. DC/RT. Never individually boxed but packed in boxes of six.	—	£65	£35
No. 36G Taxi without Rear Window Maroon and black, light green and black or dark green and black. Also brown and black or red and black (rare colours worth treble). Price 2/9. Issued 1947. Deleted 1949. 72mm. DC/RT.	—	£55	£25

TAXIS	MB	MU	GC

No. 40H Austin Taxi
Blue or yellow. 'Taxi' sign on roof. Price 3/10. Issued
November 1951. Renumbered 254 in 1955. 94mm.
DC/RT. Early models never individually boxed but
packed in boxes of six.

Box of six	£850	—	—
Model without box	—	£125	£45
Model with box	£95	£50	£25

No. 115 UB Taxi
One of the last do or die efforts by Dinky in 1978 to try
and get some sales. Chassis was adapted from Nos. 475
and 485; and No. 109 Model T Ford and made for export
only. Boxes of 12 but packed in plain cardboard boxes.
Body with gold trim on all doors, bonnet and rear. 'Taxi'
on door in medium or dark blue. Solid yellow wheels and
black tyres. Price £1.35. Issued 1978. Deleted 1978. 86mm.
DC/P. Good investment considering it was the last taxi,
and one of the last models, ever made by Dinky. £150 £80 £30

No. 115 UB Taxi
Dark blue and black with yellow mudguards and solid
yellow wheels, gold headlights and radiator.
Promotional taxi issued by the Taxi Biscuit Company.
Another rather vain event to try and get Dinky out of
serious trouble near the end of 1979. One had to collect
biscuit wrappers to acquire this model and therefore
there is no original price, but it has a high value in the
collector's world since it is quite rare. Issued and deleted
1979. 86mm. DC/P. If the box has a 25th Anniversary of
the Coronation and is franked by an official GPO stamp,
the model is worth more.

Normal GPO stamped box	£150	—	—
Coronation stamped box	£350	—	—

No. 120 Happy Cab
Made from same mould as UB Taxi. Solid wheels in
yellow with yellow mudguard, gold radiator and
bumper. Base of body is white with upper part in light
blue with white roof and 'Happy Cab' in blue, red and
yellow. Decked with flowers on bonnet and sides. Price
£1.35. Issued 1978. Deleted 1980. 86mm. DC. £65 £20 £10

No. 254 Austin Taxi
Dark blue or yellow. 'Taxi' sign on roof. Price 3/5. Issued
1954. Deleted 1956. 94mm. DC/RT. £65 £30 £15

No. 254 Austin Taxi Two-Tone
Green and yellow. 'Taxi' sign on roof. Price 3/5. Issued
January 1956. Deleted 1962/63. 94mm. DC/RT. £75 £45 £20

TAXIS	MB	MU	GC

No. 254 Austin Taxi
Black with silver hubs. This was the last issue of No. 254.
Price 4/11. Issued 1960. Deleted 1961. 94mm. DC/RT.   £275   £100   £50

No. 265 Plymouth US Taxi with Windows
Yellow and mustard with dark or medium red roof. 'Taxi'
sign on roof and fare information on sides. Price 5/9.
Issued October 1960. Deleted 1964. Replaced by No. 266
in 1965. 108mm. DC/TP/P/RT/LHD/SW/SS/S/W.   £75   £35   £15

No. 266 Plymouth Metro Cab
Yellow with red roof. Canadian version of No. 265. '450
Metro Cab' on doors. Price 5/11. Issued 1965. Deleted
1967. 108mm. DC.   £75   £35   £15

No. 268 Renault Dauphine Mini-Cab
Red with windows and adverts. This was French Dinky
casting Nos. 24E/524 but with English wheels and
baseplate. Mini-cab version made only in England. Price
3/3. Issued June 1962. Deleted 1967. 12mm.
DC/TP/P/RT.   £65   £30   £15

No. 278 Plymouth Yellow Cab
Bright yellow with red interior. 'Yellow Cab' transfers on
doors and roof sign plus aerial. Price £1.49. Issued 1978.
Deleted 1980. 134.5mm. DC/RT/P.   £75   £30   £15

No. 282 Austin 1800 Taxi
Medium blue with red interior and 'Taxi' sign on roof.
White opening bonnet and boot. Price 6/11. Issued 1966.
Deleted 1969. 101mm.   £65   £30   £15

No. 284 London Taxi
Black with silver trim and opening doors. All-plastic
Speediwheels. Metal wheels and rubber tyre
Speediwheels from 1978. Price £1.25. Issued 1972. Deleted
1980. 112mm.   £65   £30   £15

No. 284/SJ Silver Jubilee Taxi Special
Silver with royal crest on the doors. Issued in 1977 to
commemorate the Silver Jubilee. Only a limited number
were made available and were soon snapped up by
tourists and eager collectors. Price £1.55. 112mm. DC/P.
Very rare and a good investment.   £150   £75   £35

TRAINS

No. 19 Mixed Goods Train Set

MODEL	MB	MU	GC
No. 16 LNER Train Set Price 4/11. Issued 1946. Deleted 1950.	£100	£50	£25
No. 16 Silver Jubilee Set Price 1/6. Issued 1935. Deleted 1940.	£100	£50	£25
No. 16 Train Set in British Rail Colours Price 12/6. Issued 1954. Deleted 1959.	£150	£75	£25
No. 16z Streamlined Diesel Articulated Train Imported French Dinky in 1935. Price 2/11. Deleted 1940.	£95	£50	£25
No. 17 Diecast Passenger Train Set Contains miniature diecast model No. 17A Locomotive and Tender with a Coach and Guards Van. Price 2/3. Issued 1935. Deleted 1940.	£65	£30	£15
No. 18 Goods Train Set Contains tank locomotive and three wagons. Price 1/9. Issued 1935. Deleted 1940.	£65	£30	£15
No. 19 Mixed Goods Train Set Contains tank locomotive, wagon, petrol tanker and lumber wagon. Price 1/11. Issued 1935. Deleted 1940.	£75	£40	£20
No. 20 Passenger Train Set Contains tank locomotive, two coaches and guard's van. Price 2/6. Issued 1935. Deleted 1940.	£150	£75	£35

TRAINS	MB	MU	GC
No. 21 Modelled Miniatures Set Price 1/11. Issued 1935. Deleted 1940.	£145	£75	£25
No. 26 GWR Rail Car Red with cream roof. Runs on small plastic bobbins. Price 6d. Issued April 1934. Deleted 1948. 106mm. DCP. Never individually boxed.	—	£125	£45
No. 26z Diesel Rail Car Cream and orange or white and yellow. Runs on small bobbin stand. Price 5d. Issued in France 1934. Imported from France 1937. Deleted 1940.	—	£125	£45
No. 784 Dinky Goods Train Set Non-motorised and no track required but may be used on OO or HO track. Blue engine with 'GER' on side, 115mm long. Yellow truck and red trucks, each 92mm long. Price £1.55. Issued 1972. Deleted 1975.	£55	£30	£15
No. 798 Express Passenger Set Price 10/6. Issued 1954. Deleted 1959.	£75	£50	£20

VANS

No. 514   Spratts Guy Van

Many of these models were never individually boxed. Hence only prices for mint unboxed and good condition are given in such instances.

Many vans were used as promotional items by companies and show organisers as well as by various toy shops etc., and two of the favourite Dinky products for this purpose were the '407' and the '410' series. Regardless of what name the van may have connected with it and whatever colour schemes are introduced, whether by individuals or by Dinky itself, the models are worthwhile investments. No one can say definitely what is worth paying in this field. Therefore, I have set out my own prices for these models combined with my extensive experience and research. Any model is worth only whatever a collector will pay for it, but any collector should get the indicated prices for the promotional items. Please feel free to write to me c/o the publishers about any model you may have. I will be pleased to give private valuations to any person who may wish to have them.

MODEL	MB	MU	GC
No. 14z Three Wheeled Delivery Van			
Green with opening and driver cast in. White tyres in rubber stamped 'Dunlop'. Made in France from 1935 to 1939 with black or white Dunlop tyres on metal hubs. From 1940 to 1949 made with all-metal wheels and from 1950 to 1952 with black 'M' tyres. Price 10d. First version only imported 1937/40. 70mm. DC/RT.			
First version	—	£125	£50
Second version	—	£95	£35
Third version	—	£65	£25

No. 22d Delivery Van

Various colours schemes, of which the best known are grey or blue and blue and yellow two-tone with no headlights on tinplate radiator. Metal wheels. Two distinct types of model: Hornby series between December 1933 and April 1934, and Dinky from 1935 to 1936. Price 8d. 83mm. DC/TP.

First version	—	£650	£250
Second version	—	£550	£150

No. 22d Delivery Van with Morris Cab

Meccano type in green with 'Meccano Engineering for Boys' on sides in gold and red or blue and yellow with red lettering on sides (extremely rare). Metal wheels and tinplate radiator without headlights. Strictly speaking, this model is of the '28' series Type 1 class as it appeared in the '28/2' Dinky set of delivery vans. Although Gibson actually mentions the '28' Type 1 vans as having rubber tyres on metal hubs, as distinct from the '22' series van, which had solid metal wheels, I dispute this. All the '26' Type 1 vans I have come across and valued have had the same solid metal wheels as the '22' series and are definitely cast in lead. Consequently, no fatigue is possible. With regard to the Meccano van, I would be surprised if many collectors have the model in blue and yellow as these were snapped up a very fortunate few. I have seen only one. This is one of the most precious items in the whole Dinky range. Price 9d. Issued May 1934. Deleted 1936. 83mm. DC/TP. Sold in a set of six as well as being sold in the '28/2' set of six.

Green	—	£550	£350
Blue and yellow	—	£1000	£500

No. 25b Meccano Covered Wagon

Gold with red on sides. 'Meccano Engineering for Boys' in black. Open chassis and diecast radiator with lights as Type 2. Price 6d. Issued 1938/39. Deleted 1940. Reissued 1946. Deleted 1956. 105mm. DC/TP/RT.

Pre-war	—	£1750	£450
Post-war	—	£750	£300

No. 25f Market Gardener's Van

Although I use the term 'van', this model is an open lorry with slatted sides and its successor is called a farm produce wagon. Various colours, including dark blue, light green, dark green and very dark green (quite rare and worth double). Black open chassis and tinplate radiator without lights as Type 1. Price 9d. Issued April 1934. Deleted October 1938. 107mm. DC/QT/TP.

	—	£350	£150

No. 25f Market Gardener's Van
Yellow body. Open green or black chassis with diecast
radiator and lights as Type 2. Type 2 trucks also appeared
briefly after the war in 1946 until they were replaced by
Type 3, where only the axle thicknesses were different.
Price 9d. Issued 1938. Deleted 1940. 105mm. DC/RT.

Pre-war	—	£200	£100
Post-war	—	£150	£75

No. 25F Market Gardener's Van
Green with plain black chassis and diecast radiator with
lights as Type 3. Price 9d. Issued 1946. Deleted 1947.
110mm. DC/RT.

	—	£75	£25

No. 25F Market Gardener's Van
Yellow with black moulded chassis, bumper and diecast
radiator with lights as Type 4. Price 9d. Issued 1947.
Deleted 1950. 110mm. DC/RT.

	—	£65	£15

No. 28a Delivery Van
See No. 22d Delivery Van with Morris Cab for general
details on '28' series. 'Hornby Trains British and
Guaranteed' in gold on sides and Hornby train in yellow.
Type 1 has tinplate radiator. Price 9d. Issued April 1934.
Deleted 1936. 84mm. Type 2 is a Ford 7 model with rubber
tyres and cast in Zamac so suffers badly from fatigue.
Divide price by five for fatigued examples in mint
unboxed or good condition. Price 6d. Issued August 1935.
Deleted 1938. 81mm. Both models DC/RT/TP.

Type 1	—	£550	£350
Type 2	—	£750	£200

No. 28a Delivery Van
Yellow. 'Golden Shred Marmalade' with design in red
and blue. Price 6d. Issued April 1936. Deleted 1940.
84mm. DC/RT/TP.

	—	£750	£250

No. 28b Delivery Van, Pickfords Type 1
Blue with 'Pickfords Removals and Storage. 'Over 100
Branches' in gold. Price 9d. Issued 1934. Deleted 1936.
84mm. DC/RT.

	—	£750	£250

No. 28b Delivery Van, Pickfords Type 2
Blue with words as on Type 1. Price 6d. Issued 1935.
Deleted 1938. 81mm. DC/RT.

	—	£550	£250

No. 28b Delivery Van, Seccotine Type 2
Blue with 'Seccotine Sticks Everything' in gold. Price 6d.
Issued 1936. Deleted 1940. 81mm. DC/RT.

	—	£550	£250

VANS	MB	MU	GC

No. 28b Delivery Van, Bedford Seccotine Type 3
Words as on Type 2. Price 6d. Issued early 1939. Deleted
late 1939. 83mm. DC/RT. Liable to fatigue.

	—	£450	£200

No. 28c Delivery Van, Manchester Guardian Type 1
Red and brown with 'Manchester Guardian' in gold.
Price 9d. Issued April 1934. Deleted August 1935. 84mm.
DC/RT

	—	£800	£350

No. 28c Delivery Van, Manchester Guardian Type 2
Brown or reddish brown (worth double). Words as on
Type 1. Price 9d. Issued August 1935. Deleted 1940.
84mm. DC/RT.

	—	£450	£200

No. 28d Delivery Van, Oxo Type 1
Blue with 'Oxo, Beef in Brief' on the left side and 'Oxo,
Beef at Its Best' on the right side in gold. Made in very
small production numbers and being more expensive
were found in middle class homes only. Very hard to find
in perfect condition. Price 9d. Issued April 1934. Deleted
August 1935. 81mm. DC/RT.

	—	£1000	£350

No. 28d Delivery Van, Oxo Type 2
Blue with words as on Type 1. Price 6d. Issued August
1935. Deleted 1939. 81mm. DC/RT.

	—	£450	£200

No. 28d Delivery Van, Oxo Type 3
Blue with words as on Types 1 and 2. Price 6d. Issued
1939. Deleted 1940. 83mm. DC/RT.

	—	£350	£200

No. 28e Delivery Van, Ensign Type 1
Grey and dark green with 'Ensign Cameras' on each side
and photograph of camera on doors. Other colours exist.
Price 9d. Issued and deleted 1934. Few models issued in
Type 2 range but most destroyed in warehouse fire.
84mm. DC/RT/TP.

	—	£900	£350

No. 28e Delivery Van, Firestone Type 1
Dark blue with 'Firestone Tyres' in red. Price 9d. Issued
September 1934. Deleted August 1935. 84mm. DC/RT.

	—	£700	£300

No. 28e Delivery Van, Firestone Type 2
Dark blue with words as on Type 1. Price 6d. Issued
August 1935. Deleted 1939. 81mm. DC/RT.

	—	£450	£200

No. 28e Delivery Van, Firestone Type 3
Dark blue. Price 6d. Issued 1939. Deleted 1940. 83mm.
DC/RT.

	—	£450	£200

No. 28f Delivery Van, Palethorpes Type 1
Light green with 'Palethorpes Royal Cambridge' on sides
and design 'Palethorpes Model Factory Tipton' on rear.
Price 9d. Issued April 1934. Deleted August 1935. 84mm.
DC/RT.   —   £650   £350

No. 28f Delivery Van, Palethorpes Type 2
Light green with words as on Type 1. Price 6d. Issued
August 1935. Deleted 1937. 81mm. DC/RT.   —   £450   £250

No. 28f Delivery Van, Virol Type 2
Yellow with 'Give Your Child a Virol Constitution' and
Virol design on sides. Price 6d. Issued 1937. Deleted 1940.
81mm. DC/RT.   —   £450   £200

No. 28g Delivery Van, Kodak Type 1
Red and blue with 'Use Kodak Film' and 'To be Sure' on
sides etc. Price 9d. Issued May 1934. Deleted August 1935.
84mm. DC/RT.   —   £950   £350

No. 28g Delivery Van, Kodak Type 2
Yellow with words as on Type 1. Price 6d. Issued August
1935. Deleted 1939. 84mm. DC/RT.   —   £350   £200

No. 28g Delivery Van, Kodak Type 3
Yellow with words as on Types 1 and 2. Price 6d. Issued
May 1939. Deleted 1940. 83mm. DC/RT.   —   £450   £250

No. 28h Delivery Van, Sharps Type 1
Blue or black and white with 'Sharps Toffees' in gold.
Other colours do exist, but I have seen only those listed.
Price 9d. Issued 1934. Deleted 1935. 84mm. DC/RT.   —   £850   £350

No. 28h Delivery Van, Dunlop Type 2
Red with 'Dunlop Tyres' in gold on sides. Price 6d. Issued
August 1935. Deleted 1939. 81mm. DC/RT.   —   £450   £250

No. 28h Delivery Van, Dunlop Type 3
Red with words as on Type 2. Price 6d. Issued 1939.
Deleted 1940. 83mm. DC/RT.   —   £350   £200

No. 28k Delivery Van, Marsh's Type 2
Dark green with 'Marsh's Sausages' and gold design.
Price 6d. Issued August 1935. Deleted 1939. 81mm.
DC/RT.   —   £800   £350

No. 28k Delivery Van, Marsh's Type 3
Dark green with words and design as on Type 2. Price 6d.
Issued 1939. Deleted 1940. 83mm. DC/RT.   —   £450   £250

| --- | --- | --- | --- |

No. 281 Delivery Van, Ensign Cameras Type 1
Black with design and 'Ensign Cameras' in red and gold
on sides. Price 9d. Issued April 1934. Deleted 1934/35.
84mm. DC/RT. — £900 £350

No. 281 Delivery Van, Crawfords Type 1
Red with 'Crawfords Biscuits' in gold. Price 9d. Issued
May 1934. Deleted 1935. 84mm. DC/RT. — £900 £350

No. 281 Delivery Van, Crawfords Type 2
Red or very dark red (rare and worth double). Words as
on Type 1. Price 6d. Issued 1935. Deleted 1939. 81mm.
DC/RT. — £450 £250

No. 281 Delivery Van, Crawfords Type 3
Dark red with words as on Type 2. Price 6d. Issued 1939.
Deleted 1940. 83mm. DC/RT. — £350 £200

No. 28m Delivery Van, Wakefield's Type 1
Green with 'Wakefield's Castrol Motor Oil' in red. Price
9d. Issued May 1934. Deleted 1935. 84mm. DC/RT. — £1300 £500

No. 28m Delivery Van, Wakefield's Type 2
Green with words as on Type 1. Price 6d. Issued August
1935. Deleted 1939. 81mm. DC/RT. — £450 £250

No. 28m Delivery Van, Wakefield's Type 3
Green or dark green (worth more). Price 6d. Issued 1939.
Deleted 1940. 83mm. DC/RT. — £350 £200

No. 28n Delivery Van, Marsh & Baxters Type 1
Green with 'Marsh & Baxters Sausages Make a Fine
Meal'. Price 9d. Issued May 1934. Deleted 1935. 84mm.
DC/RT. — £800 £350

No. 28n Delivery Van, Atco Type 2
Green and dark green with 'Atco Sales and Service' in
gold and 'Motor Mowers' in red. Price 6d. Issued August
1935. Deleted 1938. 81mm. DC/RT. — £500 £200

No. 28o Delivery Van, Raleigh Type 2
Green or green with black roof (worth more). With
'Raleigh – the All Steel Bicycle'. Price 6d. Issued 1936.
Deleted 1937. 81mm. DC/RT. — £650 £350

No. 28p Delivery Van, Crawfords Type 2
Maroon with 'Crawfords Biscuits' in gold. Price 6d.
Issued August 1935. Deleted 1936. 81mm. DC/RT. — £500 £200

No. 28r Delivery Van, Swans Type 2
Black with 'Swans Pens' and design in gold. Price 6d.
Issued May 1936. Deleted 1939. 81mm. DC/RT. — £500 £200

No. 28r Delivery Van, Swans Type 3
Black with words and design as on Type 2. Price 6d.
Issued April 1939. Deleted 1940. 83mm. DC/RT. — £450 £200

No. 28s Delivery Van, Fry's Type 2
Dark brown or chocolate with 'Fry's Chocolate' and
design in gold. Price 6d. Issued May 1936. Deleted 1940.
81mm. DC/RT. — £650 £350

No. 28t Delivery Van, Ovaltine Type 2
Red with 'Drink Ovaltine for Health' in green and black.
Price 6d. Issued May 1936. Deleted 1939. 81mm. DC/RT. — £650 £350

No. 28t Delivery Van, Ovaltine Type 3
Red with words as on Type 2. Price 6d. Issued 1939.
Deleted 1940. 83mm. DC/RT. — £450 £200

No. 28u Delivery Van, Carter's Type 2
Red or black with 'Carter's Little Liver Pills' and design.
Price 6d. Issued May 1936. Deleted 1937. 81mm. DC/RT.
Very rare. — £650 £350

No. 28v Delivery Van, Rington's Type 2
Black with 'Rington's Tea' in green and gold. Specially
produced for the Rington's Tea Company at Newcastle
upon Tyne and is extremely rare. Price 6d. Issued 1936.
81mm. DC/RT. — £650 £350

No. 28w Delivery Van, Osram Type 2
Yellow with 'Osram Lamps, a GEC Product'. Price 6d.
Issued May 1936. Deleted 1939. 81mm. DC/RT. — £650 £350

No. 28w Delivery Van, Osram Type 3
Yellow with words as on Type 2. Price 6d. Issued 1939.
Deleted 1940. 83mm. DC/RT. — £450 £200

No. 28x Delivery Van, Hovis Type 2
White with 'Hovis' in gold. Price 6d. Issued May 1936.
Deleted 1939. 81mm. DC/RT. — £650 £350

No. 28y Delivery Van, Exide Type 2
Red with 'Drydex Batteries' on left side and 'Exide
Batteries' on right side in gold. Price 6d. Issued May 1936.
Deleted 1940. 81mm. DC/RT. — £650 £350

No. 28y Delivery Van, Bentalls Type 3
Green with yellow sides and cream roof. With 'Bentalls
Kingston upon Thames Phone Kin 1001'. Price 6d. Issued
July 1936. Deleted 1940. 81mm. DC/RT. Very rare.

	MB	MU	GC
	—	£650	£350

No. 30e Bedford Breakdown Van
Red, green or grey with black wings. Also blue with dark
blue wings. Open window in cab (briefly) post-war; only
the axle thicknesses differ. Wire hook on crane. Price 9d.
Issued August 1935. Deleted 1940. Reissued 1946. Deleted
1948.

	MB	MU	GC
Pre-war	—	£500	£250
Post-war	£450	£300	£100

No. 30V NCB Electric Dairy Van
Cream and red. Price 3/6. Issued 1949. Renumbered 491
in 1954. Deleted 1960. 85mm. DC/RT. Rarer of the two
dairy vans.

	MB	MU	GC
	£450	£300	£100

No. 30V Express Electric Dairy Van
Grey and blue or red and cream (worth double). 'Express
Dairy' on nose. Price 3/-. Issued April 1951. Renumbered
490 in 1954. Deleted 1956. 85mm. DC/RT.

	MB	MU	GC
	£250	£100	£50

No. 31 Holland Coachcraft Van
Blue or green with white line trim and rubber tyres.
'Holland Coachcraft Registered Design' in gold. Price 6d.
Issued January 1935. Deleted 1940. 88mm. DC/RT. One
of the rarest models ever produced by Dinky.

	MB	MU	GC
Single	—	£1000	£400
Box of six	£5000	—	—

No. 31A Esso 15cwt Trojan Van
Red with 'Esso' on sides. Price 2/6. Issued February 1951.
Renumbered 450 in 1954. Deleted 1957. 85mm.
DC/RT/TP. This model was the reason why many more
people turned to collecting diecast toys.

	MB	MU	GC
	£500	£200	£100

No. 31B Dunlop 15cwt Trojan Van
Red with 'Dunlop the World's Master Tyre' on sides.
Price 2/6. Issued June 1952. Deleted 1957. 85mm.
DC/RT/TP.

	MB	MU	GC
	£300	£100	£50

No. 31C Chivers 15cwt Trojan Van
Green with 'Chivers Jellies' and design on sides. Price
2/6. Issued October 1953. Renumbered 452 in 1954.
Deleted 1957. 85mm. DC/RT/TP.

	MB	MU	GC
	£300	£150	£50

No. 31D Oxo 15cwt Trojan Van
Blue with 'Beefy Oxo' on sides. Price 2/2. Issued October 1953. Deleted 1954. 85mm. DC/RT/TP. Model never had an individual box but was delivered to shops in boxes of six as initially were the other Trojan models; these only went into boxes from 1954, most of which are dual numbered.

— £500 £150

No. 33d Hornby Box Van Trailer
Green with 'Hornby Trains. British and Guaranteed' in gold on sides. Price 8d. Issued 1936. Deleted 1938. 70mm. DC/RT/TP.

Trailer only	—	£350	£100
With matching tug	—	£350	£100

No. 33d Meccano Box Van Trailer
Green with 'Meccano Engineering for Boys' in black, green and gold on sides. Price 8d. Issued 1938. Deleted 1939. 70mm. DC/RT/TP.

Trailer only	—	£350	£100
With matching tug	—	£400	£150

No. 33r GWR Mechanical Horse
Brown with grey or cream roof. GWR motif and '2742' on sides. Price 1/6. Issued October 1935. Deleted 1940. 65mm. DC/RT.

— £250 £75

No. 33r GWR Trailer Van
Brown with cream roof. GWR motif and 'Express Cartage Services' on sides. Price 1/6. Issued October 1935. Deleted 1940. 70mm. DC/RT/TP.

Trailer only	—	£250	£75
With GWR mechanical trailer	—	£450	£150

No. 33r SR Mechanical Horse
Green with black or white roof. '3016 M' on sides. Price 1/6. Issued October 1935. Deleted 1940. 65mm. DC/RT.

— £750 £250

No. 33r SR Trailer Van
Green and black. 'Southern Railway' and 'Express Parcels Service' on sides. Price 1/6. Issued October 1935. Deleted 1940. 70mm. DC/RT/TP.

— £350 £150

No. 33r LMS Mechanical Horse
Brown with black roof. LMS and '2246' on sides. Price 1/6. Issued October 1935. Deleted 1940. 65mm. DC/RT.

— £500 £150

No. 33r LMS Trailer Van
Brown and black with 'LMS' on sides. Price 1/-. Issued
October 1935. Deleted 1940. 70mm. DC/RT/TP.

Trailer only	—	£250	£100
With LMS mechanical horse	—	£450	£150

No. 33r LNER Mechanical Horse
Blue with black roof. 'LNER' on sides. Price 1/6. Issued
1935. Deleted 1940. 65mm. DC/RT.

	—	£250	£100

No. 33r LNER Trailer Van
Blue and black with 'LNER' on sides. Price 1/6. Issued
October 1935. Deleted 1940. 70mm. DC/RT/TP.

Trailer only	—	£150	£50
With LNER mechanical horse	—	£400	£100

No. 34a Royal Air Mail Service Car
Blue with 'Royal Air Mail Services' on sides. Price 6d.
Issued October 1935. Deleted 1938. 83mm. DC/RT.

	—	£350	£100

No. 34b Royal Mail Van
Red and black with 'Royal Mail GR' and Crown on sides.
Pre-war and early post-war models have open windows.
Set of 12. Price 10d. Issued 1938. Deleted 1940. 83mm.
DC/RT/TP.

Pre-war	—	£300	£100
Early post-war	—	£200	£75

No. 34B Royal Mail Van
Office livery and designs with 'Royal Mail GR' and
Crown on sides. No rear windows. Price 2/2. Issued 1948.
Deleted 1952. 83mm. DC/RT/TP.

	—	£30	£12

No. 34C Loudspeaker Van
Brown with black speakers; grey with black speakers; or
blue with silver speakers. Wheel colour is normally as
speaker colour. Also green with black speakers and black
wheels (rare). Price 2/2. Issued February 1948.
Renumbered 492 in 1945. Deleted 1957. 81mm. DC/RT.
Not individually boxed until number change.

Brown with black speakers	—	£150	£50
Grey with black speakers	—	£120	£40
Blue with silver speakers	—	£125	£30
Green with black speakers	—	£500	£150

No. 255 Mersey Tunnel Police Van
Red with 'Mersey Tunnel' on sides in yellow and orange
and 'Police' on roof. Price 2/10. Issued September 1955.
Deleted 1961. 77mm. DC/TP/RT.

	£250	£100	£50

No. 260 Royal Mail Van
Red with black roof. 'Royal Mail' on sides and Crown and
post office designs on sides. Price 2/10. Issued 1955.
Deleted 1961. 78mm. DC/TP/RT.

| | £250 | £100 | £50 |

No. 261 Telephone Service Van
Green with black roof and grey ladder. 'Post Office
Telephones' on door and Crown on sides. Price 2/10.
Issued March 1956. Deleted 1961. 73mm. DC/RT/TP.
Good investment.

| | £200 | £100 | £50 |

No. 262 Volkswagen Swiss Postal Van
Yellow and black with PTT crest on sides. Made for sale
only in Switzerland, although many models were bought
by holidaymakers and brought back to other countries.
Casting as No. 181 which was a Volkswagen saloon, but
this is the best section for this somewhat confusing
model. Equivalent price 5/11. Issued 1956/59. 90mm.
DC/TP/RT.

| | £500 | £150 | £75 |

No. 273 RAC Patrol Van
Blue RAC livery with red seats. 'Road Service' and RAC
badge on sides. Opening rear doors with RAC sign and
motif on roof. Early versions had blue emblem, and later
versions had white and blue emblems. Price 5/-. Issued
1965. Deleted 1970. 78mm. DC/RT.

| Early version | £250 | £100 | £50 |
| Later version | £200 | £100 | £50 |

No. 274 AA Patrol Mini-Van
Yellow and black with AA patrol wording and livery. As
with No. 273, there were two colour schemes: early
versions had all-over yellow with crested emblem, while
later versions had yellow van with white roof and square
emblem which came into production in 1968/69. Price
4/11. Issued July 1964. Deleted 1973. 78mm. DC/P/RT.

| Early version | £250 | £150 | £50 |
| Later version | £100 | £75 | £50 |

No. 275 Brinks Armoured Car
Grey and blue. Tinted green with two drivers and
opening side and rear doors with 'Brinks Security Service
1859'. Crates and imitation gold bars. Price 12/11. Issued
November 1964. Deleted 1969. 120mm.
DC/RT/SW/LHD/SS/S/W.

| | £650 | £250 | £75 |

No. 275 Brinks Armoured Car (Reissue)
Darker shade of grey than previous with a yellow tint.
Otherwise as above. Made specially for US market.
Equivalent price £2.25. Issued 1979. Deleted 1980.

| | £200 | £100 | £50 |

No. 280 Delivery Van, Type 3
Pre-war issue of the 28/280 Van Type 3, which was a
Bedford. Never had any advertising connected with it
after the war. No rear window. Price 1/-. Issued 1937.
Deleted 1940. 83mm. DC/RT.

— £250 £100

No. 280a Delivery Van, Viyella Type 2
Light blue with 'Viyella for the Nursery' in black and
white. Price 6d. Issued 1937. Deleted 1940. 81mm.
DC/RT.

— £2000 £500

No. 280a Delivery Van, Viyella Type 3
Light blue with words as on Type 2. Price 6d. Issued 1937.
Deleted 1940. 81mm. DC/RT.

— £2000 £500

No. 280b Delivery Van, Lyons Type 2
Dark blue with 'Lyons Tea' in orange and 'Always the
Best' in white. Price 6d. Issued 1937. Deleted 1940. 81mm.
DC/RT.

— £1500 £250

No. 280b Delivery Van, Hartley's Type 3
Cream with 'Hartley's is Real Jam'. Price 6d. Issued 1939.
Deleted 1940. 83mm. DC/RT.

— £1750 £300

No. 280c Delivery Van, Shredded Wheat Type 2
Cream with 'Shredded Wheat' on a red band and
'Welwyn Garden City, Herts' on side. Price 6d. Issued
1937. Deleted 1940.

— £2500 £350

No. 280d Delivery Van, Bisto Type 2
Yellow with 'Ah! Bisto' and design. Price 6d. Issued 1937.
Deleted 1938. 81mm. DC/RT. Rarer of the two Bisto vans.

— £2500 £350

No. 280d Delivery Van, Bisto Type 2
Yellow with 'Bisto' and design. Price 6d. Issued 1938.
Deleted 1940. 81mm. DC/RT.

— £1500 £250

No. 280e Delivery Van, Ekco Type 2
Green with 'Ekco Radio' in gold. Price 6d. Issued 1937.
Deleted 1940. 81mm. DC/RT.

— £1000 £200

**No. 280e Delivery Van, Yorkshire Evening News
Type 2**
Cream with 'Yorkshire Evening News, the Original Buff'
in black and gold. Price 6d. Issued 1938. Deleted 1939.
81mm. DC/RT.

— £2000 £250

No. 280e Delivery Van, Yorkshire Evening Post Type 3
Dark cream and cream with 'Yorkshire Evening Post'.
Price 6d. Issued 1939. Deleted 1940. 83mm. DC/RT.

— £1500 £250

No. 280f Delivery Van, Mackintosh's Type 2
Red with 'Mackintosh's Toffee'. Price 6d. Issued 1937.
Deleted 1940. 81mm. DC/RT.

| | — | £2000 | £350 |

No. 390 Customised Transit Van
Metallic blue with black, red and yellow stick-on
transfers (vampire plus flashes etc.). Black, grille,
chromed wide wheels, 'Side-Winder' exhaust pipes and
casting as Nos. 269, 274 and 417. Price £1.55. Issued 1978.
Deleted 1980. 133mm. DC/P.

| | £85 | £35 | £15 |

No. 407 Kenwood Ford Transit Van
Blue with white roof and 'Kenwood' on sides etc. Price
9/11. Issued 1966. Replaced in 1970 by No. 407 with
'Telefusion'. Deleted 1978. 122mm. DC/P.

| | £250 | £75 | £50 |

No. 407 Ford Transit Van
White with 'Colour TV' in colour on black strip.
'Telefusion' in black or 'T' in white on red. Price 9/11.
Issued 1970. Deleted and replaced in 1971 by No. 407 with
'Hertz Truck Rental'. Deleted 1978. 122mm. DC/P. Rare.

| | £300 | £100 | £50 |

No. 407 Ford Transit Van
Red or yellow body with 'Hertz Truck Rental' in black or
gold. Only available in prototype or Action Kit No. 1025
but still collectable in the promotional series. Price £1.55.
Issued 1972. Deleted 1978. 122mm. DC/P.

| | £250 | £75 | £40 |

No. 407 Ford Transit Van
Two-tone red with red interior and 'Avis Van Rental'.
Also made from Action Kit No. 1925. Price £1.55. Issued
1972. Deleted 1981. 122mm. DC/P.

| | £250 | £75 | £35 |

No. 410 Royal Mail Bedford Van
Red with silver bumpers, black hubs and white cab
interior. The first of the Bedfords made by Dinky itself as
a promotional model. Price £1.25. Issued 1972. Deleted
1980. 90mm. DC/P.

| | £500 | £150 | £75 |

No. 410 Promotional Bedford Van
Blue with 'John Menzies'. Genuine promotional model
sold only by John Menzies. Price £1.25. Issued 1974.
Deleted 1974. 90mm. DC/P.

| | £350 | £100 | £50 |

No. 410 Promotional Bedford Van
White with red or white interior. 'OCL' on sides. Price
£1.25. Issued and deleted 1975. 90mm. DC/P.

| | £350 | £100 | £50 |

No. 410 Promotional Bedford Van
Grey with white or grey interior. Rare as there were only 150 with 'Opel' made specially for a French collector. Issued and deleted 1975. 90mm. DC/P.   £750   £250   £100

No. 410 Promotional Bedford Van
Made specially for the French and US markets with 'Carter' on sides. Promotional model in the presidential election campaign for Jimmy Carter and although some early models were out in 1975 the majority were on sale in 1976. Very rare as only 100 were made. Price £2. Issued 1975/76. Deleted almost at once. 90mm. DC/P.   £700   £250   £100

No. 410 Promotional Bedford Van
Green with white or green interior. Only 100 with 'Parlophone' made for a French collector in 1976. Price £2. 90mm. DC/P.   £600   £250   £100

No. 410 Promotional Bedford Van
White with white or red interior with 'MJ Hire and Service'. Price £2.50. Issued 1975/76. Deleted almost at once. 90mm. DC/P.   £600   £250   £100

No. 410 Promotional Bedford Van
White. Only 200 with 'Modeller's World' on sides made specially for the Mikansue Company in 1976. Price £2.50. Almost certainly deleted the same year as made and like many promotional models can sometimes be found at swapmeets, collector's shops etc. 90mm. DC/P.   £350   £75   £35

No. 410 Promotional Bedford Van
Dark, medium or bright red with promotional stickers saying 'Simpson's'. Made specially for a large department store in Toronto, Canada, to celebrate 100 years of trading. Equivalent price £1. Issued 1972. Deleted 1985. 90mm. DC/P.   £750   £150   £50

No. 410 Promotional Bedford Van
Red with 'Marley Tiles' on sides. Promotional gimmick for the Marley Tiles Company. Price £1. Issued 1975. Deleted 1976. 90mm. DC/P.   £300   £100   £50

No. 410 Promotional Bedford Van
Brown and black with 'Relaco' on sides. Price £2. Issued 1974. Deleted 1975. 90mm. DC/P.   £350   £75   £35

No. 410 Bedford Van
Standard Dinky Toy with 'Danish Post' made for Denmark. Equivalent price £1.50. Issued 1974. Deleted 1976. 90mm.   £550   £150   £75

No. 410 Promotional Bedford Van
Red with 'Caledonian Autominologists'. Only 100 made
for members of this association. Price £2.50. Issued and
deleted 1977. 90mm. DC/P.

	£500	£150	£75

No. 410 Promotional Bedford Van
White with 'Collector's Gazette' on sides. Only 200 made.
Available from the paper's head office or at swapmeets,
but most of these have been snapped up. Price £2.50.
Issued 1979. 90mm. DC/P.

	£500	£150	£75

No. 412 AA Bedford Van
Authentic yellow and black AA colours with 'AA Service'
on sides. Price £1.45. Issued 1974. Deleted 1980. 90mm.
DC/P.

	£150	£40	£15

No. 416 Ford Transit Van
Yellow with 'Motorways' on sides. Driver's door does not
open. Warning signs, red beacon on roof and bollard
inside van. Replaced No. 407 and then replaced in 1978
by No. 417. Price £1.45. Issued 1975. Deleted 1978.
129mm. DC/P.

	£250	£100	£50

No. 417 Ford Transit Service Van
Medium or dark yellow. Opening side and rear doors and
roof light with red interior, silver bumpers, wheels etc.
Replaced No. 416. With a third grille, otherwise details as
above. Price £1.75. Issued 1978. Deleted 1980. 133mm.
DC/P.

	£75	£50	£35

No. 450 Esso Trojan Van
Red with 'Esso' on sides. One of the most sought after
ranges of models from the mid- and late 1950s. The price
of these models will rise very quickly like No. 31A and
the series renumbered 450. It is important to note that the
empty boxes of theses models are worth money as all
collectors like to hear the words 'mint boxed'. The
practice of late has been the purchase of models in one
place and the box in another. All early boxes are worth
saving as people are keen to buy them. Price 2/5. Issued
1955. Deleted 1957. 85mm. DC/TP/RT.

	£250	£100	£50

No. 450 TK Bedford Van
Metallic green and white with 'Castrol the Masterpiece
in Oils' on sides and front. Red interior and silver trim.
Opening door with 'Bedford' on front radiator. Price
10/9. Issued 1965. Deleted 1970. 143mm. DC/P.

	£350	£100	£50

VANS	MB	MU	GC

No. 451 Dunlop Trojan Van
Red with 'Dunlop the World's Master Tyre' on sides.
Renumbering of 31B. Price 2/5. Issued November 1955.
Deleted 1957. 85mm. DC/RT/TP

£250 £100 £50

No. 452 Chivers Trojan Van
Green with 'Chivers Jellies' on sides. Renumbering of
31C. Price 2/5. Issued October 1954. Deleted 1957. 85mm.
DC/RT/TP.

£300 £100 £50

No. 454 Cydrax Trojan Van
Green with 'Drink Cydrax' on sides. Price 2/9. Issued
February 1957. Deleted March 1959. 85mm. DC/RT/TP.

£250 £100 £50

No. 455 Brooke Bond Trojan Van
Red with 'Brooke Bond Tea' on sides. Price 2/5. Issued
May 1957. Deleted 1961. 85mm. DC/TP/RT. Highly
sought after.

£350 £150 £75

No. 465 Capstan Morris Van
Blue and dark blue with 'Have a Capstan' and other
designs on sides. Price 2/11. Issued March 1957. Deleted
1959. 78mm. DC/TP/RT.

£250 £100 £50

No. 470 Shell BP Austin Van
Red and green with 'Shell' and 'BP' on sides. Price 2/5.
Issued May 1954. Deleted 1956.

£100 £50 £25

No. 471 Nestlés Austin Van
Red with 'Nestlés' on sides. Price 2/5. Issued October
1955. Deleted 1960. 89mm. DC/RT/TP.

£250 £100 £50

No. 472 Raleigh Austin Van
Green with 'Raleigh Cycles' on sides. Price 2/5. Issued
April 1957. Deleted 1960. 89mm. DC/TP/RT.

£200 £100 £50

No. 480 Kodak Bedford Van
Yellow with 'Kodak Cameras and Films' on sides. Price
2/5. Issued June 1954. Deleted 1956. 83mm. DC/TP/RT.

£275 £100 £50

No. 481 Ovaltine Bedford Van
Blue with 'Ovaltine' in black or cream on sides and
'Ovaltine Biscuits' in gold, yellow or blue. Price 2/9.
Issued September 1955. Deleted 1960. 83mm.
DC/TP/RT.

£250 £100 £50

No. 482 Dinky Toys Bedford Van
Yellow with orange on lower body panels and 'Dinky
Toys' in red on sides. Price 2/9. Issued October 1956.
Deleted 1960. 83mm. DC/TP/RT.

£250 £100 £50

No. 490 Express Dairy Electric Van
Grey and blue or cream and red with 'Express Dairy' on front. Price 3/4. Issued 1954. Deleted 1956. 85mm. DC/TP/RT.

	MB	MU	GC
No. 490	£100	£50	£25

No. 491 NCB Electric Dairy Van
Cream and red with 'NCB' on front. Seen at swapmeets on the Continent, especially in Amsterdam, but very scarce in England. Price 2/11. Issued 1956 mainly for export. Deleted 1960. 85mm. DC/RT.

	£250	£100	£50

No. 492 Loudspeaker Van
Renumbering of 34C. Price 2/3. Issued 1954. Deleted 1957. 81mm. DC/RT. Boxes very rare.

	£100	£50	£25

No. 492 Election Mini-Van
White with 'Vote for Somebody' on sides. Orange loudspeaker on roof and opening rear doors plus candidate figure with microphone. Never actually appeared in any Dinky catalogue and had a very short production run. Price 7/11. Issued 1964. Deleted 1965. 78mm. DC/RT/P.

	£300	£150	£75

No. 514 Slumberland Guy Van
Red with 'Slumberland Spring Interior Mattresses' and crest on sides. Opening rear doors and four wheels. Price 5/8. Issued December 1949. Deleted 1952. 134mm. DC/TP/RT.

	£750	£250	£100

No. 514 Lyons Guy Van
'Lyons Swiss Rolls' on sides. Type 1 front with opening rear doors, four wheels and one spare. Price 7/9. Issued November 1951. Deleted 1952. 134mm. DC/TP/RT. Condition matters a great deal, especially where the transfer is concerned. A chip off a transfer can make a £10 difference in the selling price, although from what I have seen, collectors will be willing to pay high prices for models in this range.

	£2000	£350	£150

No. 514 Weetabix Guy Van
Yellow. Opening rear doors with four wheels and one spare. Price 7/9. Issued June 1952. Deleted 1954. 134mm. DC/TP/RT.

	£1000	£500	£250

No. 514 Spratts Guy Van
Red and cream with 'Spratts' on sides. Opening rear doors. Type 1 front, four wheels and one spare. Price 7/-. Issued July 1953. Deleted 1954.

	£900	£250	£100

No. 561 Citroën Delivery Van
Metallic blue with sliding door and 'Cibie' on sides. Price
5/5. Issued July 1962. Deleted 1964. 90mm. DC/TP/RT.
French Dinky Toy imported into England and actually
made in France but with different advert as well as 'Cibie'
on sides.   £300   £75   £25

No. 561 Citroën Delivery Van
Blue and white with 'Gervais' on sides. Otherwise as
above. Available only in France.   £400   £250   £100

No. 917 Spratts Guy Van
Red and cream with 'Spratts' on sides. Type 1 or 2 front,
four wheels, one spare and opening rear doors. Price 7/3.
Issued January 1955. Deleted 1956. 132mm. DC/TP/RT.   £500   £200   £50

No. 918 Ever Ready Guy Van
Blue livery with 'Ever Ready Batteries for Life' on sides.
Type 2 front, four wheels, one spare and opening rear
doors. Price 8/-. Issued December 1955. Deleted 1958.
132mm. DC/TP/RT. Although the commonest Guy van,
prices have appreciated considerably.   £350   £100   £50

No. 919 Golden Shred Guy Van
Red with 'Robertson's Golden Shred' and golliwog on
sides. Type 2 front, four wheels, one spare and opening
rear doors. Price 8/9. Issued June 1957. Deleted 1958.
132mm. DC/TP/RT.   £800   £250   £75

No. 920 Heinz Guy Warrior Van
'Heinz 57 Varieties' and tomato ketchup bottle on sides.
Rear opening doors, red cab and chassis. Because of the
short production run, this is the rarest post-war Dinky
van of all. Price 8/9. Issued 1960. Deleted 1961. 137mm.
DC/TP/RT/P.   £900   £500   £150

No. 920 Heinz Guy Warrior Van
'Heinz 57 Varieties' and tin of baked beans on sides.
Otherwise as above. Very rare.   £550   £150   £50

No. 923 Heinz Big Bedford Van
'Heinz 57 Varieties' and tin of baked beans on sides. Four
wheels, one spare, opening rear doors and no hook. Price
8/3. Issued December 1955. Deleted 1958. 146mm.
DC/TP/RT.   £400   £200   £100

No. 923 Heinz Big Bedford Van
Red and yellow with 'Heinz 57 Varieties' and tomato
ketchup bottle on sides. Price 9/6. Issued 1958. Deleted
1960. 146mm. DC/TP/RT. Much rarer than the model
with tin of baked beans on sides.   £800   £500   £150

No. 930 Bedford Pallet Jekta Van
Orange and yellow with 'Dinky Toys' on sides and
'Meccano' on front. Windows, opening rear doors and
three plastic pallets. Handle works the interior floors.
Marked No. 793 it is worth double the ordinary No. 930.
Price 14/3. Issued January 1960. Deleted 1964. 177mm.
DC/TP/RT/P. Rare.   £200   £75   £25

No. 988 ABC TV Transmitter Van
Cream and grey with red flash and 'ABC' on front.
Windows and rotating aerial on roof. Price 7/9. Issued
May 1962. Deleted 1969. 111mm. DC/TP/RT/P.   £250   £150   £75

EMPTY BOXES

An Empty Box

We have now reached a period in the world of collecting when not only diecast models but the empty boxes themselves are of considerable value. It is only common sense to realise that a model has considerably more value when it is in its correct box. For instance, an Esso tanker which is valued at £50 without a box can be worth £100 with a box. A Trojan van might bring £100 unboxed but £250 boxed. Boxes have a psychological effect and it is always easier to sell a model with a box than it is without. At one time the specialist collector who also paid the highest prices would not even consider purchasing a model unless it was boxed and in almost perfect condition.

From early 1978 I began dealing seriously in empty boxes. In both my shops at Leeds and York there was a person who dealt only with empty boxes and catalogues. It took several months before any of the boxes caught the eye of the serious collector and I had doubts about their value myself until 1979, when suddenly all the boxes were bought up in a matter of days. People began asking about the empty boxes when they were almost impossible to obtain.

Although I have done my best to give a guide to the prices of empty boxes, I would be very pleased to hear from any collector who happens to know of any rare boxes which I could include in future editions of this book.

PRE-WAR

Boxes
Plain. A box with plain covers which contains six models
is quite rare.   £10–£1000
Pictorial. Box which contained six or more models.   £50–£2000

Exhibitions
Several exhibitions were held where prominent
companies and toy makers would show their goods and
any model sold in a box would bear special dates and
details. Rare.   £25–£2000

Aircraft   £30–£300

Ambulances   £10–250

Buses and coaches
Plain   £10–£1000
Pictorial   £25–£1000
No. 27 Tram Car   £25–£1000

Caravans   £25–£250

Dublo Dinkies
No. 060 Milk Wagon   £250

Fire engines   £25–£500

French Dinkies
Plain   £25–£500
Pictorial   £50–£750

Garages   £25–£500

Gift sets
Plain   £50–£500
Pictorial   £50–£1000

Lorries, trucks and commercial vehicles
Plain   £10–£250
Pictorial   £10–£500
No. 25b Carter Paterson Covered Wagon
First transfer pre-war   £250
First transfer post-war   £100
Second transfer pre-war   £300
Second transfer post-war   £150
No. 25d Redline Glico Petrol Wagon   £150
No. 60y Thompson Aircraft Tender   £150

Military vehicles £25–£500
No. 301 Daimler Military Ambulance £100

Police cars £25–£500

Racing cars
Several models such as the Bluebird and Speed of the
Wind were placed on show at exhibitions. Famous
figures like Sir Malcolm Campbell and G. E. Eyston
would sign boxes which were specially made in limited
numbers. Such boxes are very rare and valuable. The
models might even have had accompanying material
such as letters and certificates. £100–£500

Saloon cars
Plain £25–£500
Pictorial £25–£1000
No. 32 Chrysler Airflow Saloon £250

Ships and boats £50–£500

Taxis and sports cars £25–£250

Tractors £25–£250

Trains £50–£500

Vans
Plain £30–£300
Pictorial £50–500
No. 31 Holland Coachcraft Van £250

POST-WAR

Agricultural vehicles
Yellow boxes £20–£200
Supertoy boxes £20–£500
No. 27N Field Marshall Farm Tractor £20–£500
No. 27N Promotional Tractor £10

Aircraft £2

Buses and coaches
No. 283 BOAC Coach £5
No. 293/A Swiss Postal Bus £5
No. 296 Luxury Coach £5
No. 949 Wayne School Bus Special £25
No. 952 Vega Major Luxury Coach £10
No. 953 Continental Touring Coach £4

Dublo Dinkies	£25

Gift sets
No. 307 New Avengers Set	£200

Lorries, trucks and commerical vehicles
Bedford vehicle in the '400' series	£10
No. 415 Mechanical Horse and Open Wagon	£10
No. 428 Large Trailer	£5
Guy Truck in the '400' series	£30
Tanker in the '400' series	£30
Foden Wagon in the '500' series	£50
No. 504 Mobilgas Foden 14-Ton Tanker	£100
No. 505 Foden Flat Truck with Chains	£100
Guy vehicle in the '500' series	£50
No. 582 Pullmore Car Transporter	£25
No. 908 Mighty Antar with Transformer	£200
Foden vehicle in the '900' series	£40
No. 941 Mobilgas Foden Tanker	£250
No. 942 Regent Foden Tanker	£250
Guy vehicle in the '900' series	£40
Leyland vehicle in the '900' series	£40
No. 935 Leyland Octopus Flat Truck with Chains	£250
No. 950 Car Transporter Set	£25
No. 981 Horsebox	£50
No. 983 Dinky Car Carrier and Trailer	£50
No. 984 Car Carrier	£25
No. 985 Dinky Trailer	£5
No. 991 AEC Shell Chemicals Tanker	£50

Military vehicles
Blue and white Supertoy boxes	£40–£400
No. 624 Daimler Ambulance	£50
No. 666 Missile Erector Vehicle and Corporal Missile	£25
No. 668 Foden Army Truck	£25
No. 674 Austin Champ (Promotional Special)	£100

Models from TV, space etc.
No. 281 Pathé News Camera Car	£25
No. 354 The Pink Panther	£50
No. 357 Klingon Battle Cruiser	£20
No. 358 USS Enterprise	£25
No. 602 Armoured Command Car	£25
No. 967 BBC Mobile Control Room	£10
No. 968 BBC Roving Eye Vehicle	£10
No. 969 BBC Extending Mast Vehicle	£10
No. 987 ABC Mobile control Room	£25
No. 988 ABC TV Transmitter Van	£25

Ships

Large box	£5
Medium box	£3
Small box	£2

Sports cars and saloons

No. 100 Lady Penelope's Fab 1	£10
No. 100A Lady Penelope's Fab 1	£25
No. 100B Lady Penelope's Fab 1	£50
No. 101 Thunderbird 4	£25
No. 106 Thunderbird 2	£10
No. 112 Purdey's TR7	£10
No. 157 Jaguar XK120	£5

Taxis

No. 115 UB Taxi	£10
No. 254 Austin Taxi	£5

Vans

No. 31B Dunlop 15cwt Trojan Van	£25
No. 31C Chivers 15cwt Trojan Van	£25
No. 31D Oxo 15cwt Trojan Van	£25
No. 260 Royal Mail Van	£25
No. 261 Telephone Service Van	£25
No. 262 Volkswagen Swiss Postal Van	£25
Ford Transit Promotional Van in the '400' series	£25
No. 450 Esso Trojan Van	£25
No. 452 Chivers Trojan Van	£30
No. 454 Cydrax Trojan Van	£25
No. 455 Brooke Bond Trojan Van	£40
No. 465 Capstan Morris Van	£25
No. 470 Shell BP Austin Van	£15
No. 471 Nestlés Austin Van	£15
No. 472 Raleigh Austin Van	£15
No. 480 Kodak Bedford Van	£10
No. 481 Ovaltine Bedford Van	£10
No. 482 Dinky Toys Bedford Van	£10
No. 514 Slumberland Guy Van	£50
No. 514 Lyons Guy Van	£50
No. 514 Weetabix Guy Van	£100
No. 514 Spratts Guy Van	£754
No. 918 Ever Ready Guy Van	£50
No. 919 Golden Shred Guy Van	£100
No. 920 Heinz Guy Warrior Van	£200
No. 923 Big Bedford Heinz Van	£50

CATALOGUES

It is well known that catalogues dealing with diecast models of all descriptions are sought after and therefore valuable. This is particularly true of French Dinkies. These little booklets not only show pictures and list original prices of the models when first produced but give a guide which has in many ways contributed to the publication of my book.

Again, while I have done my best to give a guide to the prices of catalogues, I would be very pleased to hear from collectors who happen to know of any rare catalogues which I could include in future editions of this book.

	Current prices
PRE-WAR	
Meccano magazine	£10–£100
Hornby or Dinky catalogue	£25–£100
POST-WAR	
Dinky catalogues	
First series	£5–£50
Second series	£3–£30
Third series	50p–£5
Complete set of Dinky catalogues	
The numbers in this set range from 1 to 14 and cover the years from 1965, when the first catalogue was produced by Lines Bros, to 1978, when the last Dinky catalogue was issued. Prices ranged from 3d in pre-decimal currency to 5p for each annual catalogue.	£50–£300

MATCHBOX DINKY
COLLECTION

Dinky was the great name for model vehicles until 1979 when manufacturing stopped. In its 46 years of business the company produced a huge range of models, but the post-war ones were the most successful. From the late 1970s collectors and enthusiasts were asking for models from the post-war era, with the nostalgia boom and the lack of supply serving only to increase this demand.

I always hoped that one day the greatest name in diecast toys would be revived, and it happened at the end of the 1980s when the Matchbox Group of Companies began the Dinky Collection. The authenticity and careful attention to detail have meant that all the models have been very successful. I have included colour details in my description, but collectors should watch out for any unusual colour that may appear in retail outlets. Such colours will be worth double or even treble the value of the normal colours. Incidentally colour variants often arise through the manufacturer having to make up an order using paints which have not been used for the bulk of the order. However, collectors should be aware of people painting models themselves. The only true prices are for genuine factory models.

At Matchbox I would like to give particular thanks to Nick Austin, Managing Director, and Chris Livesey, Sales and Marketing Director, for their fine work and to all the wonderful staff without whose help this section of the book would have been infinitely the poorer.

MODEL	MB	MU	GC
No. DY-1 1967 E-Type Jaguar			
Introduced in 1961, the series 1 E-type Jaguar sports car was developed from the Le Mans winning D-type of 1955/57. The wheelbase is 2.44m and the 6 cylinder engine of 4235cc develops 265bhp which gave a top speed of 145mph with its revised headlights and windscreen. The 1968 car is referred to by enthusiasts as the 1½ series model in green with silver spoked wheels, bumpers, windscreen and trim. Dark green or black hood. Price £4.95. Issued December 1988. 112mm.	£50	£30	£10
No. DY-1 1967 E-Type Jaguar			
Limited edition. Black with 'Dinky' on baseplate. Price £14.95. Issued and deleted 1995.	£50	£15	£10

No. DY-1B 1967 E-Type Jaguar
Limited edition. Silver with opening dark blue hood, silver-blue trim, spoked wheels, bumpers, windscreen and headlights. Price £9.95. Issued and deleted 1990. 100mm.

£750 £250 £100

No. DY-1C 1967 E-Type Jaguar
Deep lemon or mustard with black opening hood. Silver lights, bumpers, grill and screen. Silver spoked wheels with whitewalled tyres. Price £7.25. Issued 1991. 100mm.

£40 £20 £10

No. DY-2 1957 Chevrolet Bel Air
Pink and cream with silver trim, wheels, bumpers, windscreen, lights and radiator. An American car classic. The customer could choose from 5 engines from 140 to 283hp. It was fitted with the Turboglide 3 speed automatic gear box which gave a speed of 77mph over a quarter mile. Very popular in the US in its day, it is the epitome of an American car of the 1950s. Price £5.75. Issued February 1989. 121mm.

£50 £30 £10

No. DY-3 1965 MGB GT
Dark or mid-green with silver trim, bumpers, grille, windscreen and hubs. The MGB was developed from the 1955/62 MGA. It was powered by a 4 cylinder OHV engine of 1798cc with twin carburettors which gave 98bhp at 5400rpm. In 1965 the GT was introduced which, although heavier, had a higher top speed and better road holding. It was regarded as the ideal sports car. Price £4.95. Issued January 1989. 52mm.

£50 £30 £10

No. DY-3B 1965 MGB GT
Orange with grey or black interior. Silver trim, wheels, lights, grille and bumpers. Price £7.25. Issued 1992. 90mm.

£40 £20 £10

No. DY-4 1950 Ford E83W 10cwt Van
Mustard yellow with 'Heinz 57 Varieties' on side. Yellow wheels, black tyres, grille, bumpers and roof. The van first appeared in 1938 and used the 1172cc engine from the 10hp car. Offsetting the units and placing the driving controls beside the engine gave this van a load length of 2032mm and 3.12cm capacity on a vehicle with a 2286mm wheelbase. This vehicle was very popular and appeared in many emergency and civilian versions until production stopped in 1957. Price £4.95. Issued April 1989. 90mm.

£100 £30 £15

No. DY-5 1949 Ford V8 Pilot
Black with silver grille, bumpers, wheels and headlights. The Ford V8 Pilot was introduced in 1947 to satisfy the great demand for private cars in the late 1940s and early 1950s. The 3.6 litre engine produced 83bhp which, although modest, enabled this heavy car (1540kg) to travel at 80mph. Price £4.95. Issued May 1989. 101mm. £50 £25 £10

No. DY-5B 1949 Ford V8 Pilot
Metallic blue with matching trim, bumpers, lights, grille, wheels and black tyres. Price £7.25. Issued 1991. 100mm. £40 £20 £10

No. DY-5C 1949 Ford V8 Pilot
Fawn with silver hubs, lights, screen, trim, grille and bumpers. Dark opening hatch. Price £7.25. Issued 1992. 90mm £40 £20 £10

No. DY-6 1951 Volkswagen De Luxe Sedan
Blue with grey roof, blue wheels, black tyres, silver trim and bumpers. The Volkswagen was designed by Dr F. Porsche in 1936 to provide transportation for the masses. Production started in 1938, but it was not until 1945 that it started on a large scale. The VW was given the nickname 'The Beetle' because of its shape and was in production throughout the world until the early 1980s. The 1951 VW was powered by a 1131cc rear mounted air cooled engine developing 25bhp. Price £4.95. Issued June 1989. 100mm. £75 £30 £15

No. DY-6B Volkswagen De Luxe Sedan
Black with opening light or mid-blue roof cover and matching blue bumper. Silver wheels, bumpers, trim, lights and grille. Price £7.25. Issued 1991. 90mm. £40 £20 £10

No. DY-6C Volkswagen Sedan
Red with opening grey roof cover and red wheels. Silver bumpers, grille, lights, trim and hubs. Price £7.25. Issued 1992. 90mm. £50 £25 £15

No. DY-7 1959 Cadillac Coupe de Ville
Red and cream with silver trim, grille, bumpers, spoked wheels and lights. The Cadillac's reputation grew to the extent that it became the most prestigious American car available. The 1959 Coupe de Ville was no exception and continued the reputation with its distinctive styling and extraordinary rear fins. This large car was powered by a 6539cc V8 engine developing 325bhp to provide a very smooth ride. An American car classic. Price £4.95. Issued November 1989. 133mm. £50 £25 £15

No. DY-7B 1959 Cadillac Coupe de Ville
Brilliant pink with white roof and trim. White or satin
interior. Silver grille, lights, bumpers and wheels. Price
£8.50. Issued 1991. 133mm.

£75 £35 £15

No. DY-8 1948 Commer 8cwt Van
Red with authentic Sharps Toffee motif and adverts.
Silver grille bumpers, lights and wheels. The Commer
8cwt Van was produced by the Rootes Motor Company
which included such famous marques as the Humber,
Hillman and Sunbeam. The Commer was developed
using the same mechanical units as the Hillman Minx. It
featured hydraulic brakes and an efficient engine. Price
£5.50. Issued July 1989. 84mm.

£50 £30 £15

No. DY-8 1948 Commer 8cwt Van
Limited edition of 2000 with 'Classic Toys' logo and
colour. The box has received worldwide acclaim for its
original design of Binns Road, Liverpool, Supertoys.
Special numbered certificate. Issued mid-October 1994.

£250 £100 £50

No. DY-8 1948 Commer 8cwt Van
Limited edition issued for Bentalls Department Store,
Kingston upon Thames. Green with white roof, black
tyres, silver bumpers and headlights. Yellow spots on
back windows and above headlights. 'C' in black and '13'
on white discs. Price £19. Issued 1995. 84mm.

£50 £30 £20

No. DY-8B 1948 Commer 8cwt Van
Dark blue with matching wheels. The wheels are in blue
matching livery with 'His Master's Voice Radio and
Records' in black and white with brown or chocolate
background on sides. HMV logo with dog and
gramophone on doors. Silver bumpers and lights. Price
£7.25. Issued 1991. 84mm.

£50 £25 £15

No. DY-9 1949 Land Rover Series 1
Green with yellow cover. Silver trim and bumper. Spare
wheel on bonnet. The Rover Company recognised the
need for light 4 wheel drive vehicles which were used so
effectively during the Second World War. The company
developed these for farming and in the colonies where
roads were poor. By 1948 the Land rover was introduced.
This robustly built vehicle had a 4 cylinder 1595cc engine
with a 4 speed gearbox + 2 radio transfer box to the axles
providing the vehicle with 4 wheel drive. Price £5.50.
Issued September 1989. 90mm.

£60 £30 £15

No. DY-9B 1949 Land Rover
Yellow AA van services livery with logo on doors and
fawn cover. Black wheels with spare on bonnet. Matching
grille and side and front wheel panels. Price £7.25. Issued
1991. 90mm.

£50 £25 £15

No. DY-10 Mercedes Benz 03500 Stuttgart Bus
Cream with black bonnet, mudguards and tyres.
'Reisebüro Ruoff Stuttgart'. Superb never to be repeated
model of an original bus which was powered by a 4.6 litre
6 cylinder diesel and was capable of 52mph. Seating for
29, plus fold away seating for extra 7 passengers when
required. Price £15.95. Issued October 1989. 164mm.
Hardly advertised and only a few were released, so one
to look out for as a good future investment. Its value may
be much higher than given in the prices.

£350 £100 £40

No. DY-11 1948 Tucker Torpedo
Red with silver wheels, bumpers, lights, grille, lights.
Whitewalled tyres. Price £5.95. Issued 1990. 112mm.

£40 £20 £10

No. DY-11B 1948 Tucker Torpedo
Metallic blue with whitewalled tyres, silver trim, grille,
bumpers and hubs. Price £7.25. Issued 1992. 133mm.

£75 £35 £15

No. DY-12 1955 Mercedes Benz 300SL Gullwing
White or cream with silver wheels, bumpers, lights, hubs,
grille, bumpers and trim. Windscreen wipers and black
tyres. Price £7.25. Issued 1990. 121mm.

£40 £20 £10

No. DY-12C Mercedes Benz 300SL
Rich dark green with matching wheels. Silver trim, grille,
bumpers, hubs and screen. Price £7.25. Issued 1992.
112mm.

£50 £25 £10

No. DY-13 1955 Bentley R Continental
Metallic blue with silver wheels, bumpers, grille, lights
and trim. Issued 1990. Price £7.25. 121mm.

£50 £25 £15

No. DY-13B Bentley R Continental
Blue with silver trim, grille, bumpers, lights and wheels.
Price £7.25. Issued 1992. 123mm.

£40 £20 £10

No. DY-14 1946 Delahaye
Black or dark blue with silver trim, spoked wheels,
bumpers and lights. Black grille with trim. Price £5.95.
Issued 1990. 119mm.

£40 £20 £10

No. DY-14B 1946 Delahaye
Rich dark red with grey interior. Silver trim, lights, bumpers, running boards and wheels. Price £7.25. Issued 1992. 90mm.

£40 £20 £10

No. DY-15 1952 Austin A40 Van
Bright yellow with silver wheels, bumpers and lights. 'Dinky Toys' in red with white background on sides and 'Binns Road Liverpool 13' in black on doors. Price £7.25. Issued 1990. 84mm.

£75 £35 £20

No. DY-15 1952 Austin A40 Van
Special version made for the 1990 Earls Court Toy Fair. Resin with 'Brooke Bond Tea'. Display box and case. Issued 1990.

£150 £50 £20

No. DY-15B 1952 Austin A40 Van
Dark yellow or mustard. 'Dinky Toys' on white background on sides and 'Binns Road Liverpool 13' in black or dark blue (worth double) on doors. Silver-grey solid wheels with matching bumpers and grille. Price £7.25. Issued 1991. 84mm.

£40 £20 £10

No. DY-16 1967 Mustang Fastback 2 + 2
Metallic green with silver trim, spoked wheels, bumpers, grille, lights and wipers. The biggest selling motor car in the history of American production and the favourite of James Bond in the film Diamonds are Forever. Price £7.25. Issued 1990. 119mm.

£50 £25 £15

No. DY-16B Ford Mustang
White or cream (rare and worth treble) with red interior. Silver wheels, bumpers, grille, lights and trim. Price £7.25. Issued 1992. 119mm.

£50 £25 £10

No. DY-17 1939 Triumph Dolomite
Red with red wheels, black hood, silver bumpers and lights, trim and black seats. Special limited edition. Price £10.50. Issued November 1990. Worth finding.

£75 £35 £15

No. DY-17 MGB V8
Limited edition. Orange-red. Price £9.95. Issued 1995.

£25 £15 £10

No. DY-18 1967 E-Type Jaguar
Open tourer in red with black hood. Silver spoked wheels, bumpers, trim, windscreen and lights. Price £7.25. Issued 1990. 100mm.

£40 £15 £10

No. DY-19 1973 MGB GT V8
Red with silver trim, bumpers, lights and windscreen.
Black spoked wheels or solid wheels (rare and worth
double) with black tyres. Price £5.50. Issued 1990. 100mm.

£40   £20   £10

No. DY-20 1965 Triumph TR4A-IRS
Pale blue with black interior (open sports type), silver
wheels, bumpers, trim, screen and lights. Also made with
matching blue trim, lights, bumpers etc. Price £7.25.
Issued 1991. 119mm.

£50   £30   £15

No. DY-21 1964 Mini-Cooper S
White with black roof, silver grille, bumpers, lights and
trim. Red or orange indicators. One of the most popular
cars ever sold in the large type. Price £7.25. Issued 1991.
84mm. Good investment.

£100   £50   £25

No. DY-21 Mini-Cooper Police Car
Limited edition in authentic police livery and markings.
Price £19. Issued 1995. 84mm.

£50   £30   £20

No. DY-21B Mini-Cooper
This is a rally version of the car which raced in the 1966
Bathurst Hardy 500 mile rally. Limited edition in
authentic rally livery and numbers, prepared by
Automodels of Sydney, Australia. Modifications have
been carried out to lower the suspension of the model in
line with the real car. Price £19. Issued 1995. 84mm. Will
be much sought after.

£75   £40   £25

No. DY-22 1952 Citroën 15cv
Black livery with silver solid wheels, grille, lights,
bumpers and trim. Well known as the car in the TV series
Maigret. Price £7.25. Issued 1991. 119mm.

£60   £30   £15

No. DY-22B Citroën 15cv
White with matching interior and wheels. Silver trim,
bumpers, lights, screen and grille. Price £7.25. Issued
1992. 119mm.

£50   £25   £15

No. DY-23 1956 Chevrolet Corvette
Metallic red with white or cream side panels, opening
hood, silver wheels, trim, bumpers and black
whitewalled tyres. Price £7.25. Issued 1991. 98mm.

£40   £20   £10

No. DY-23B 1956 Corvette
Metallic gold. Silver spoked wheels with whitewalled
tyres. Silver bumpers, grille, lights and screen. Brilliant
white side panels. Price £7.25. Issued 1992. 113mm.

£50   £25   £15

No. DY-24 1973 Ferrari Dino 246 GTS
Dark or medium red with black roof, silver spoked wheels, bumpers and lights. Price £7.25. Issued 1991. 90mm.

	MB	MU	GC
	£30	£15	£10

No. DY-25 1958 Porsche 365A Coupé
Metallic blue or green with matching bumpers, lights, wheels and silver trim. Price £7.25. Issued 1991. 90mm.

	£35	£20	£10

No. DY-26 1957 Studebaker Golden Hawk
Greenish bronze with silver wheels, trim, bumpers, lights and fins. Price £7.25. Issued 1991. 90mm.

	£30	£15	£10

No. DY-27 1957 Chevrolet Bel Air
Open sports car in blue with blue and white interior, white hood, silver spoked wheels, trim, lights, bumpers and fins. Beige and blue seats or brown and blue seats (rare). Price £7.25. Issued 1991. 100mm. Good investment.

	MB	MU	GC
With beige and blue seats	£40	£20	£10
With brown and blue seats	£100	£40	£20

No. DY-28 Triumph Stag
White with red seats. Opening hood in black, red or matching white (rare). Silver wheels, bumpers, trim and lights. Price £7.25. Issued 1992. 84mm.

	£30	£15	£10

No. DY-28B Triumph Stag
Limited edition. Super metallic green. Price £9.95. Issued 1995.

	£25	£15	£10

No. DY-29 Buick Skylark
Tourer with opening hood in white, red or black. White and blue interior, silver trim, wheels, bumpers and lights. Price £7.25. Issued 1992. 84mm.

	£30	£15	£10

No. DY-30 Austin Healey
Tourer in metallic green with opening hood in black, white or red. Silver spoked wheels, trim, lights, bumpers, grille and screen. Price £7.25. Issued 1992. 84mm.

	£30	£15	£10

No. DY-31 1955 Ford T Bird
Tourer in red with opening hood and light matching interior. Silver spoked or solid wheels, trim, lights, bumpers, grille and screen. Price £7.25. Issued 1992. 84mm.

	£30	£15	£10

No. DY-32 Citroën 2cv
Grey-blue or greenish with silver-grey bumpers, wheels, trim and lights. Price £7.25. Issued 1992. 90mm.

	£30	£15	£10

No. DY-903 Special Limited Edition, Three Classic Sports Cars

Contains three classic cars: 1965 Triumph TR4A-IRS in red with black interior; 1967 Series 1½ E-Type Jaguar in white with red interior; and 1956 Austin Healey 100 BN2 in blue with dark blue hood. All open sports models on dark stand with gold name-plates. Price £21.50. Issued 1992. Worthwhile investment.

£100 £25 £10

PREMIERE COLLECTION
The next four models formed this collection.

No. DY-921 Jaguar E-Type

Silver livery with all-matching parts. On dark stand with gold name-plate in centre, giving date and name of model. Price £17.95. Issued 1992. 112mm.

£75 £40 £20

No. DY-922 Ferrari 246

Silver with all-matching parts. On dark stand with gold name-plate in centre, giving date and name of model. Price £17.50. Issued 1992. 100mm.

£75 £25 £10

No. DY-923 Chevrolet Corvette

Silver with all-matching parts. On dark stand with gold name-plate in centre, giving date and name of model. Price £17.50. Issued 1992. 121mm.

£75 £35 £15

No. DY-924 Mercedes Benz 300SL Gullwing

Silver with all-matching parts. On dark stand with gold name-plate in centre, giving date and name of model. Price £17.50. Issued 1992. 121mm.

£75 £30 £10

No. DY Special Issue Jaguar XK150

Limited edition. Authentic Jaguar livery with silver trim. Price £12.95. Issued 1995.

£25 £15 £10

No. DY Special Issue Karmann Ghia

Limited edition. Red with black interior, silver trim, wheels, lights and bumpers. Price £12.95. Issued 1995.

£25 £15 £10

No. DY Special Issue Mercedes 300 Convertible

Limited edition. Authentic Mercedes livery with silver trim, headlights, bumpers and windscreen. Price £12.95. Issued 1995.

£35 £20 £10

RECENT CLASSICS

Dinky Display Stand

Smart stand made in Germany to hold 50 Dinky Classics and called 'The Dinky Dream'.

£100 £50 —

Dinky No. 001 Police Mini
Limited edition. Police livery and decals. Price £19.95.
Issued 1994 and sold out within a short time.   £50   £25   £10

Dinky No. 002 1948 Commer Van
Limited edition. Bentalls Department Store livery and
decals. Price £19.95. Issued April 1995.   £50   £20   £10

Dinky No. 003 Bathurst Mini
Limited edition. Bathurst livery and decals. Price £19.95.
Issued May 1995.   £50   £20   £10

GOLDEN AGE OF SPORTS CARS COLLECTION

Limited edition. Six of Europe's finest sports cars in a
collection of classic Dinky replicas. Available
individually or as a set in special box at £75. Custom-
designed display stand (330mm long x 203mm wide)
given with each set. Good investment which will quickly
treble in price.

1957 Jaguar XK 150
Cream with open black hood, red interior, spoked wheels
and bumpers. Price £12.50. Issued 1995.

1957 Mercedes Benz 300 Roadster
Mid-blue with open top, red interior, silver trim and
bumpers. Price £12.50. Issued 1995.

1967 Jaguar E-Type
Black with hood, red interior, spoked wheels and
bumpers. Price £12.50. Issued 1995.

1968 Karmann Ghia
Red with open fawn hood, fawn interior, silver trim and
bumpers. Price £12.50. Issued 1995.

1969 Triumph Stag
Dark green with fawn interior, silver trim and bumpers.
Classic design by the famous Turin coach builder,
Micholotti. Carried one of the first T bars in British
automotive design. Price £12.50. Issued 1995.

1973 MGB GT
Red with dark interior, silver trim and bumpers. Price
£12.50. Issued 1995.